THE MASSIVE

"*THE MASSIVE* HAS BEEN ONE OF MY FAVORITE BOOKS OF THE YEAR—ONE THAT I LOOK FORWARD TO EACH MONTH. IT'S JUST REALLY DAMN ENGROSSING."
—CRAVE ONLINE

"As we consumers become more embedded in the world that Wood and his fellow creators build; as we dig deeper into the people he writes and the incredibly complicated and morally compromised panoply that Wood designed, we are slowly, gradually changed. Good fiction has the power to subtly affect our perceptions, forcing our minds to progress in new directions."
—Comics Bulletin

"*THE MASSIVE* IS CONTINUING ITS RUN OF BEING AN INTERESTING AND CAPTIVATING STORY FULL OF TERRIFIC CHARACTERS AND A STORY THAT IS INCREDIBLY UNIQUE . . . THERE IS NO QUESTION THAT THIS IS A GREAT SERIES."
—DIGITAL NOOB/EGM NOW

8/14 Ingram 2000

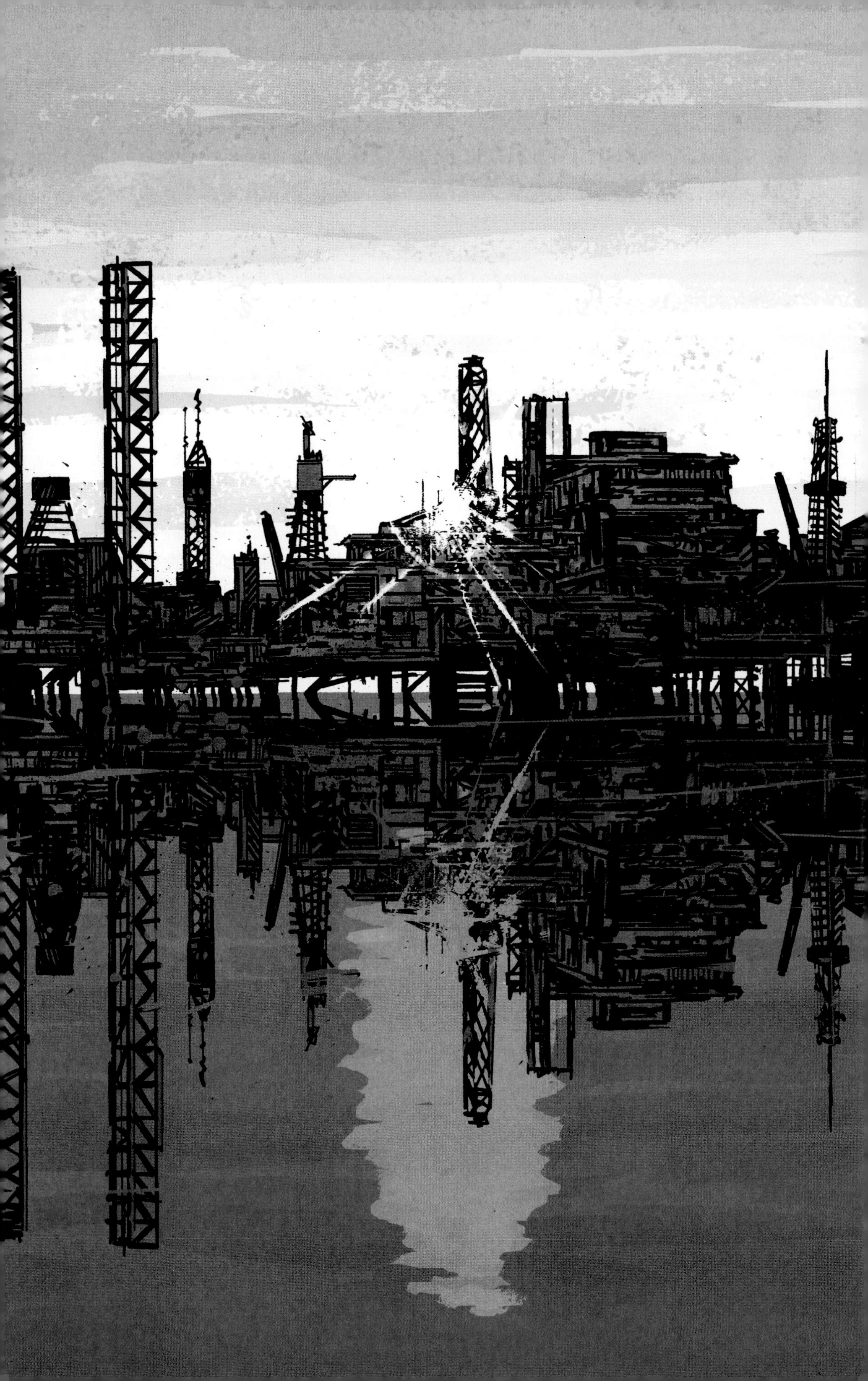

BRIAN WOOD
STORY

Subcontinental

GARRY BROWN
ART

DAVE STEWART
COLORS

Polaris

GARY ERSKINE
"BREAKER" ART

DECLAN SHALVEY
"MEGALODON" ART

DANIJEL ZEZELJ
"NUNATAK" ART

JORDIE BELLAIRE
COLORS

JARED K. FLETCHER
LETTERING

J. P. LEON
COVER ART

THE MASSIVE

SUBCONTINENTAL

DARK HORSE BOOKS

GN SUBCONTINENTAL V.2

MIKE RICHARDSON
PRESIDENT & PUBLISHER

SIERRA HAHN
EDITOR

JIM GIBBONS
ASSOCIATE EDITOR

JUSTIN COUCH
COLLECTION DESIGNER

Special thanks to Meredith, Audrey, and Ian.

Published by **DARK HORSE BOOKS**

A division of Dark Horse Comics, Inc.

10956 SE Main Street, Milwaukie, OR 97222

DARKHORSE.COM

First edition: December 2013
ISBN 978-1-61655-316-6

1 3 5 7 9 10 8 6 4 2

To find a comics shop in your area, call the
Comic Shop Locator Service toll-free at (888) 266-4226.
International Licensing: (503) 905-2377

Neil Hankerson Executive Vice President · Tom Weddle Chief Financial Officer · Randy Stradley Vice President of Pub-
lishing · Michael Martens Vice President of Book Trade Sales · Anita Nelson Vice President of Business Affairs · Scott
Allie Editor in Chief · Matt Parkinson Vice President of Marketing · David Scroggy Vice President of Product Develop-
ment · Dale LaFountain Vice President of Information Technology · Darlene Vogel Senior Director of Print, Design, and
Production · Ken Lizzi General Counsel · Davey Estrada Editorial Director · Chris Warner Senior Books Editor · Diana
Schutz Executive Editor · Cary Grazzini Director of Print and Development · Lia Ribacchi Art Director · Cara Niece
Director of Scheduling · Tim Wiesch Director of International Licensing · Mark Bernardi Director of Digital Publishing

This volume reprints the comic-book series *The Massive* #7–#12 from Dark Horse Comics.

BEFORE NINTH WAVE, THERE WAS SEA SHEPHERD
CAPTAIN PETER HAMMARSTEDT

Prior to the Crash, Ninth Wave routinely harassed illegal whaling vessels in the Barents Sea, using innovative tactics, like the deployment of propeller entanglement devices, to obstruct whale poachers from conducting their bloody business. In an altercation depicted in *Dark Horse Presents*, the whalers fire upon a rigid-hull inflatable belonging to the *Kapital*, in a desperate attempt to dissuade the direct-action conservationists. Captain Callum Israel asks his trusted chief officer Mag Nagendra, "Since when does the whaling fleet take shots at us?" to which Mag replies, "It's their seventh year of decimated profits." Ninth Wave was considered a tangible threat by the whalers because they spoke the only language that those poachers understood—profit and loss.

The Massive, that elusive behemoth of a boat for which icebergs are routinely mistaken, was originally donated to Ninth Wave as an antiwhaling vessel, and it is likely that Ninth Wave campaigned against whaling in the wake of successful Antarctic whale defense campaigns by Sea Shepherd Conservation Society. Perhaps the actions of Sea Shepherd, dogging the Japanese whaling fleet for nine consecutive years, bankrupting the whaling industry for three years in a row, and saving 932 whales from slaughter in the 2012/13 whaling season, inspired Ninth Wave to take direct action of their own. Or maybe the two organizations act independently of one another, in different universes, one Dark Horse's and one our very own, to be the only defense for whales against unlawful slaughter.

But unlike Ninth Wave, Sea Shepherd would not need to search all seven seas for the cause of the Crash. In our universe, the cause would so obviously have been our own greed. The human species has been on course for a crash since it first took to the sea. Our economies are based on models where infinite growth is a necessity, in a world where there are natural limits to growth. The planet Earth has a limited production capacity (there are only so many fish), absorbent capacity (it can only process so much pollution), and carrying capacity (it can only support so many people).

More species of plants and animals will disappear between 2000 and 2065 than have gone extinct in the last 65 million years. The crisis facing the world's oceans, where by 2048 it is predicted that all of the world's major fisheries will have collapsed, is the tragedy of the commons, the depletion of fish populations in an extractive free-for-all fueled by the reality that if one fishing vessel doesn't exploit an area to the fullest, then another one will. Threatened, endangered, and protected whales are being hunted in the most cruel and barbaric slaughter of any animal in order to satiate markets that measure the value of the lives of these beautiful social creatures by economic units rather than by ethical consideration.

But thankfully we have many of the laws in place needed to protect the oceans. What is missing is somebody to enforce those laws. Sea Shepherd works to uphold international conservation law when the governments of the world lack either the political will or the economic means to protect the marine environment. We measure our success by the number of lives that we save and the number of criminal operations that we shut down, and since we started campaigning to stop whaling in the Antarctic, our direct-action interventions have saved over 4,500 whales.

Captain Callum Israel would have a lot in common with Captain Paul Watson, the founder of Sea Shepherd, as both fight for order in a lawless world where chaos sets the course. Both walk a thin line between what is legal and what is not, never crossing it, while taking action that is aggressive, but nonviolent, in a quest for a different reality, one that is not dictated by the greedy corporations of insidious poachers but rather by all of us whose very survival depends on healthy oceans.

As Sea Shepherd's campaigns to stop whaling continue in the Southern Ocean Whale Sanctuary, we maintain our search for our own *Massive*. But our target just over the horizon is not an intermittent blip on the radar that does not respond to our frequent attempts to hail it on radio. Our goal is another world, one where the laws put in place to protect the Earth's oceans are enforced and where the creatures who call this watery realm home swim free of the harpoon. By recognizing that our environmental problems do not simply go away by just hoping that they will disappear, our direct intervention is critical crash prevention.

Captain Peter Hammarstedt is master of the marine conservation vessel M/Y *Bob Barker* and director of ship operations for the Sea Shepherd Conservation Society. Sea Shepherd is wholly dependent on donations from the public to directly save whales, sharks, seals, bluefin tuna, and all other oceanic life from slaughter. You can find out more and donate at SeaShepherd.org.au.

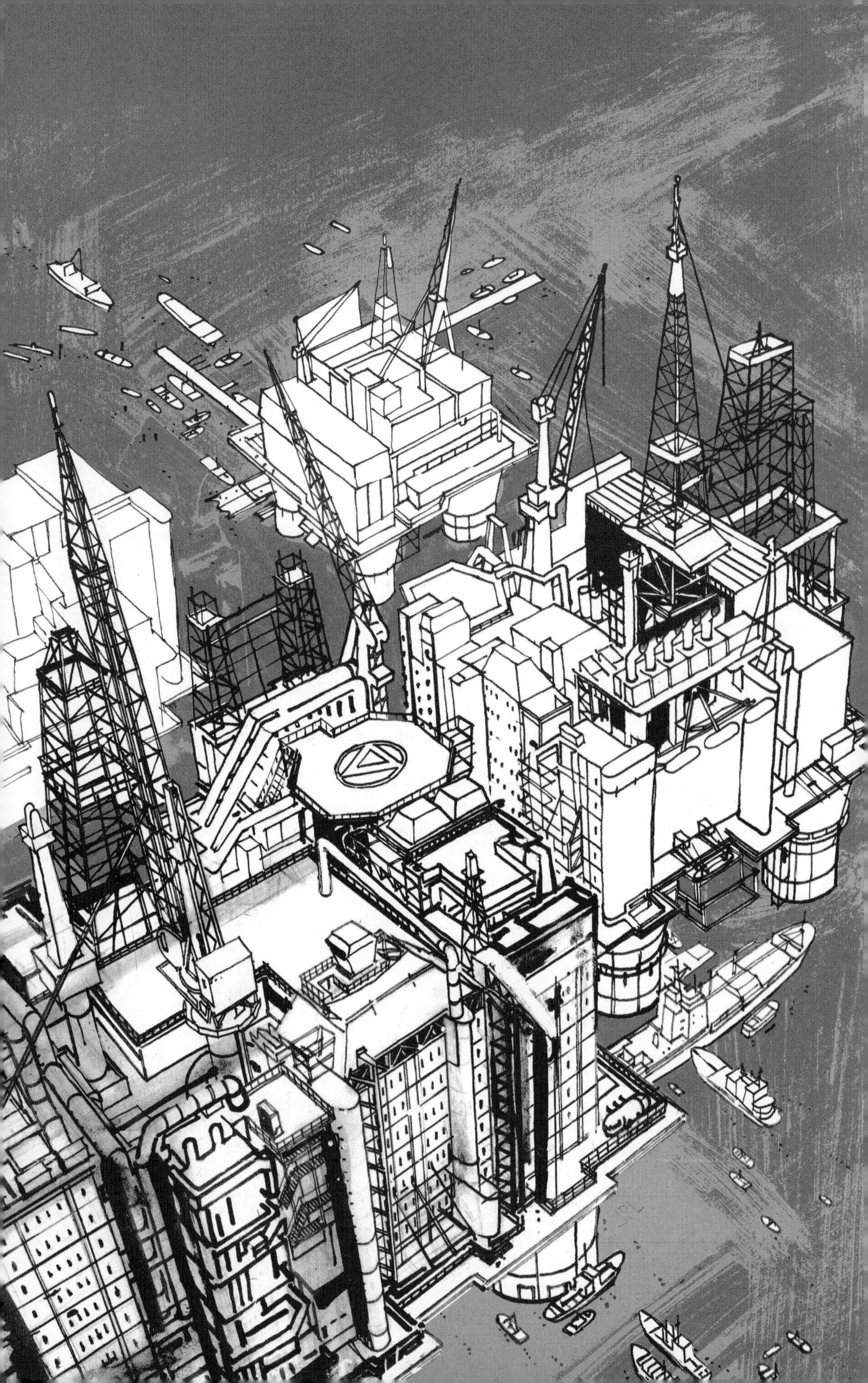

beep beep beep beep beep

...beep beep

BIP!

...SHIPPING BULLETIN FOR MET AREA EIGHT, SOUTH OF EQUATOR, AUTOMATED FOR THE EAST CENTRAL BAY OF BENGAL AREA OFFSHORE WEST TO INDIA...

...TIME ZONE GREENWICH MEAN PLUS FIVE HOURS...

...HIGH SEAS FORECAST VALID FOR 24/48 HOURS. WEATHER SEASONAL TO MODERATE, AT TIMES VARIABLE...

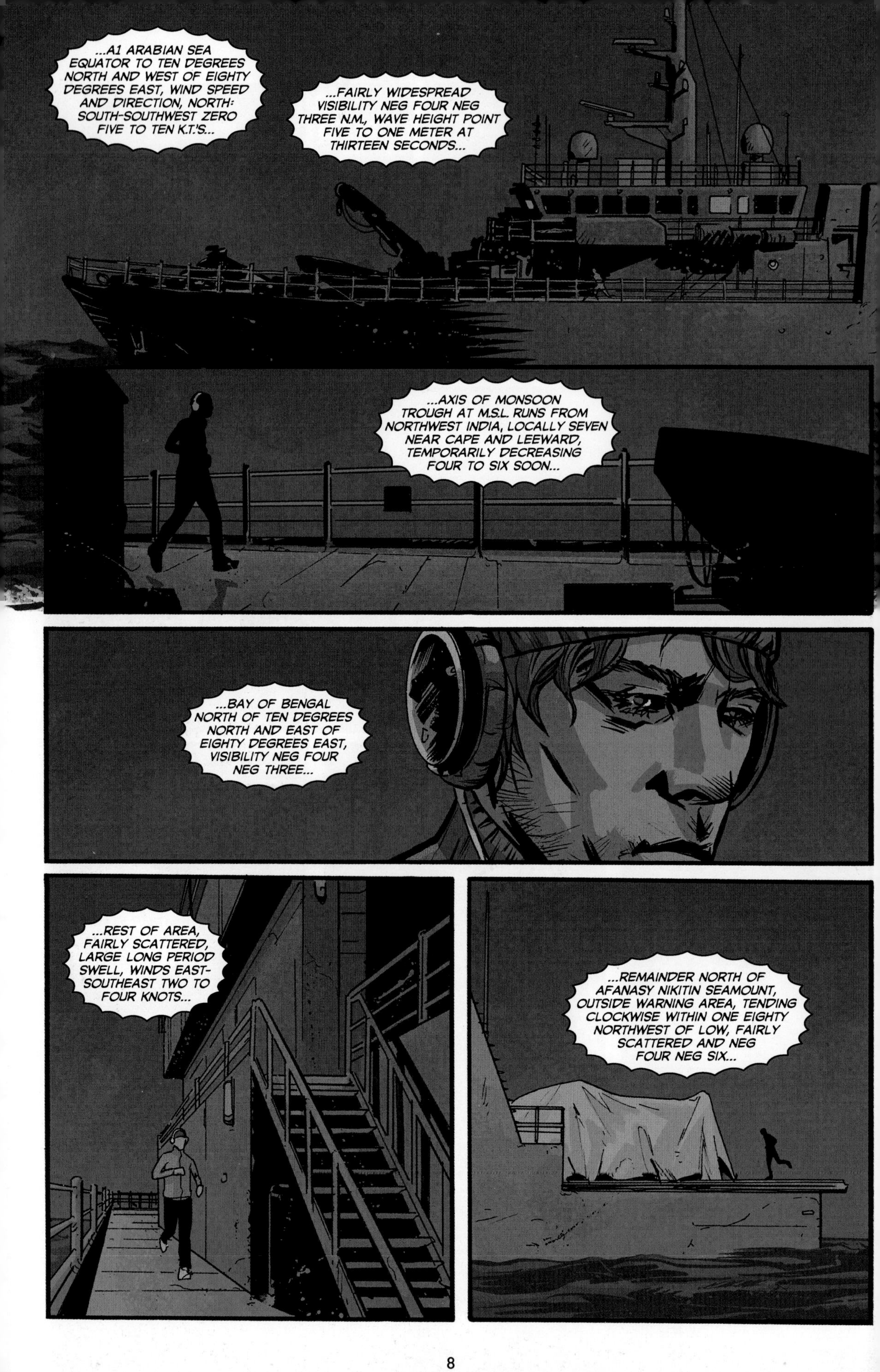
...A1 ARABIAN SEA EQUATOR TO TEN DEGREES NORTH AND WEST OF EIGHTY DEGREES EAST, WIND SPEED AND DIRECTION, NORTH: SOUTH-SOUTHWEST ZERO FIVE TO TEN K.T.'S...
...FAIRLY WIDESPREAD VISIBILITY NEG FOUR NEG THREE N.M., WAVE HEIGHT POINT FIVE TO ONE METER AT THIRTEEN SECONDS...
...AXIS OF MONSOON TROUGH AT M.S.L. RUNS FROM NORTHWEST INDIA, LOCALLY SEVEN NEAR CAPE AND LEEWARD, TEMPORARILY DECREASING FOUR TO SIX SOON...
...BAY OF BENGAL NORTH OF TEN DEGREES NORTH AND EAST OF EIGHTY DEGREES EAST, VISIBILITY NEG FOUR NEG THREE...
...REST OF AREA, FAIRLY SCATTERED, LARGE LONG PERIOD SWELL, WINDS EAST-SOUTHEAST TWO TO FOUR KNOTS...
...REMAINDER NORTH OF AFANASY NIKITIN SEAMOUNT, OUTSIDE WARNING AREA, TENDING CLOCKWISE WITHIN ONE EIGHTY NORTHWEST OF LOW, FAIRLY SCATTERED AND NEG FOUR NEG SIX...

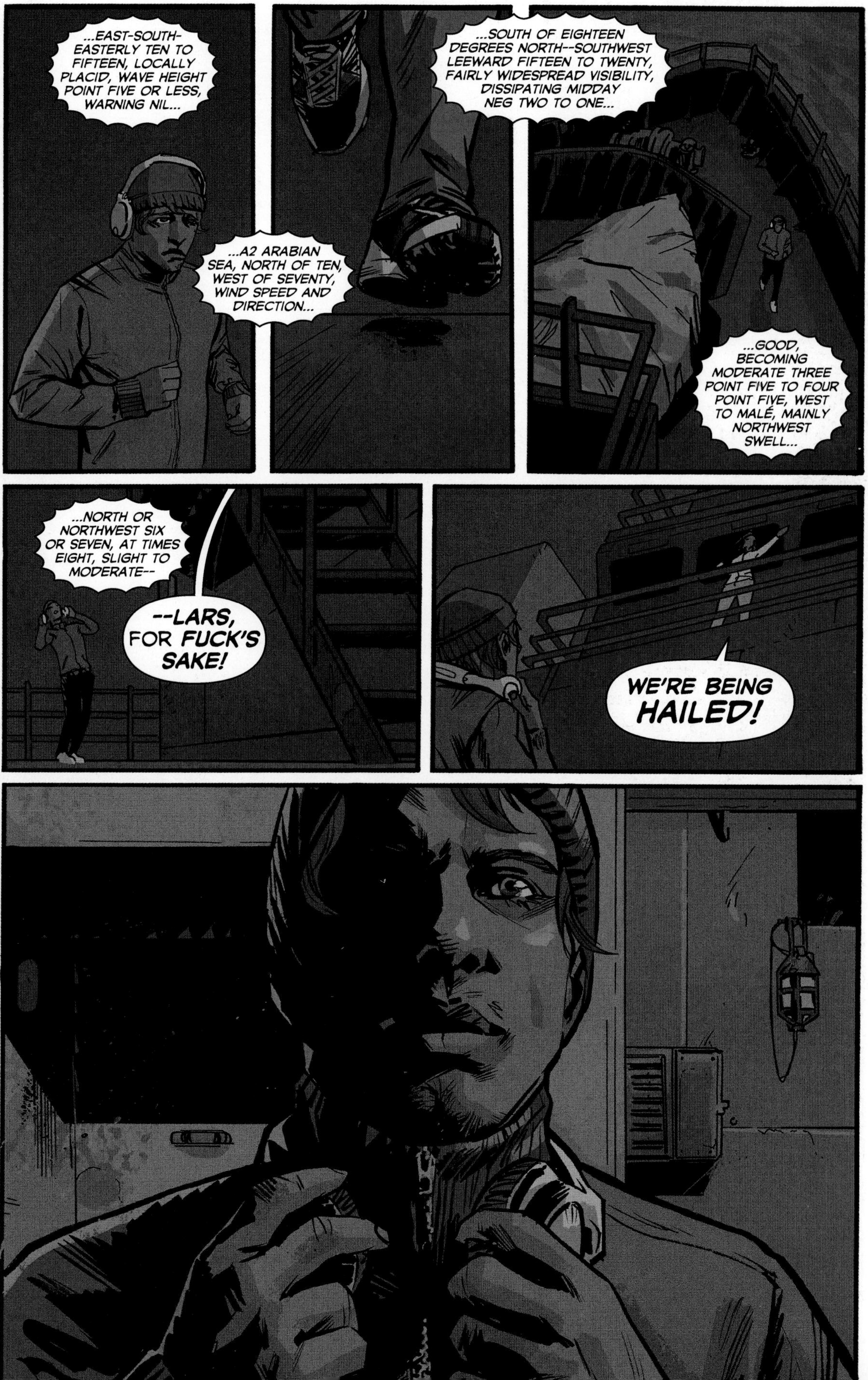
...EAST-SOUTH-EASTERLY TEN TO FIFTEEN, LOCALLY PLACID, WAVE HEIGHT POINT FIVE OR LESS, WARNING NIL...
...A2 ARABIAN SEA, NORTH OF TEN, WEST OF SEVENTY, WIND SPEED AND DIRECTION...
...SOUTH OF EIGHTEEN DEGREES NORTH--SOUTHWEST LEEWARD FIFTEEN TO TWENTY, FAIRLY WIDESPREAD VISIBILITY, DISSIPATING MIDDAY NEG TWO TO ONE...
...GOOD, BECOMING MODERATE THREE POINT FIVE TO FOUR POINT FIVE, WEST TO MALÉ, MAINLY NORTHWEST SWELL...
...NORTH OR NORTHWEST SIX OR SEVEN, AT TIMES EIGHT, SLIGHT TO MODERATE--
--LARS, FOR FUCK'S SAKE!
WE'RE BEING HAILED!

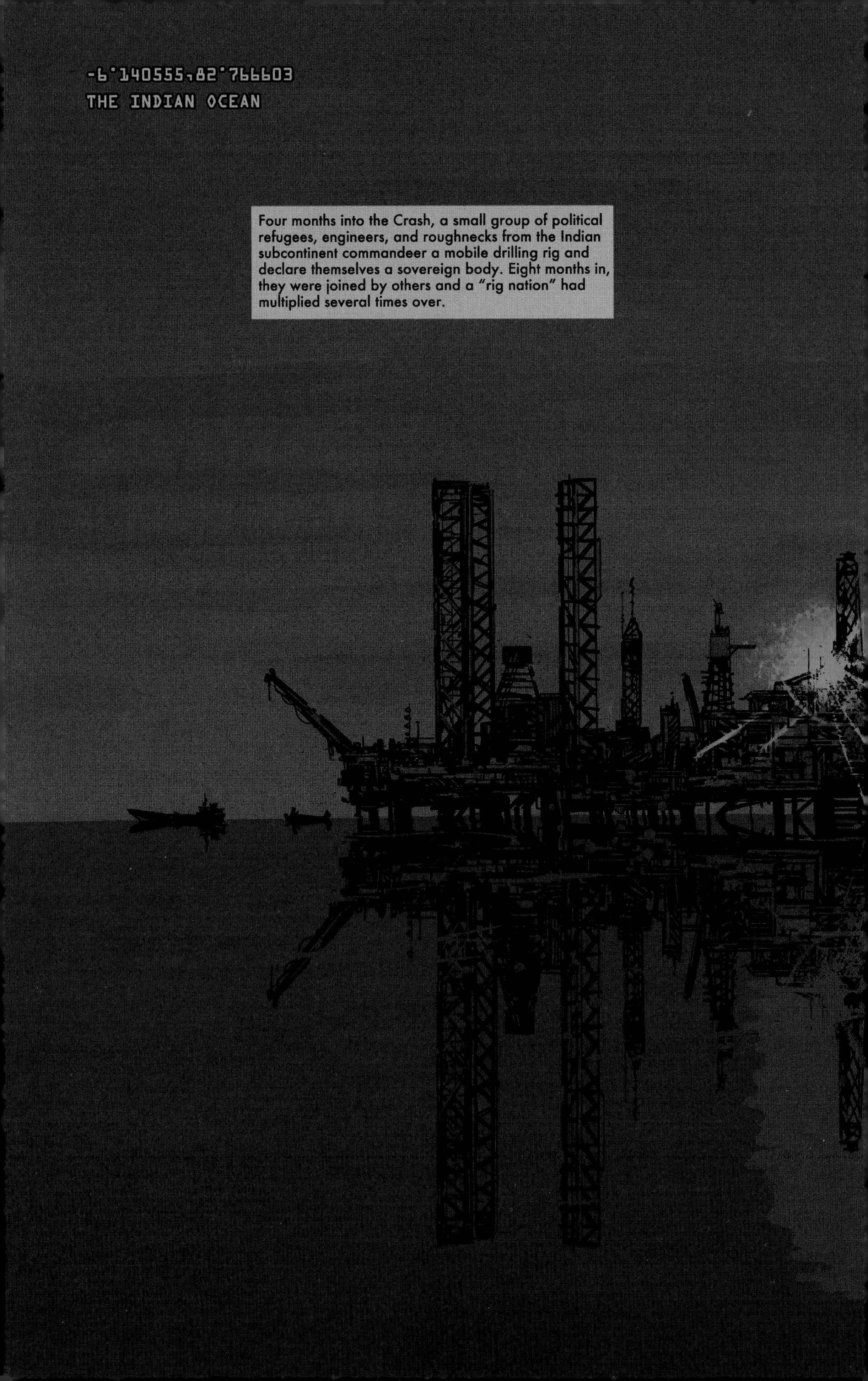
-6°140555,82°766603
THE INDIAN OCEAN
Four months into the Crash, a small group of political refugees, engineers, and roughnecks from the Indian subcontinent commandeer a mobile drilling rig and declare themselves a sovereign body. Eight months in, they were joined by others and a "rig nation" had multiplied several times over.

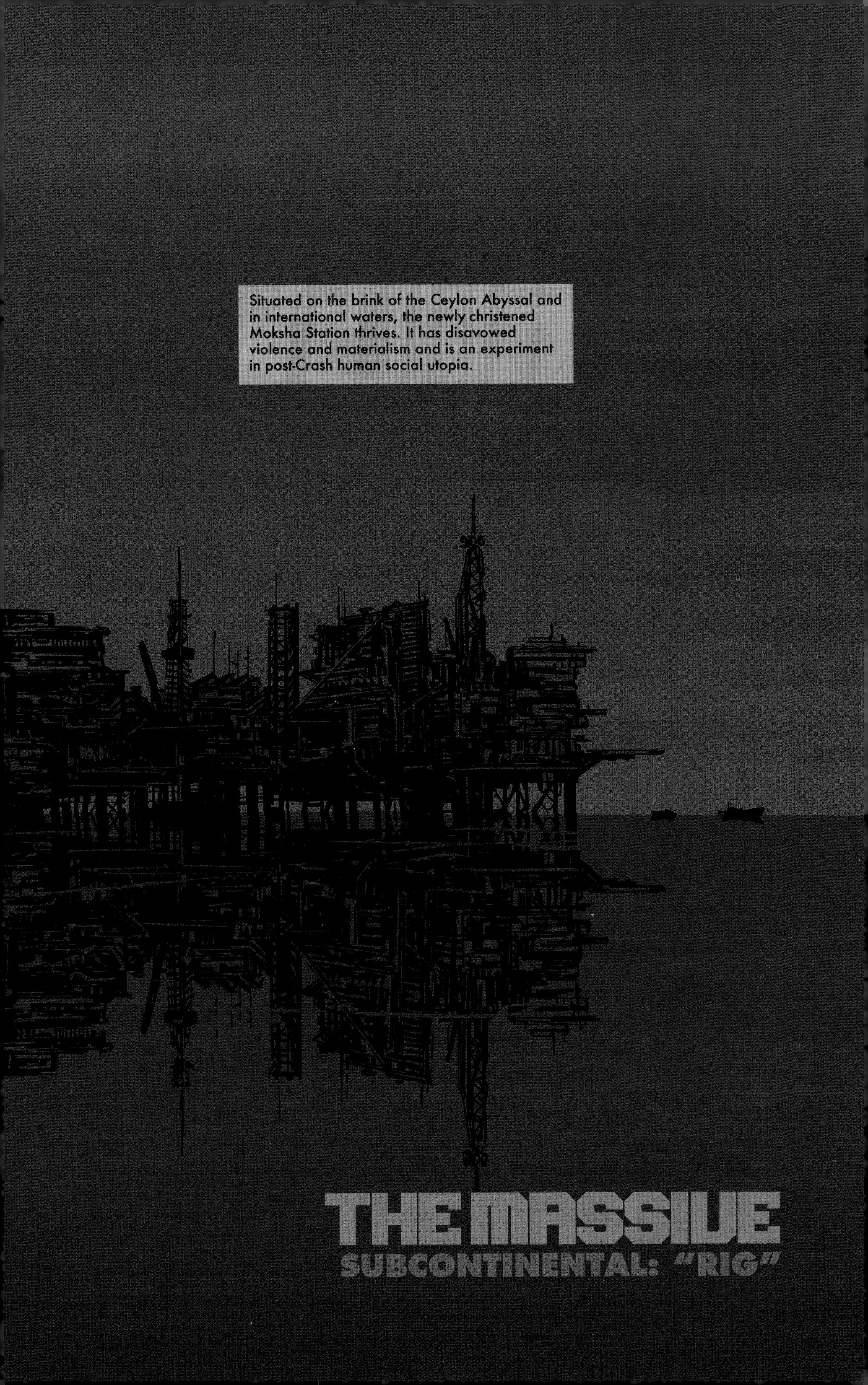
Situated on the brink of the Ceylon Abyssal and in international waters, the newly christened Moksha Station thrives. It has disavowed violence and materialism and is an experiment in post-Crash human social utopia.
THE MASSIVE
SUBCONTINENTAL: "RIG"

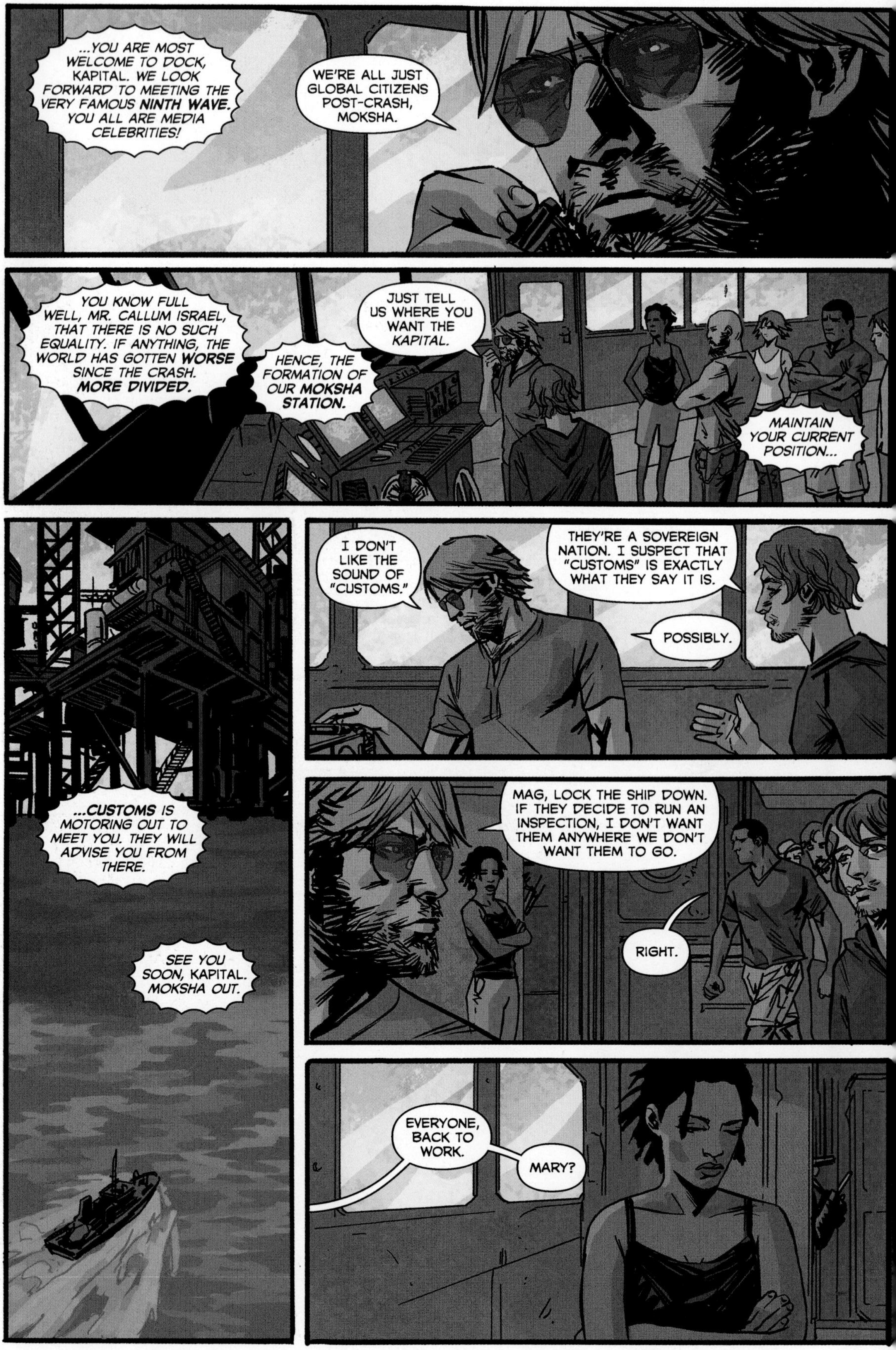
...YOU ARE MOST WELCOME TO DOCK, KAPITAL. WE LOOK FORWARD TO MEETING THE VERY FAMOUS **NINTH WAVE.** YOU ALL ARE MEDIA CELEBRITIES!
WE'RE ALL JUST GLOBAL CITIZENS POST-CRASH, MOKSHA.
YOU KNOW FULL WELL, MR. CALLUM ISRAEL, THAT THERE IS NO SUCH EQUALITY. IF ANYTHING, THE WORLD HAS GOTTEN **WORSE** SINCE THE CRASH. **MORE DIVIDED.**
HENCE, THE FORMATION OF OUR **MOKSHA STATION.**
JUST TELL US WHERE YOU WANT THE KAPITAL.
MAINTAIN YOUR CURRENT POSITION...
...CUSTOMS IS MOTORING OUT TO MEET YOU. THEY WILL ADVISE YOU FROM THERE.
SEE YOU SOON, KAPITAL. MOKSHA OUT.
I DON'T LIKE THE SOUND OF "CUSTOMS."
THEY'RE A SOVEREIGN NATION. I SUSPECT THAT "CUSTOMS" IS EXACTLY WHAT THEY SAY IT IS.
POSSIBLY.
MAG, LOCK THE SHIP DOWN. IF THEY DECIDE TO RUN AN INSPECTION, I DON'T WANT THEM ANYWHERE WE DON'T WANT THEM TO GO.
RIGHT.
EVERYONE, BACK TO WORK.
MARY?

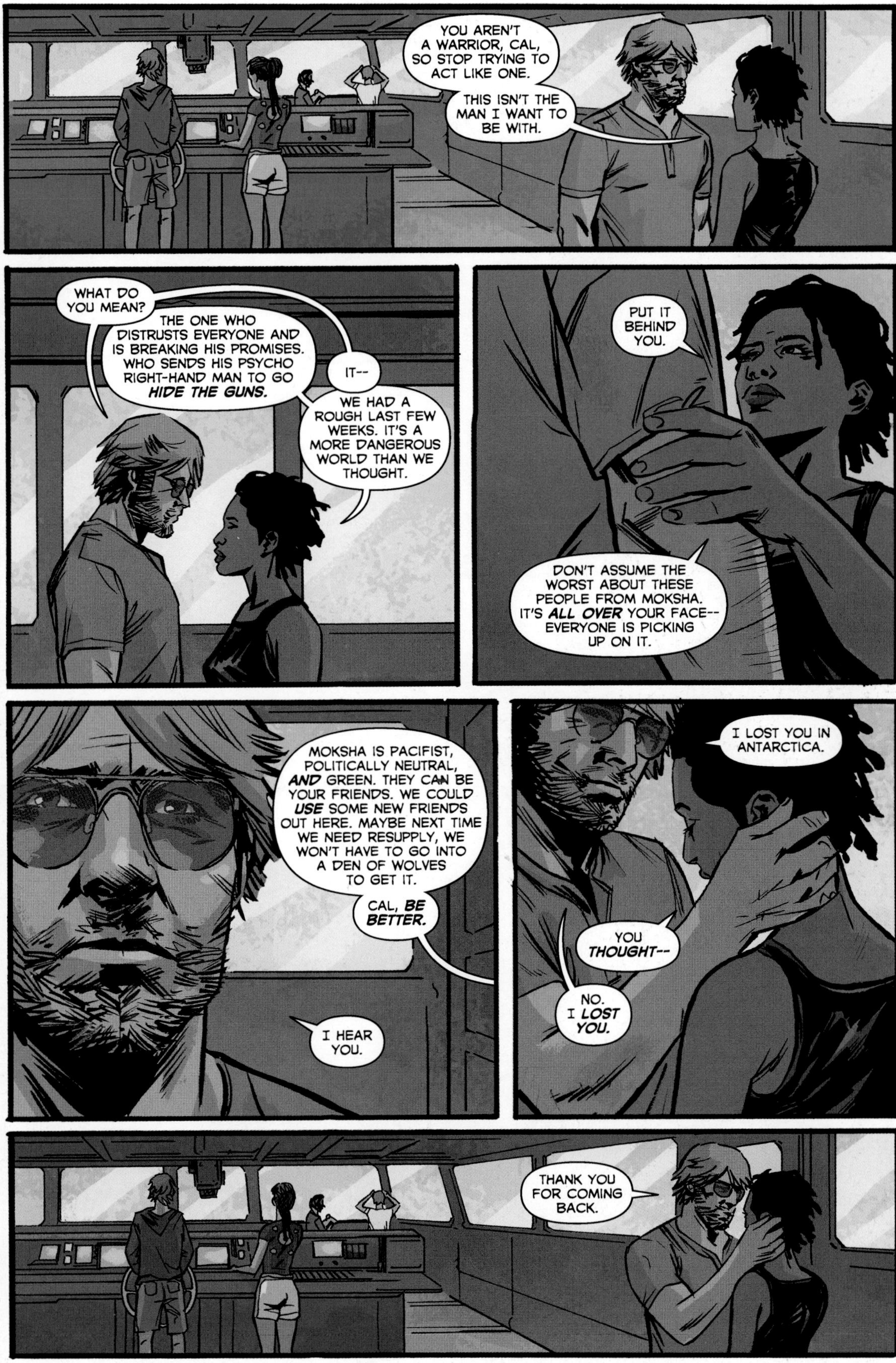
YOU AREN'T A WARRIOR, CAL, SO STOP TRYING TO ACT LIKE ONE.
THIS ISN'T THE MAN I WANT TO BE WITH.
WHAT DO YOU MEAN?
THE ONE WHO DISTRUSTS EVERYONE AND IS BREAKING HIS PROMISES. WHO SENDS HIS PSYCHO RIGHT-HAND MAN TO GO HIDE THE GUNS.
IT--
WE HAD A ROUGH LAST FEW WEEKS. IT'S A MORE DANGEROUS WORLD THAN WE THOUGHT.
PUT IT BEHIND YOU.
DON'T ASSUME THE WORST ABOUT THESE PEOPLE FROM MOKSHA. IT'S ALL OVER YOUR FACE-- EVERYONE IS PICKING UP ON IT.
MOKSHA IS PACIFIST, POLITICALLY NEUTRAL, AND GREEN. THEY CAN BE YOUR FRIENDS. WE COULD USE SOME NEW FRIENDS OUT HERE. MAYBE NEXT TIME WE NEED RESUPPLY, WE WON'T HAVE TO GO INTO A DEN OF WOLVES TO GET IT.
CAL, BE BETTER.
I HEAR YOU.
I LOST YOU IN ANTARCTICA.
YOU THOUGHT--
NO. I LOST YOU.
THANK YOU FOR COMING BACK.

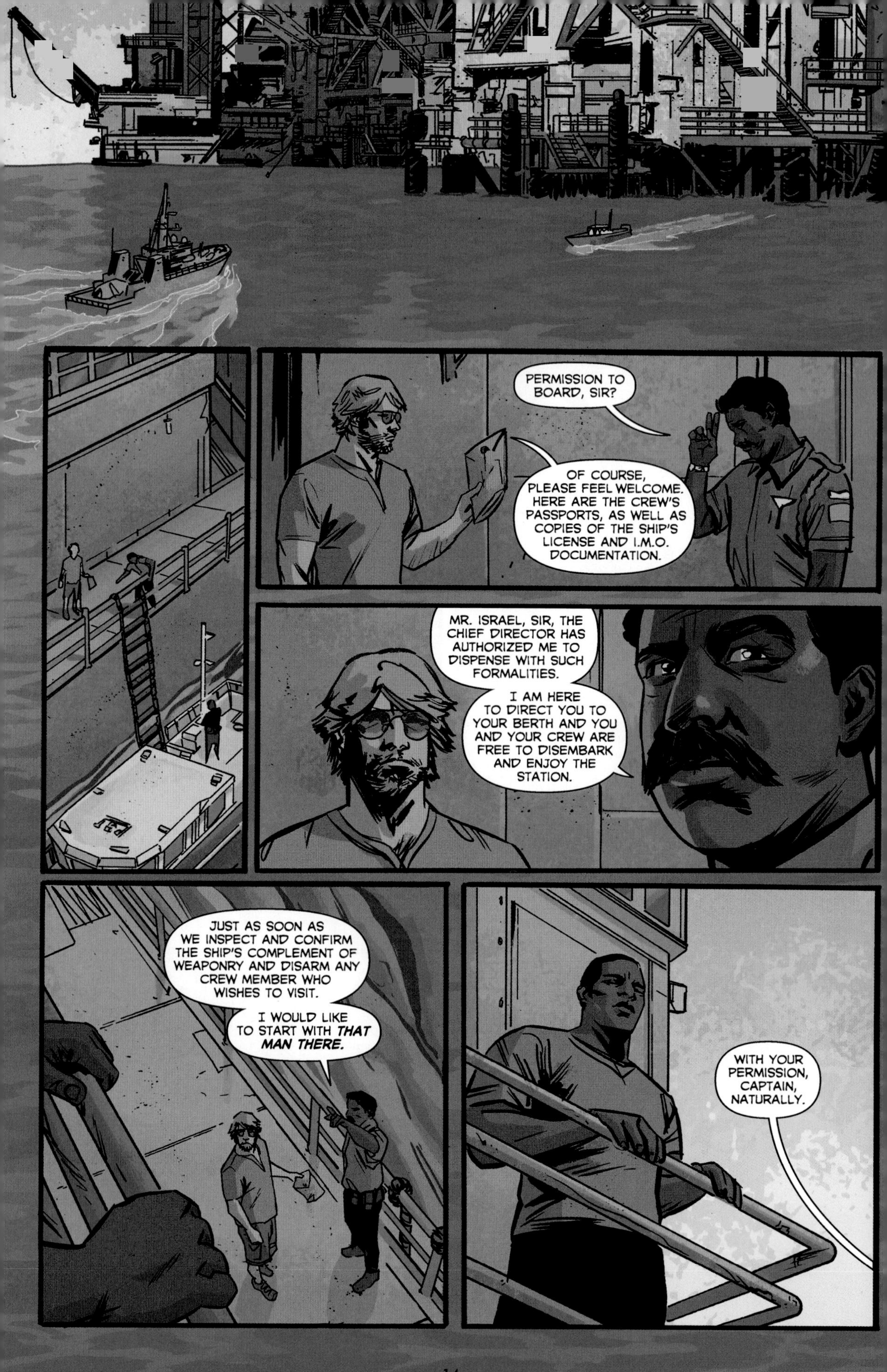
PERMISSION TO BOARD, SIR?
OF COURSE, PLEASE FEEL WELCOME. HERE ARE THE CREW'S PASSPORTS, AS WELL AS COPIES OF THE SHIP'S LICENSE AND I.M.O. DOCUMENTATION.
MR. ISRAEL, SIR, THE CHIEF DIRECTOR HAS AUTHORIZED ME TO DISPENSE WITH SUCH FORMALITIES.
I AM HERE TO DIRECT YOU TO YOUR BERTH AND YOU AND YOUR CREW ARE FREE TO DISEMBARK AND ENJOY THE STATION.
JUST AS SOON AS WE INSPECT AND CONFIRM THE SHIP'S COMPLEMENT OF WEAPONRY AND DISARM ANY CREW MEMBER WHO WISHES TO VISIT.
I WOULD LIKE TO START WITH *THAT MAN THERE.*
WITH YOUR PERMISSION, CAPTAIN, NATURALLY.

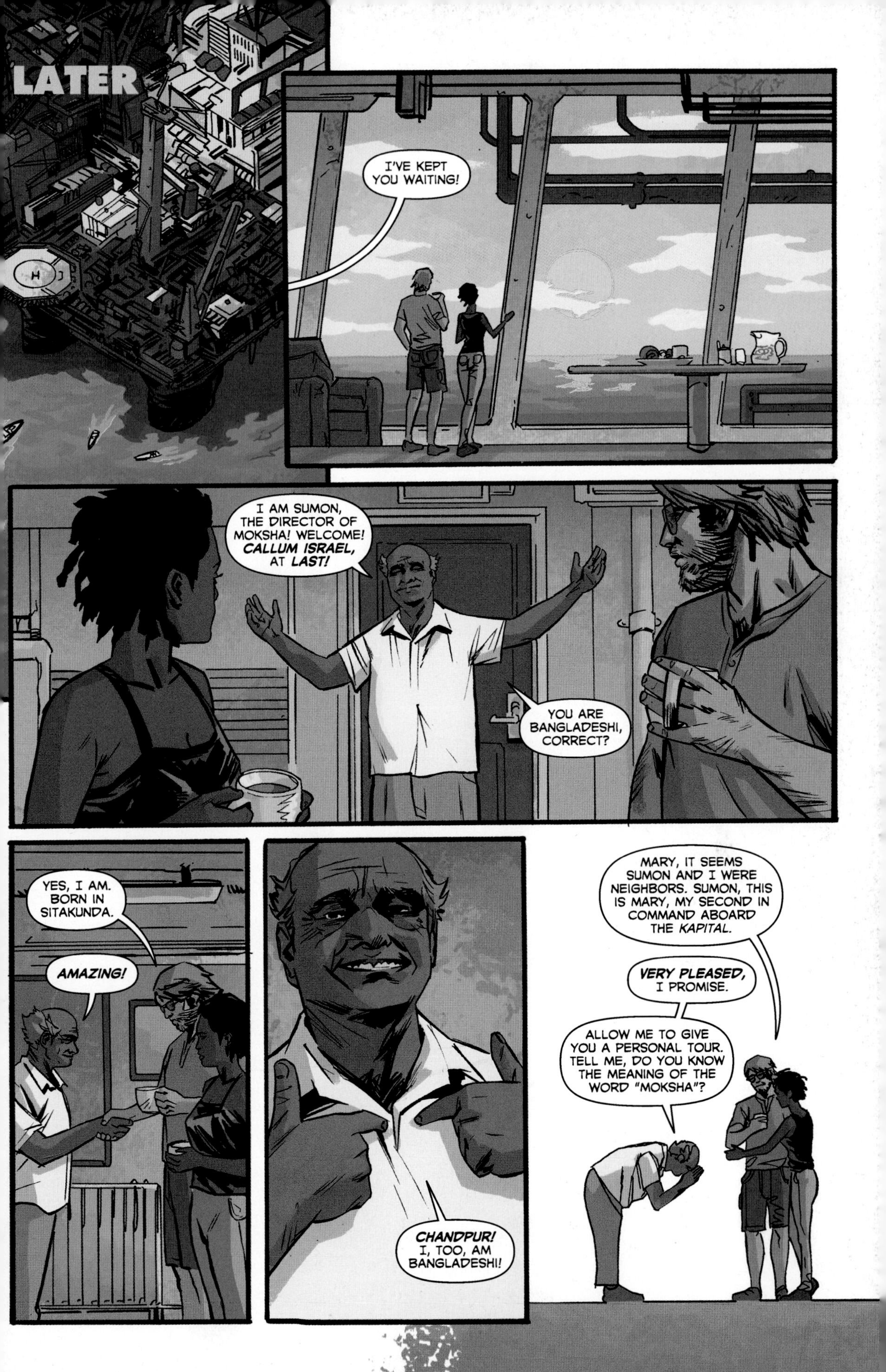
LATER
I'VE KEPT YOU WAITING!
I AM SUMON, THE DIRECTOR OF MOKSHA! WELCOME! CALLUM ISRAEL, AT LAST!
YOU ARE BANGLADESHI, CORRECT?
YES, I AM. BORN IN SITAKUNDA.
AMAZING!
CHANDPUR! I, TOO, AM BANGLADESHI!
MARY, IT SEEMS SUMON AND I WERE NEIGHBORS. SUMON, THIS IS MARY, MY SECOND IN COMMAND ABOARD THE KAPITAL.
VERY PLEASED, I PROMISE.
ALLOW ME TO GIVE YOU A PERSONAL TOUR. TELL ME, DO YOU KNOW THE MEANING OF THE WORD "MOKSHA"?

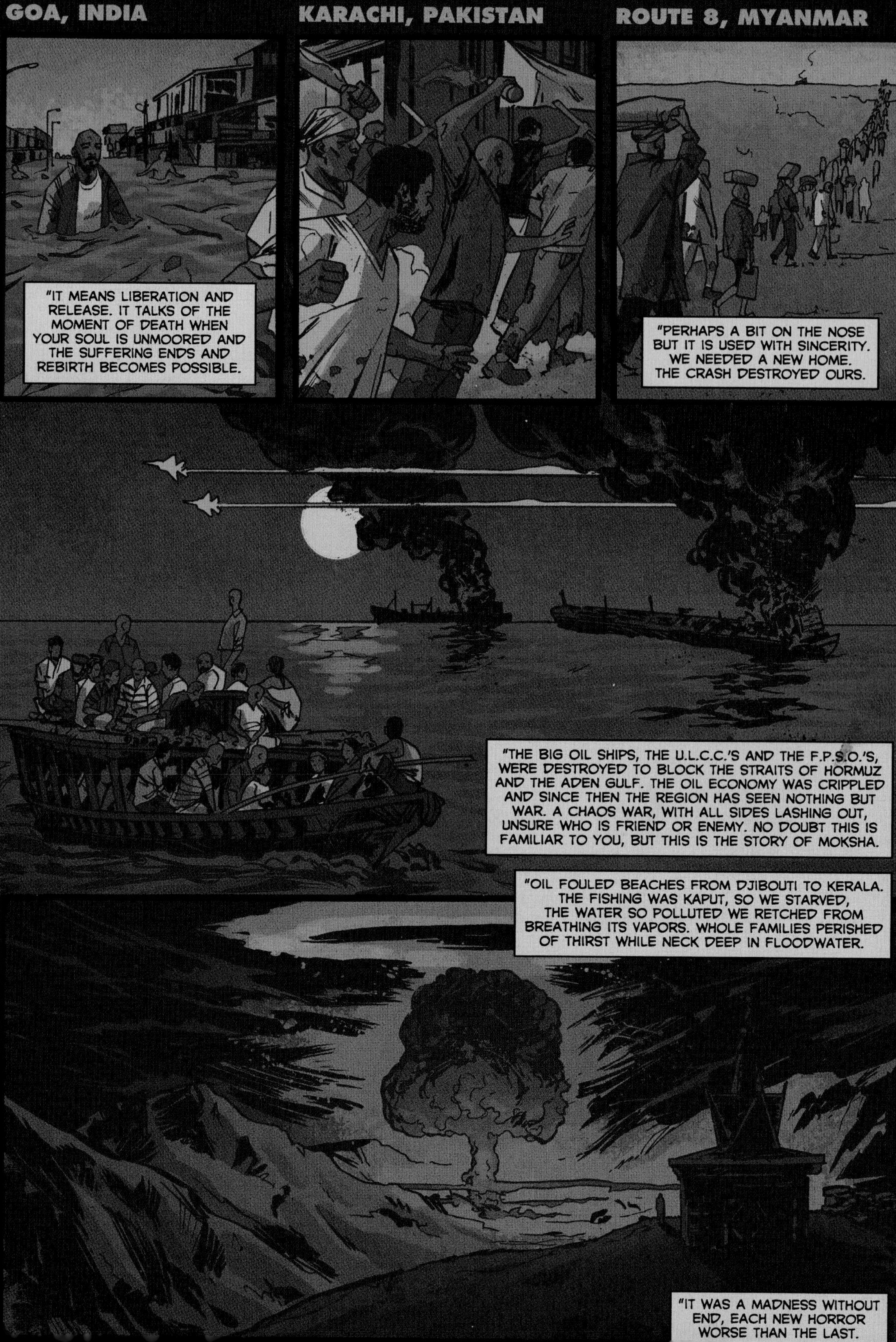
GOA, INDIA
"IT MEANS LIBERATION AND RELEASE. IT TALKS OF THE MOMENT OF DEATH WHEN YOUR SOUL IS UNMOORED AND THE SUFFERING ENDS AND REBIRTH BECOMES POSSIBLE.
KARACHI, PAKISTAN
ROUTE 8, MYANMAR
"PERHAPS A BIT ON THE NOSE BUT IT IS USED WITH SINCERITY. WE NEEDED A NEW HOME. THE CRASH DESTROYED OURS.
"THE BIG OIL SHIPS, THE U.L.C.C.'S AND THE F.P.S.O.'S, WERE DESTROYED TO BLOCK THE STRAITS OF HORMUZ AND THE ADEN GULF. THE OIL ECONOMY WAS CRIPPLED AND SINCE THEN THE REGION HAS SEEN NOTHING BUT WAR. A CHAOS WAR, WITH ALL SIDES LASHING OUT, UNSURE WHO IS FRIEND OR ENEMY. NO DOUBT THIS IS FAMILIAR TO YOU, BUT THIS IS THE STORY OF MOKSHA.
"OIL FOULED BEACHES FROM DJIBOUTI TO KERALA. THE FISHING WAS KAPUT, SO WE STARVED, THE WATER SO POLLUTED WE RETCHED FROM BREATHING ITS VAPORS. WHOLE FAMILIES PERISHED OF THIRST WHILE NECK DEEP IN FLOODWATER.
"IT WAS A MADNESS WITHOUT END, EACH NEW HORROR WORSE THAN THE LAST.

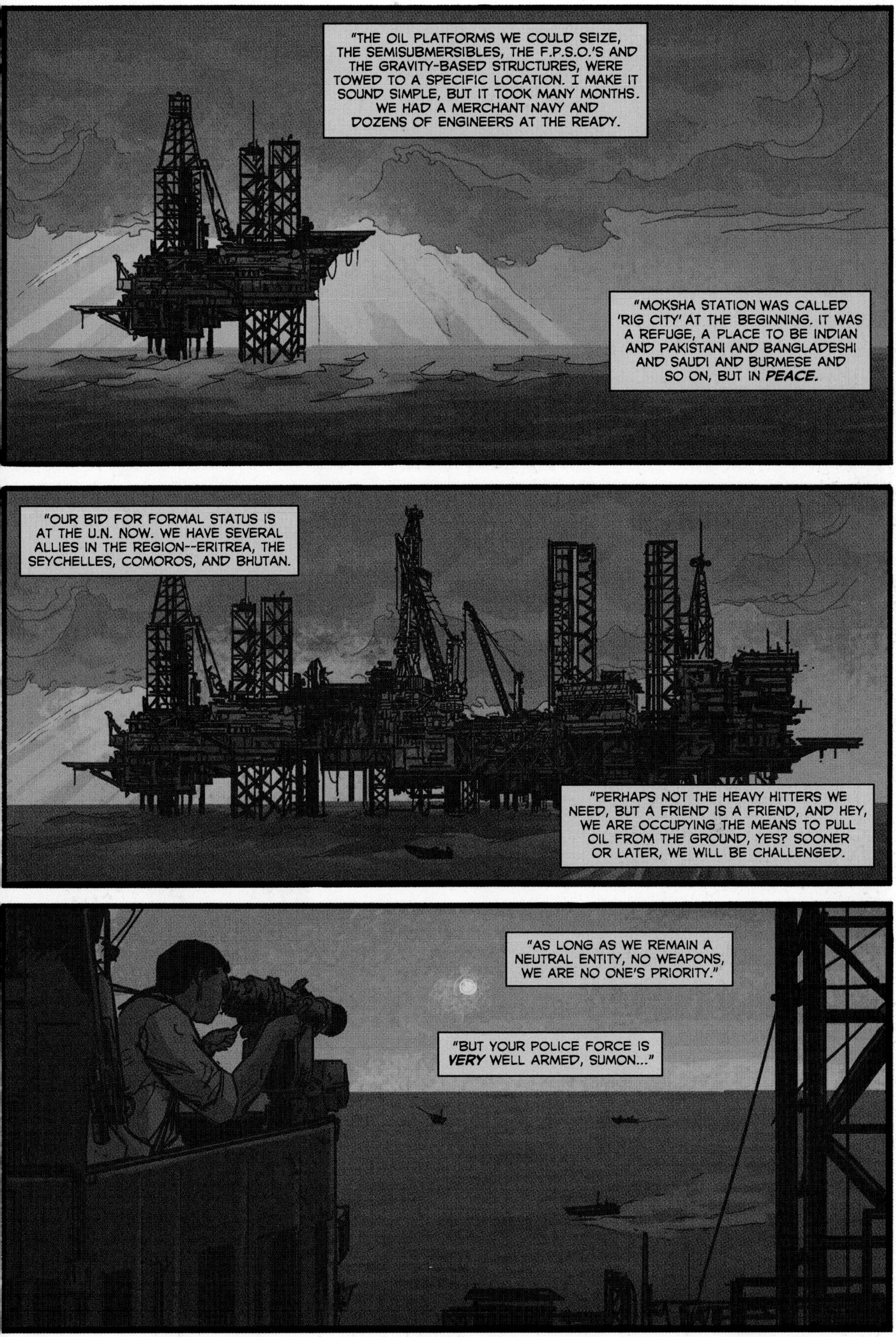
"THE OIL PLATFORMS WE COULD SEIZE, THE SEMISUBMERSIBLES, THE F.P.S.O.'S AND THE GRAVITY-BASED STRUCTURES, WERE TOWED TO A SPECIFIC LOCATION. I MAKE IT SOUND SIMPLE, BUT IT TOOK MANY MONTHS. WE HAD A MERCHANT NAVY AND DOZENS OF ENGINEERS AT THE READY.
"MOKSHA STATION WAS CALLED 'RIG CITY' AT THE BEGINNING. IT WAS A REFUGE, A PLACE TO BE INDIAN AND PAKISTANI AND BANGLADESHI AND SAUDI AND BURMESE AND SO ON, BUT IN ***PEACE.***
"OUR BID FOR FORMAL STATUS IS AT THE U.N. NOW. WE HAVE SEVERAL ALLIES IN THE REGION--ERITREA, THE SEYCHELLES, COMOROS, AND BHUTAN.
"PERHAPS NOT THE HEAVY HITTERS WE NEED, BUT A FRIEND IS A FRIEND, AND HEY, WE ARE OCCUPYING THE MEANS TO PULL OIL FROM THE GROUND, YES? SOONER OR LATER, WE WILL BE CHALLENGED.
"AS LONG AS WE REMAIN A NEUTRAL ENTITY, NO WEAPONS, WE ARE NO ONE'S PRIORITY."
"BUT YOUR POLICE FORCE IS ***VERY*** WELL ARMED, SUMON..."

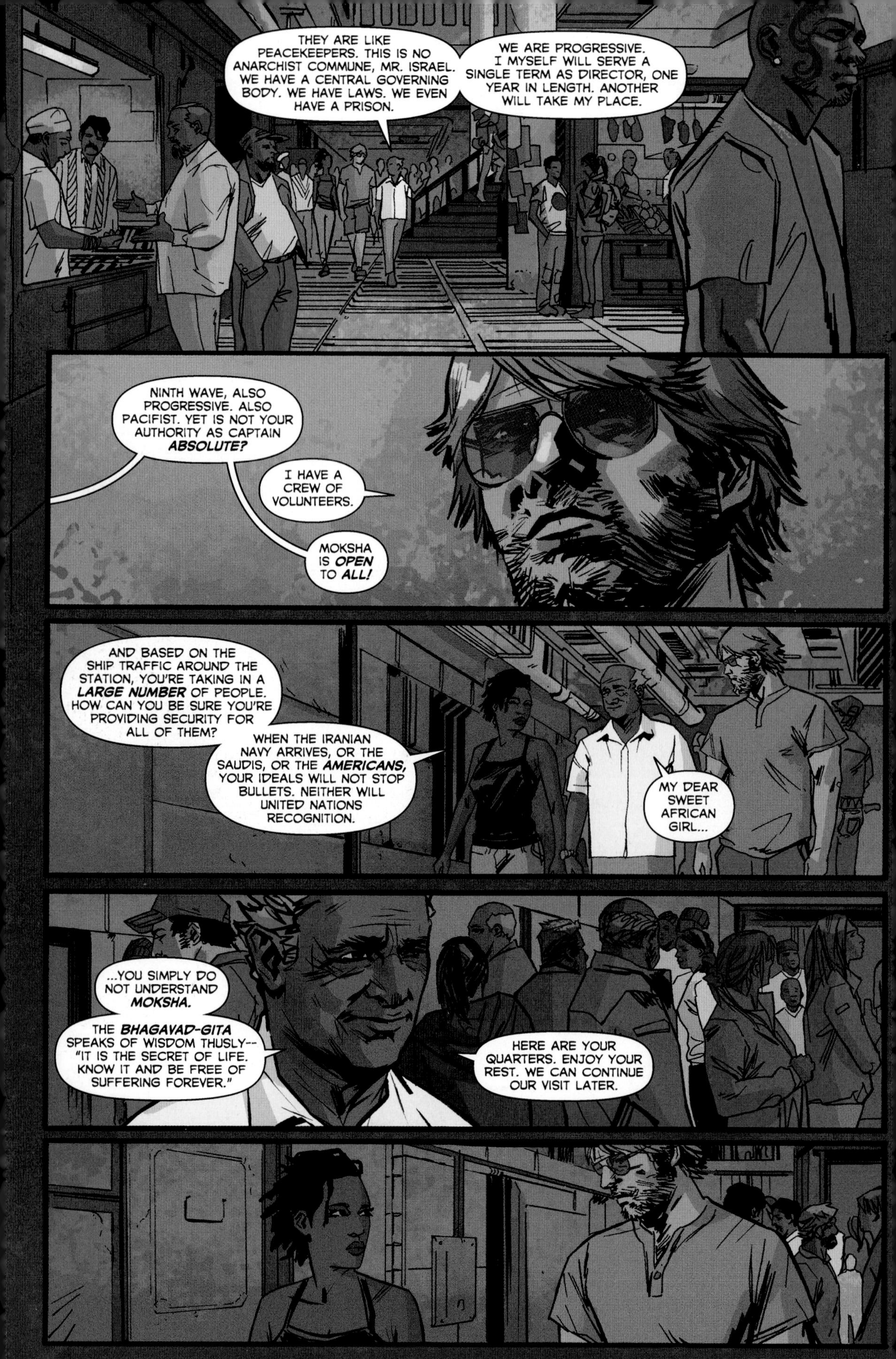
THEY ARE LIKE PEACEKEEPERS. THIS IS NO ANARCHIST COMMUNE, MR. ISRAEL. WE HAVE A CENTRAL GOVERNING BODY. WE HAVE LAWS. WE EVEN HAVE A PRISON.
WE ARE PROGRESSIVE. I MYSELF WILL SERVE A SINGLE TERM AS DIRECTOR, ONE YEAR IN LENGTH. ANOTHER WILL TAKE MY PLACE.
NINTH WAVE, ALSO PROGRESSIVE. ALSO PACIFIST. YET IS NOT YOUR AUTHORITY AS CAPTAIN ***ABSOLUTE?***
I HAVE A CREW OF VOLUNTEERS.
MOKSHA IS ***OPEN*** TO ***ALL!***
AND BASED ON THE SHIP TRAFFIC AROUND THE STATION, YOU'RE TAKING IN A ***LARGE NUMBER*** OF PEOPLE. HOW CAN YOU BE SURE YOU'RE PROVIDING SECURITY FOR ALL OF THEM?
WHEN THE IRANIAN NAVY ARRIVES, OR THE SAUDIS, OR THE ***AMERICANS,*** YOUR IDEALS WILL NOT STOP BULLETS. NEITHER WILL UNITED NATIONS RECOGNITION.
MY DEAR SWEET AFRICAN GIRL...
...YOU SIMPLY DO NOT UNDERSTAND ***MOKSHA.***
THE ***BHAGAVAD-GITA*** SPEAKS OF WISDOM THUSLY-- "IT IS THE SECRET OF LIFE. KNOW IT AND BE FREE OF SUFFERING FOREVER."
HERE ARE YOUR QUARTERS. ENJOY YOUR REST. WE CAN CONTINUE OUR VISIT LATER.

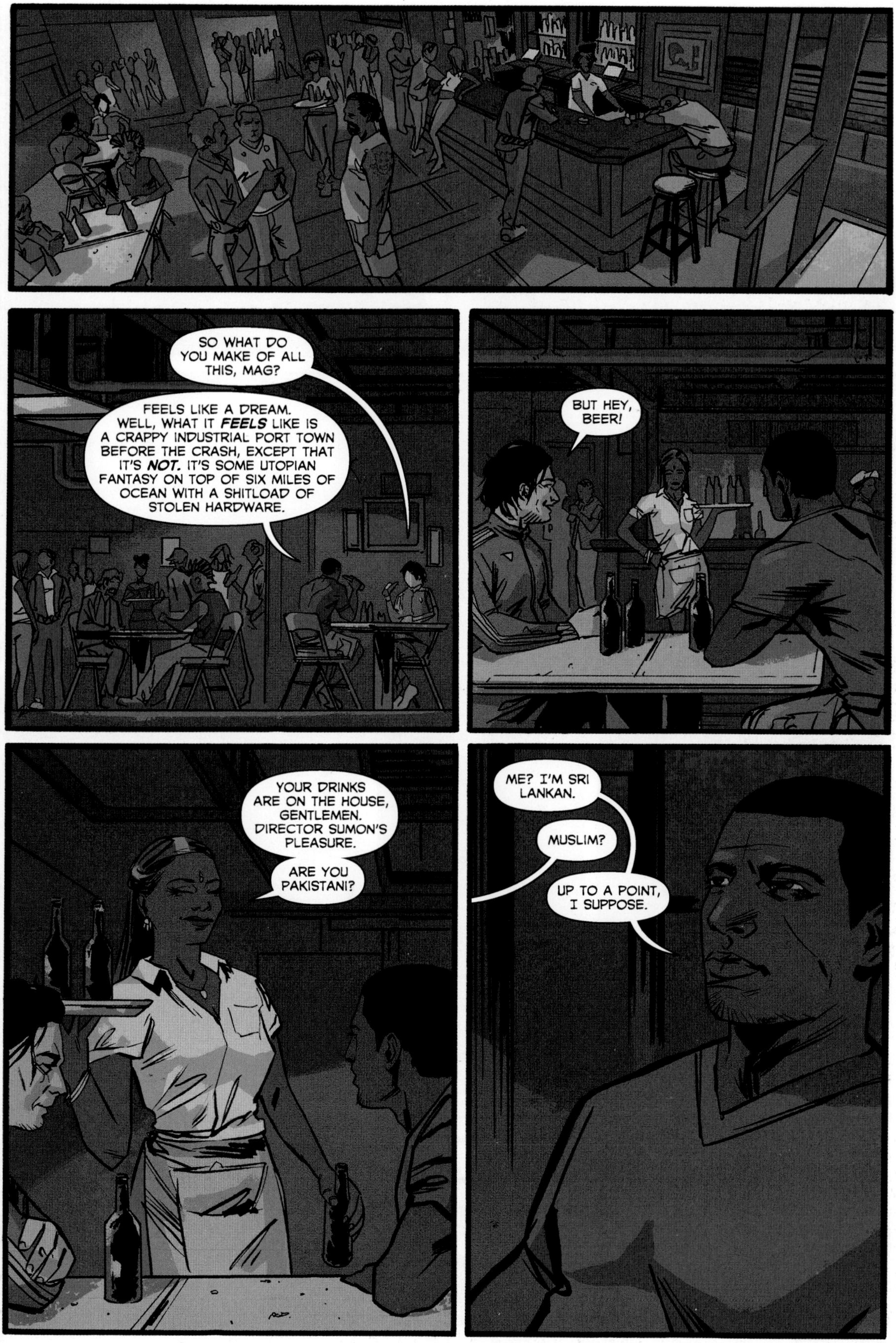
SO WHAT DO YOU MAKE OF ALL THIS, MAG?
FEELS LIKE A DREAM. WELL, WHAT IT FEELS LIKE IS A CRAPPY INDUSTRIAL PORT TOWN BEFORE THE CRASH, EXCEPT THAT IT'S NOT. IT'S SOME UTOPIAN FANTASY ON TOP OF SIX MILES OF OCEAN WITH A SHITLOAD OF STOLEN HARDWARE.
BUT HEY, BEER!
YOUR DRINKS ARE ON THE HOUSE, GENTLEMEN. DIRECTOR SUMON'S PLEASURE.
ARE YOU PAKISTANI?
ME? I'M SRI LANKAN.
MUSLIM?
UP TO A POINT, I SUPPOSE.

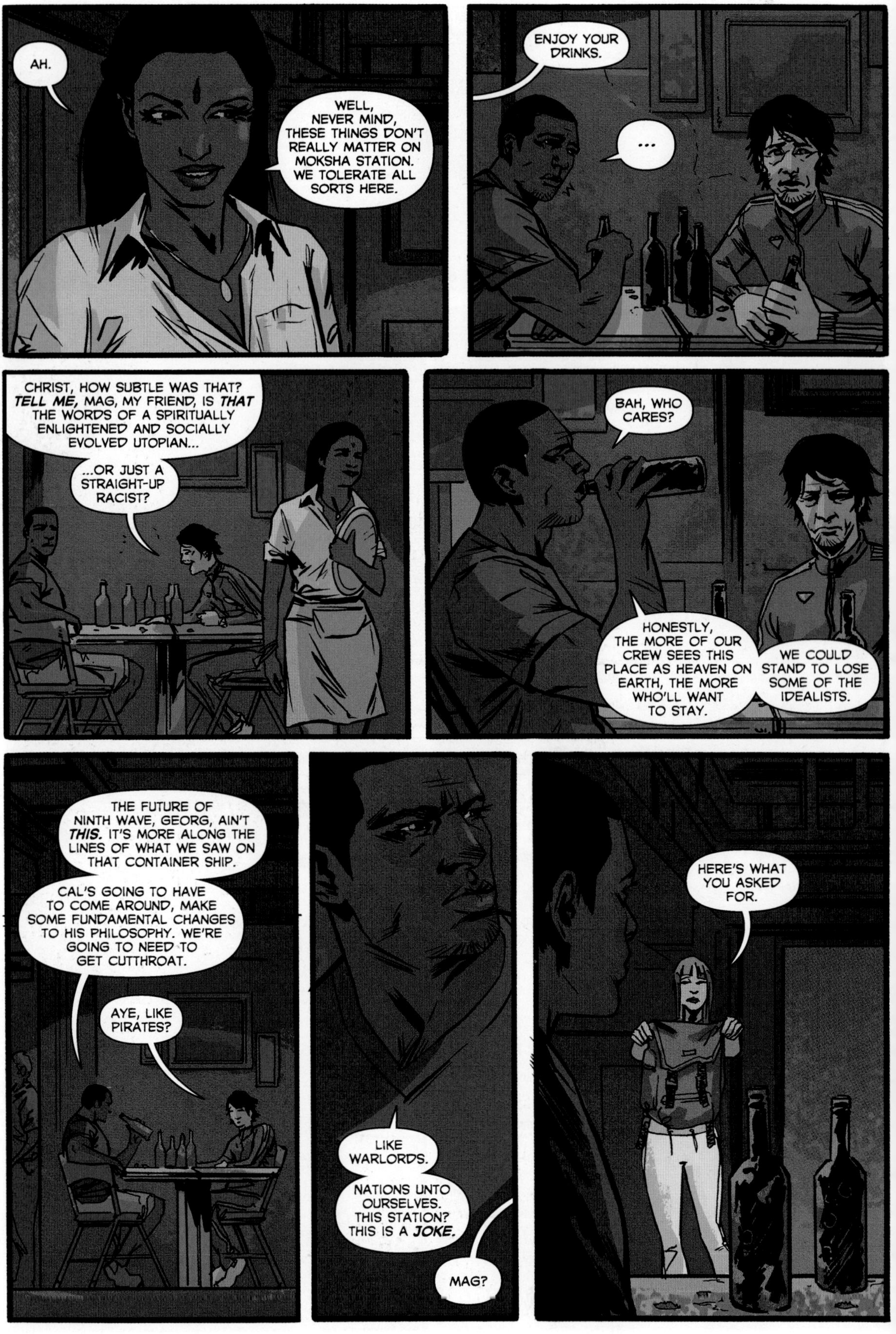
AH.
WELL, NEVER MIND, THESE THINGS DON'T REALLY MATTER ON MOKSHA STATION. WE TOLERATE ALL SORTS HERE.
ENJOY YOUR DRINKS.
...
CHRIST, HOW SUBTLE WAS THAT? *TELL ME,* MAG, MY FRIEND, IS *THAT* THE WORDS OF A SPIRITUALLY ENLIGHTENED AND SOCIALLY EVOLVED UTOPIAN...
...OR JUST A STRAIGHT-UP RACIST?
BAH, WHO CARES?
HONESTLY, THE MORE OF OUR CREW SEES THIS PLACE AS HEAVEN ON EARTH, THE MORE WHO'LL WANT TO STAY.
WE COULD STAND TO LOSE SOME OF THE IDEALISTS.
THE FUTURE OF NINTH WAVE, GEORG, AIN'T *THIS.* IT'S MORE ALONG THE LINES OF WHAT WE SAW ON THAT CONTAINER SHIP.
CAL'S GOING TO HAVE TO COME AROUND, MAKE SOME FUNDAMENTAL CHANGES TO HIS PHILOSOPHY. WE'RE GOING TO NEED TO GET CUTTHROAT.
AYE, LIKE PIRATES?
LIKE WARLORDS.
NATIONS UNTO OURSELVES. THIS STATION? THIS IS A *JOKE.*
MAG?
HERE'S WHAT YOU ASKED FOR.

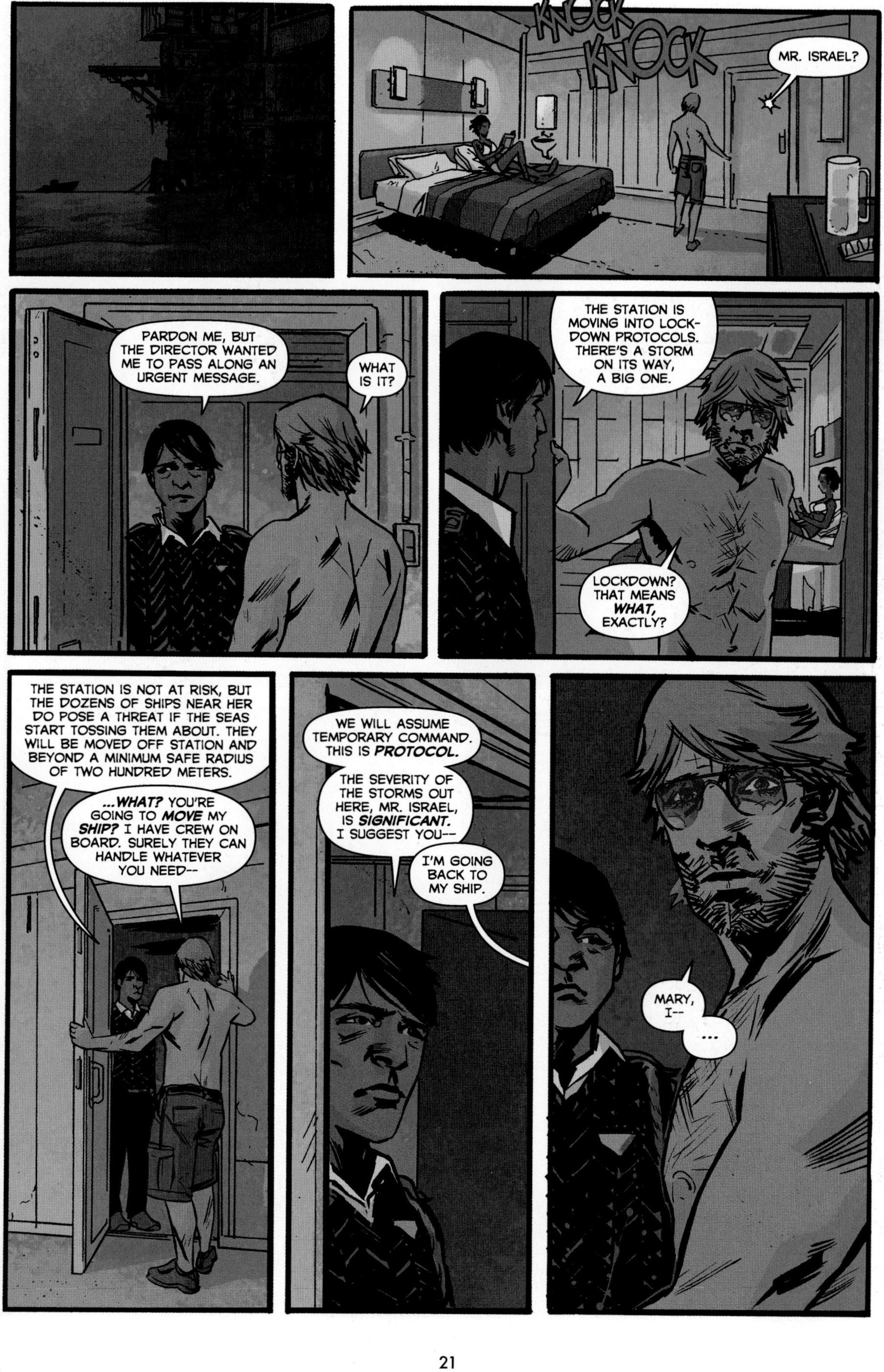
KNOCK KNOCK
MR. ISRAEL?
PARDON ME, BUT THE DIRECTOR WANTED ME TO PASS ALONG AN URGENT MESSAGE.
WHAT IS IT?
THE STATION IS MOVING INTO LOCK-DOWN PROTOCOLS. THERE'S A STORM ON ITS WAY, A BIG ONE.
LOCKDOWN? THAT MEANS WHAT, EXACTLY?
THE STATION IS NOT AT RISK, BUT THE DOZENS OF SHIPS NEAR HER DO POSE A THREAT IF THE SEAS START TOSSING THEM ABOUT. THEY WILL BE MOVED OFF STATION AND BEYOND A MINIMUM SAFE RADIUS OF TWO HUNDRED METERS.
...WHAT? YOU'RE GOING TO MOVE MY SHIP? I HAVE CREW ON BOARD. SURELY THEY CAN HANDLE WHATEVER YOU NEED--
WE WILL ASSUME TEMPORARY COMMAND. THIS IS PROTOCOL.
THE SEVERITY OF THE STORMS OUT HERE, MR. ISRAEL, IS SIGNIFICANT. I SUGGEST YOU--
I'M GOING BACK TO MY SHIP.
MARY, I--
...

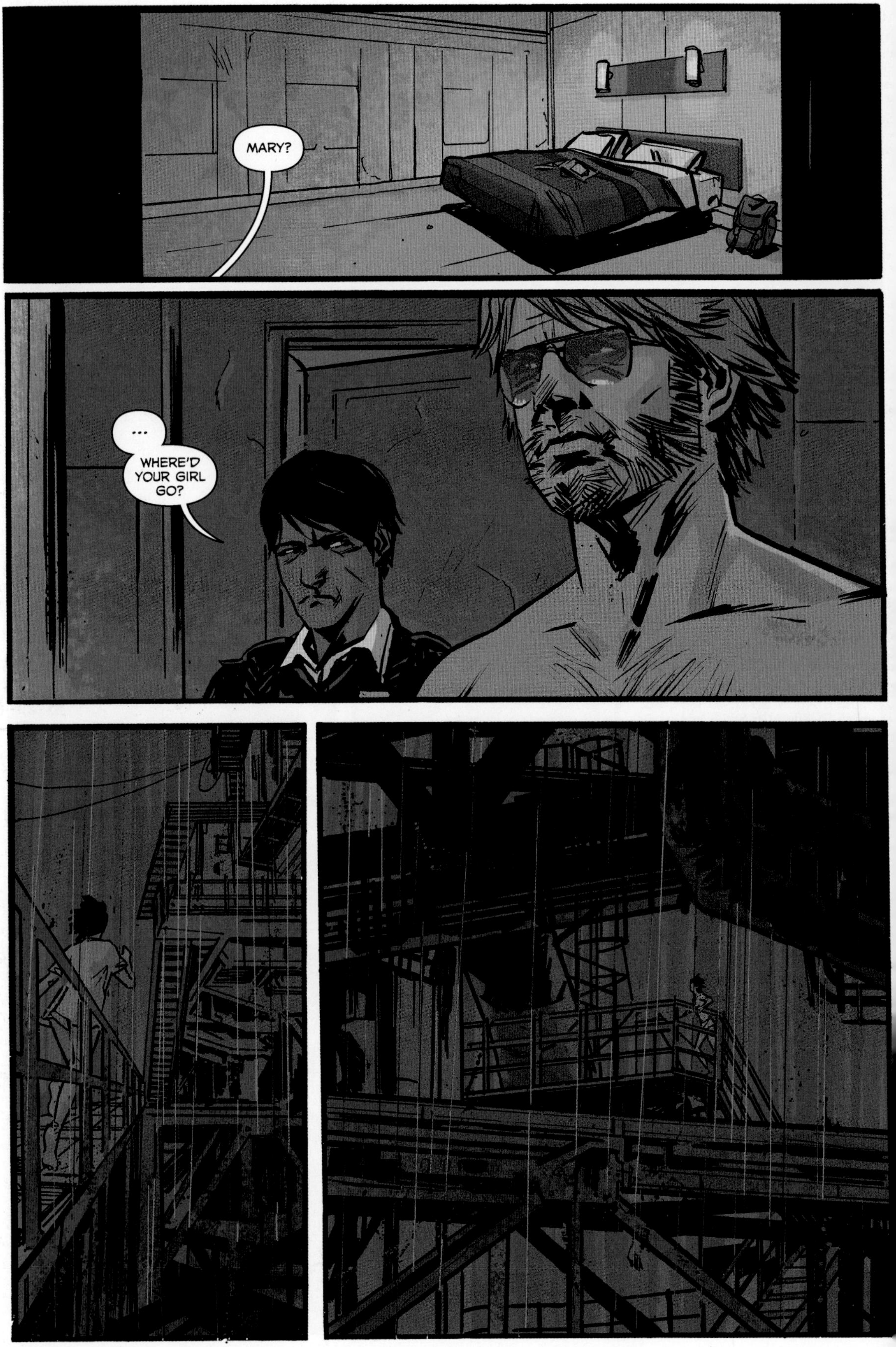
MARY?
...
WHERE'D YOUR GIRL GO?

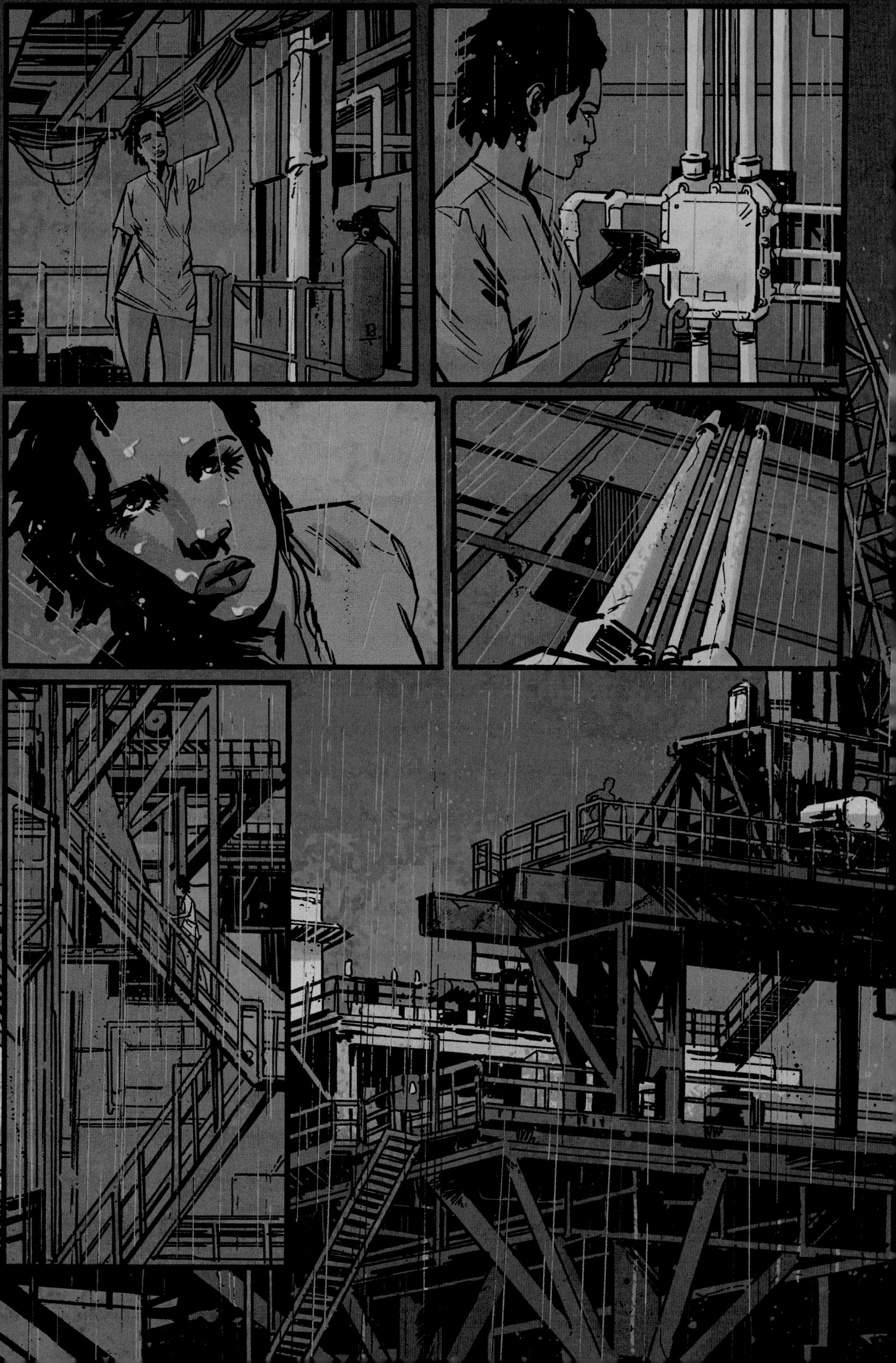

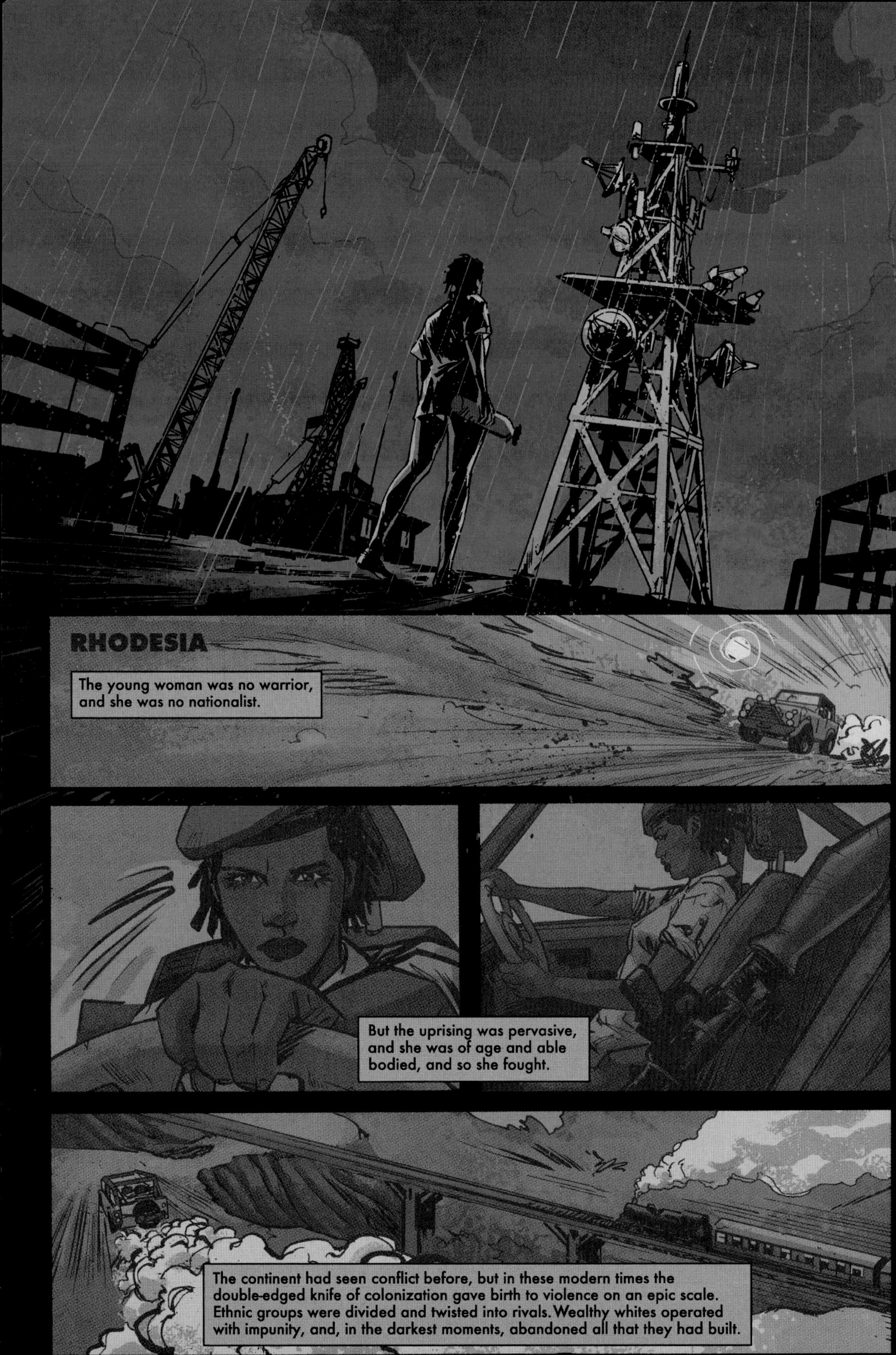
RHODESIA
The young woman was no warrior, and she was no nationalist.
But the uprising was pervasive, and she was of age and able bodied, and so she fought.
The continent had seen conflict before, but in these modern times the double-edged knife of colonization gave birth to violence on an epic scale. Ethnic groups were divided and twisted into rivals. Wealthy whites operated with impunity, and, in the darkest moments, abandoned all that they had built.

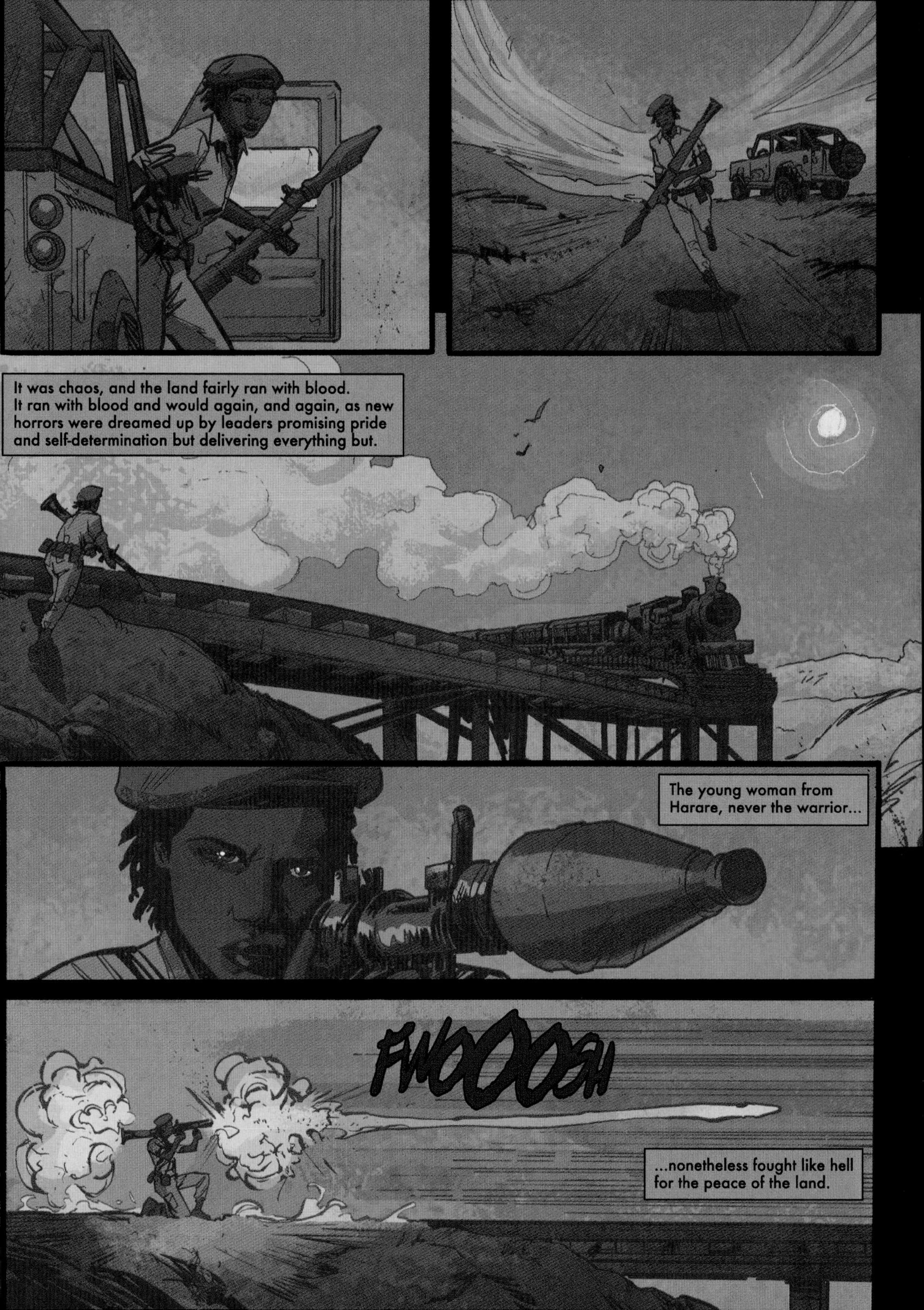
It was chaos, and the land fairly ran with blood.
It ran with blood and would again, and again, as new horrors were dreamed up by leaders promising pride and self-determination but delivering everything but.
The young woman from Harare, never the warrior...
FWOOOOSH
...nonetheless fought like hell for the peace of the land.

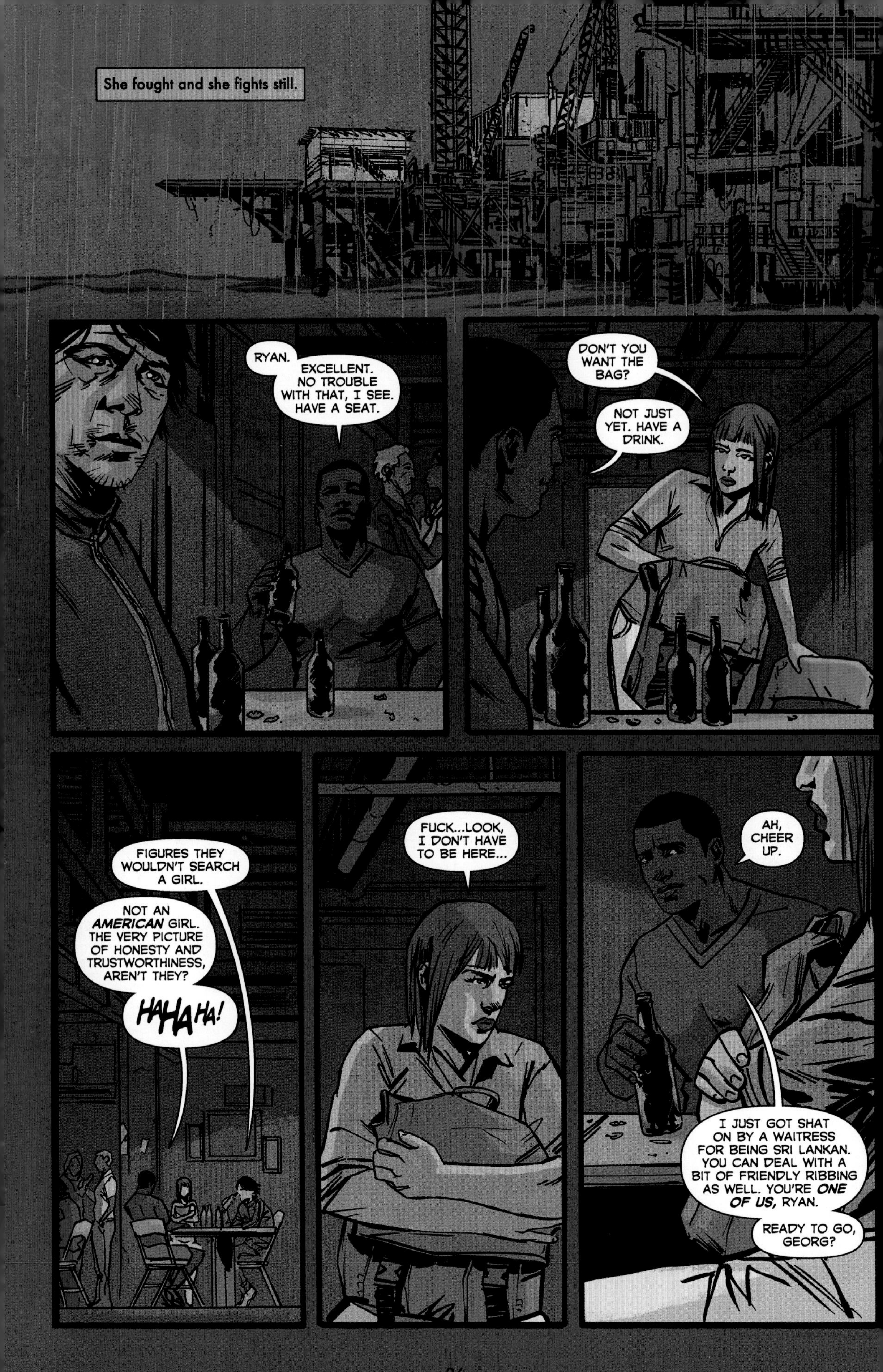

She fought and she fights still.
RYAN.
EXCELLENT. NO TROUBLE WITH THAT, I SEE. HAVE A SEAT.
DON'T YOU WANT THE BAG?
NOT JUST YET. HAVE A DRINK.
FIGURES THEY WOULDN'T SEARCH A GIRL.
NOT AN AMERICAN GIRL. THE VERY PICTURE OF HONESTY AND TRUSTWORTHINESS, AREN'T THEY?
HAHAHA!
FUCK...LOOK, I DON'T HAVE TO BE HERE...
AH, CHEER UP.
I JUST GOT SHAT ON BY A WAITRESS FOR BEING SRI LANKAN. YOU CAN DEAL WITH A BIT OF FRIENDLY RIBBING AS WELL. YOU'RE ONE OF US, RYAN.
READY TO GO, GEORG?

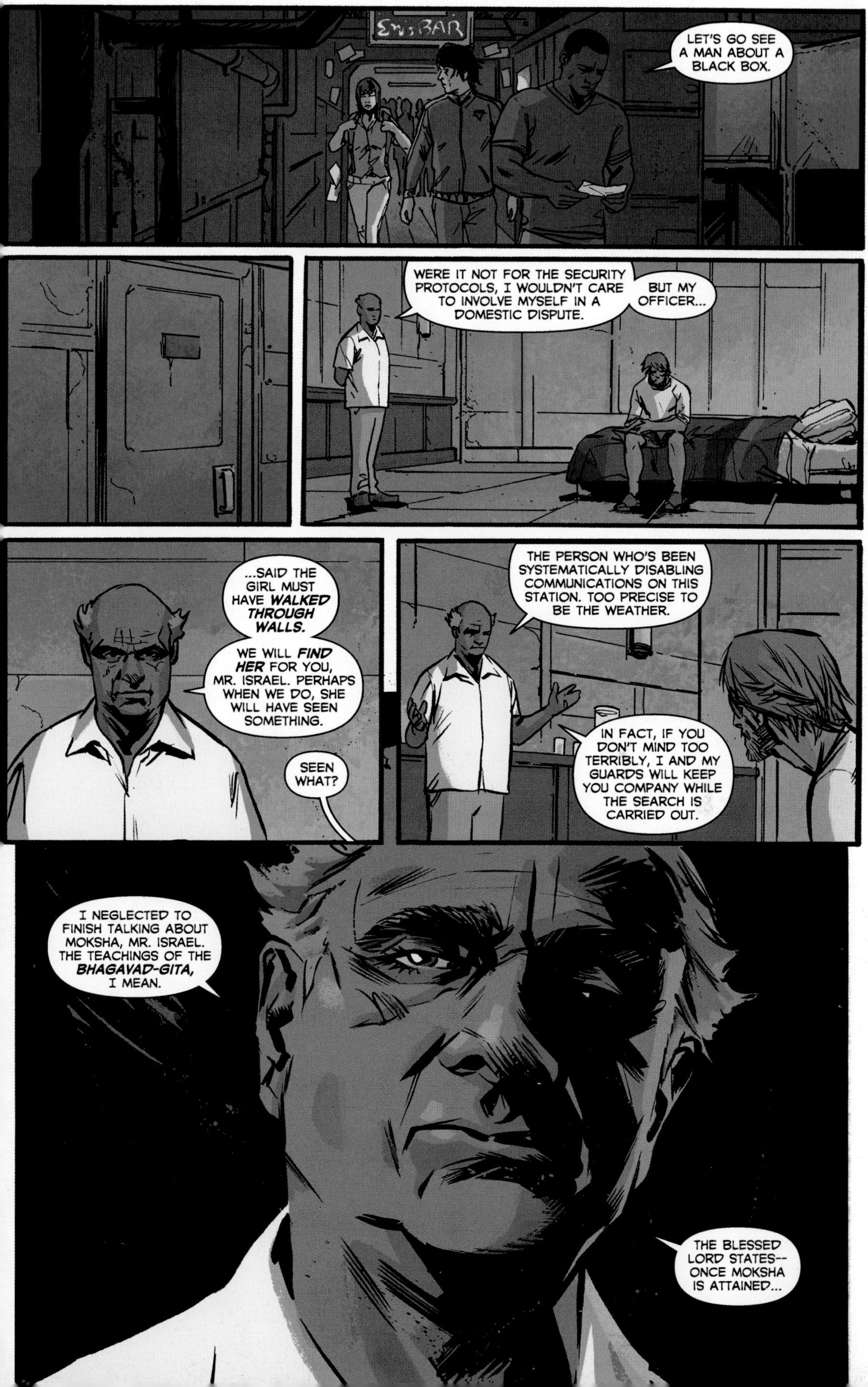

LET'S GO SEE A MAN ABOUT A BLACK BOX.
WERE IT NOT FOR THE SECURITY PROTOCOLS, I WOULDN'T CARE TO INVOLVE MYSELF IN A DOMESTIC DISPUTE.
BUT MY OFFICER...
...SAID THE GIRL MUST HAVE *WALKED THROUGH WALLS.*
WE WILL *FIND HER* FOR YOU, MR. ISRAEL. PERHAPS WHEN WE DO, SHE WILL HAVE SEEN SOMETHING.
SEEN WHAT?
THE PERSON WHO'S BEEN SYSTEMATICALLY DISABLING COMMUNICATIONS ON THIS STATION. TOO PRECISE TO BE THE WEATHER.
IN FACT, IF YOU DON'T MIND TOO TERRIBLY, I AND MY GUARDS WILL KEEP YOU COMPANY WHILE THE SEARCH IS CARRIED OUT.
I NEGLECTED TO FINISH TALKING ABOUT MOKSHA, MR. ISRAEL. THE TEACHINGS OF THE *BHAGAVAD-GITA,* I MEAN.
THE BLESSED LORD STATES-- ONCE MOKSHA IS ATTAINED...

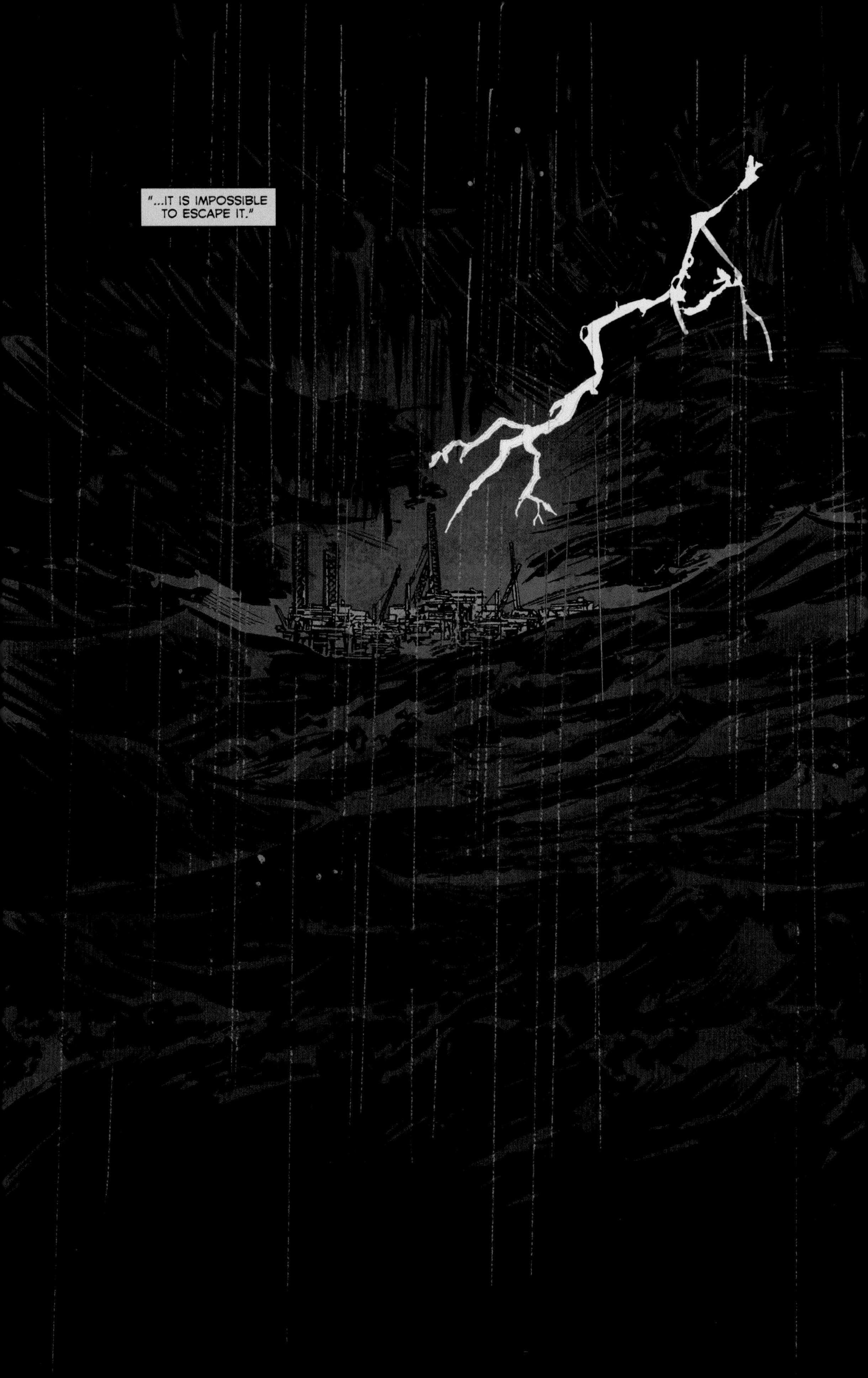
"...IT IS IMPOSSIBLE TO ESCAPE IT."

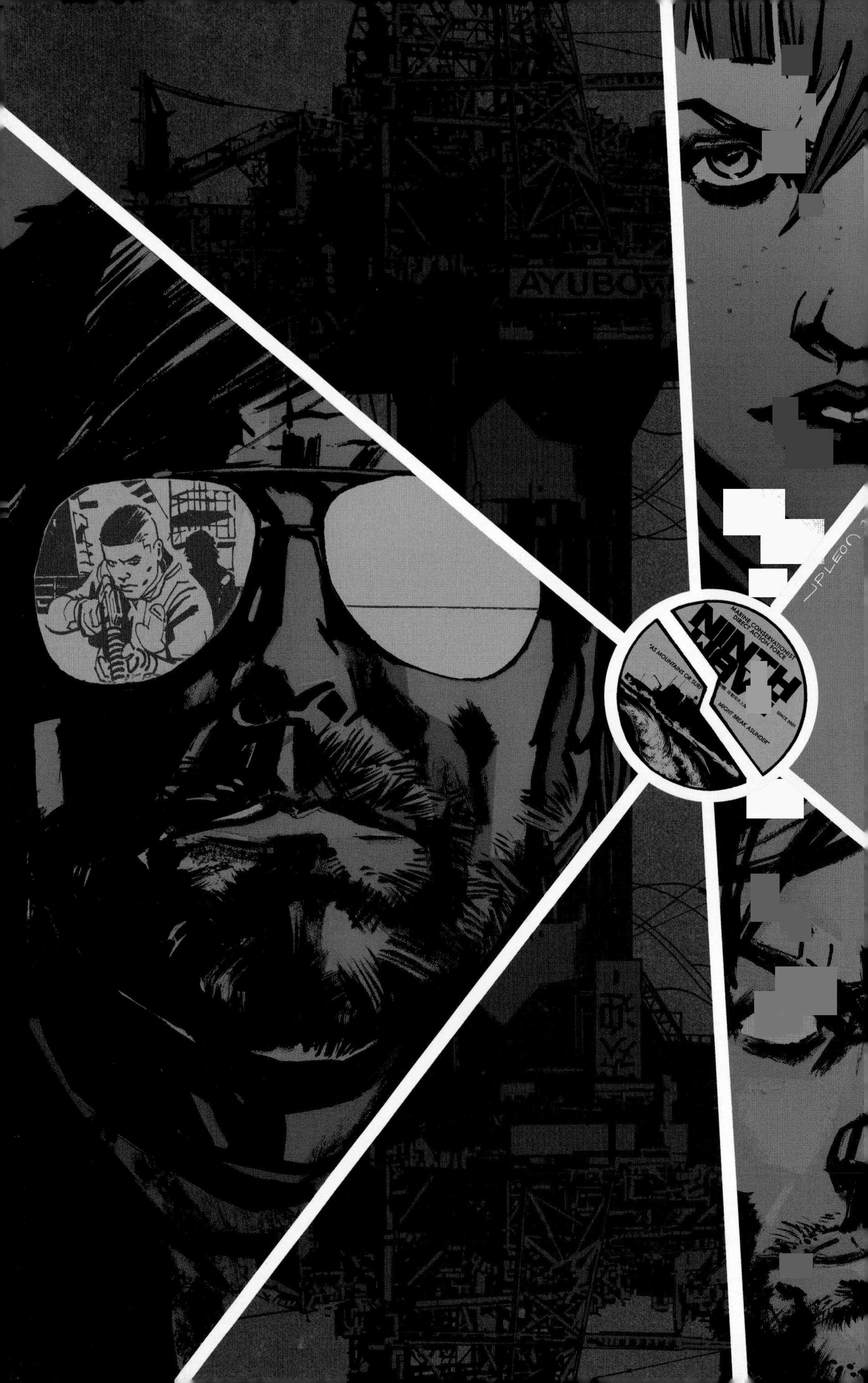
AYUBOW
MARINE CONSERVATIONIST
DIRECT ACTION FORCE
NINTH
"AS MOUNTAINS OR SURF
MIGHT BREAK ASUNDER"
SINCE 2001

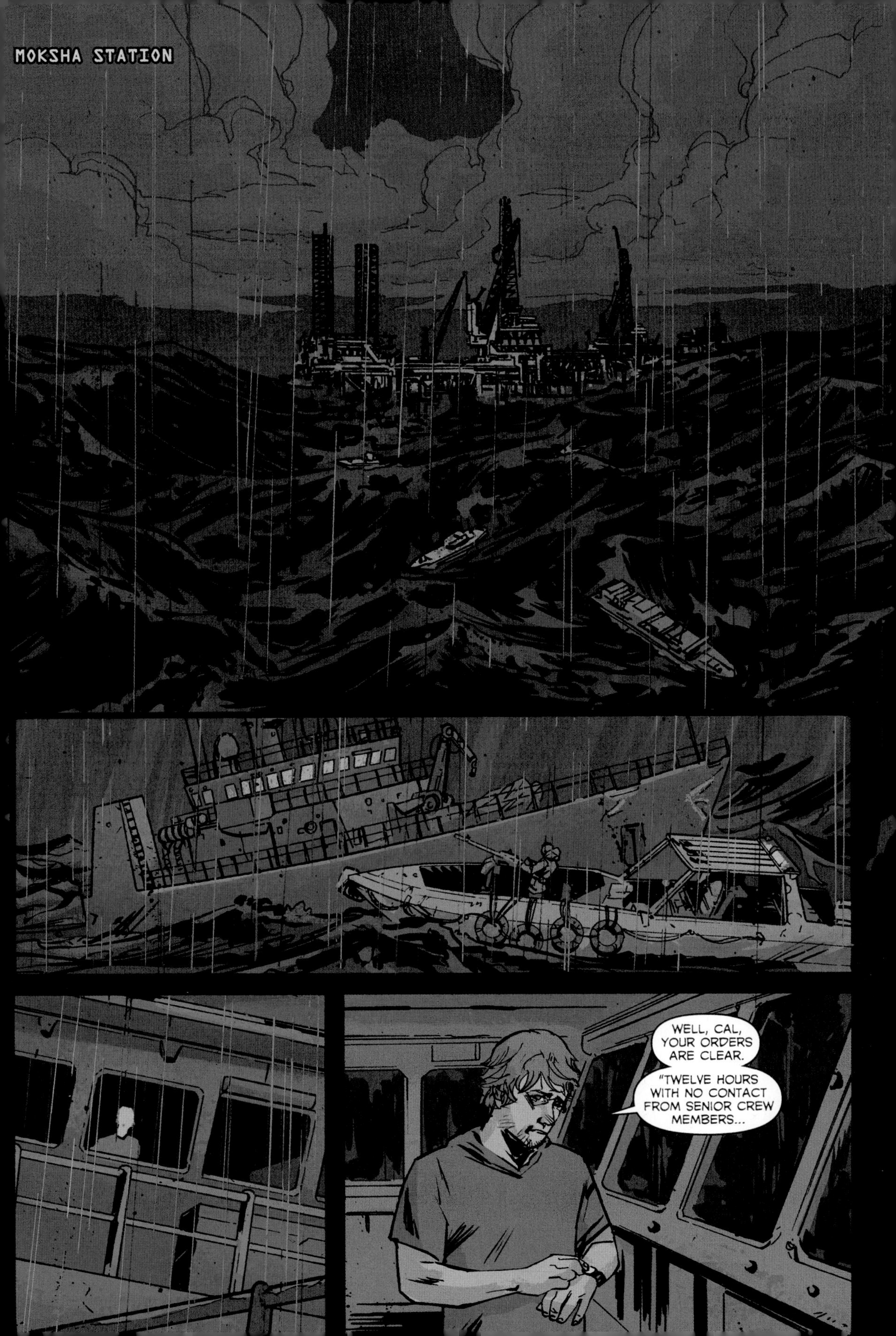
MOKSHA STATION
WELL, CAL, YOUR ORDERS ARE CLEAR.
"TWELVE HOURS WITH NO CONTACT FROM SENIOR CREW MEMBERS...

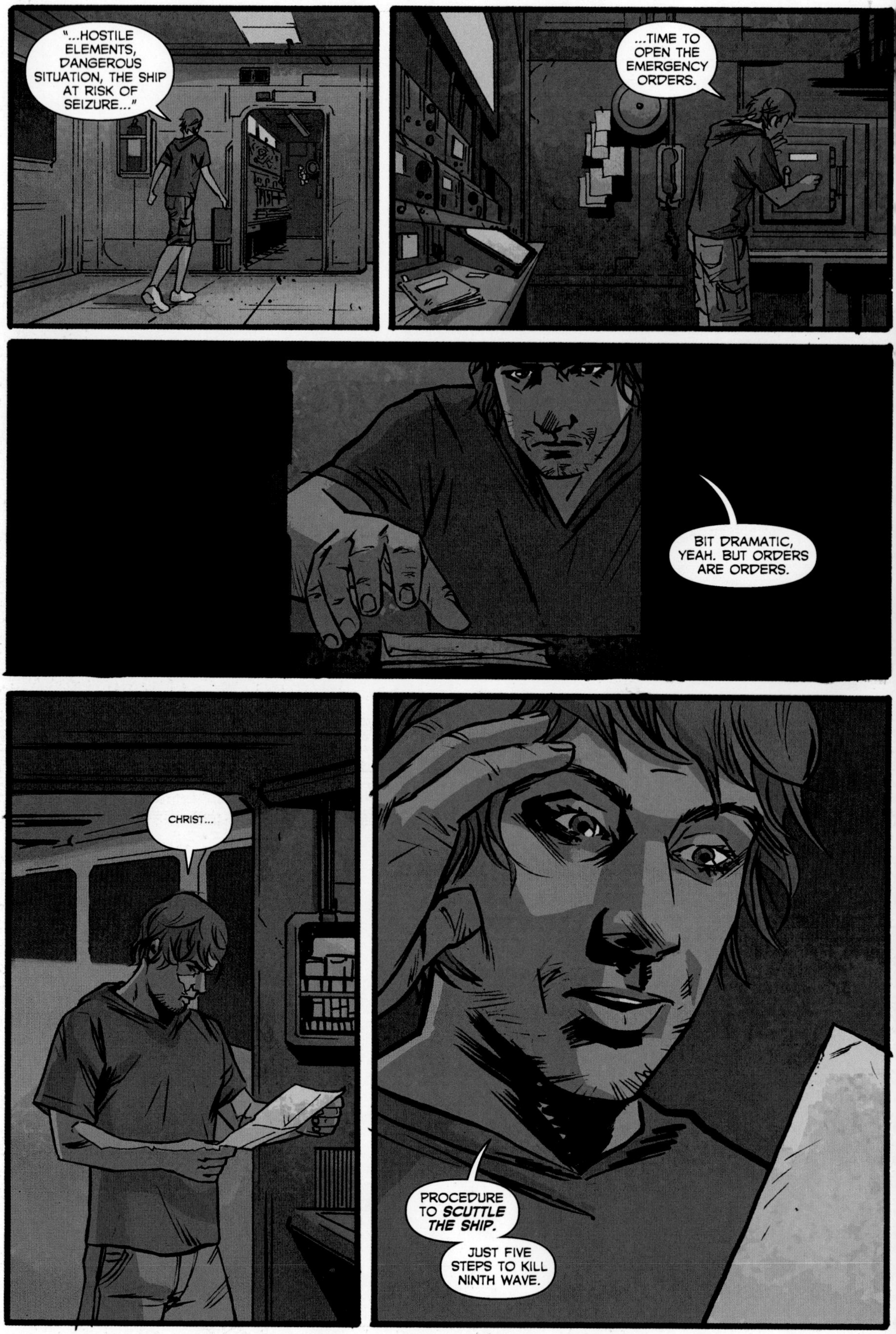
"...HOSTILE ELEMENTS, DANGEROUS SITUATION, THE SHIP AT RISK OF SEIZURE..."
...TIME TO OPEN THE EMERGENCY ORDERS.
BIT DRAMATIC, YEAH. BUT ORDERS ARE ORDERS.
CHRIST...
PROCEDURE TO *SCUTTLE THE SHIP.*
JUST FIVE STEPS TO KILL NINTH WAVE.

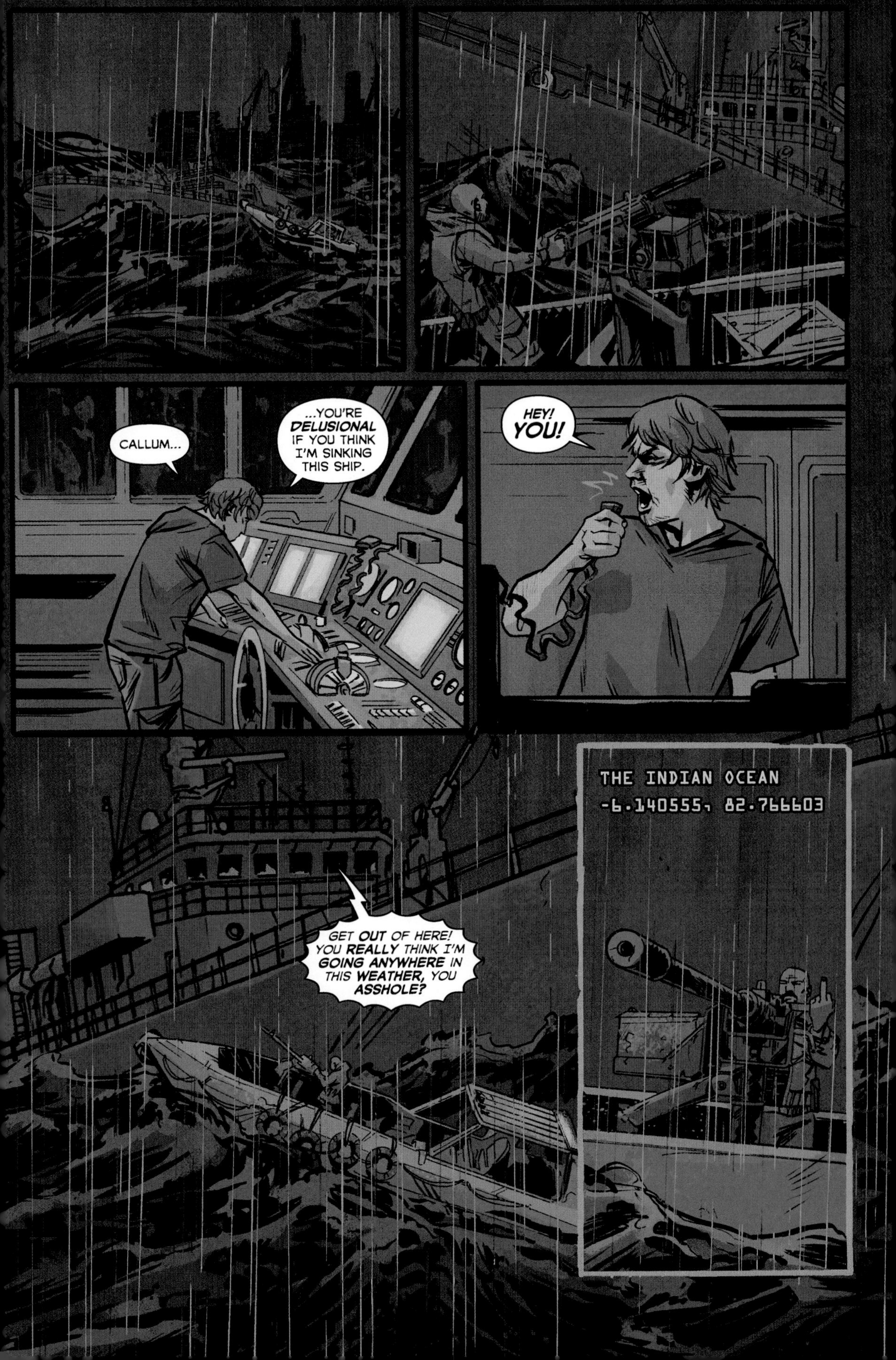
CALLUM...
...YOU'RE DELUSIONAL IF YOU THINK I'M SINKING THIS SHIP.
HEY! YOU!
THE INDIAN OCEAN
-6.140555, 82.766603
GET OUT OF HERE! YOU REALLY THINK I'M GOING ANYWHERE IN THIS WEATHER, YOU ASSHOLE?

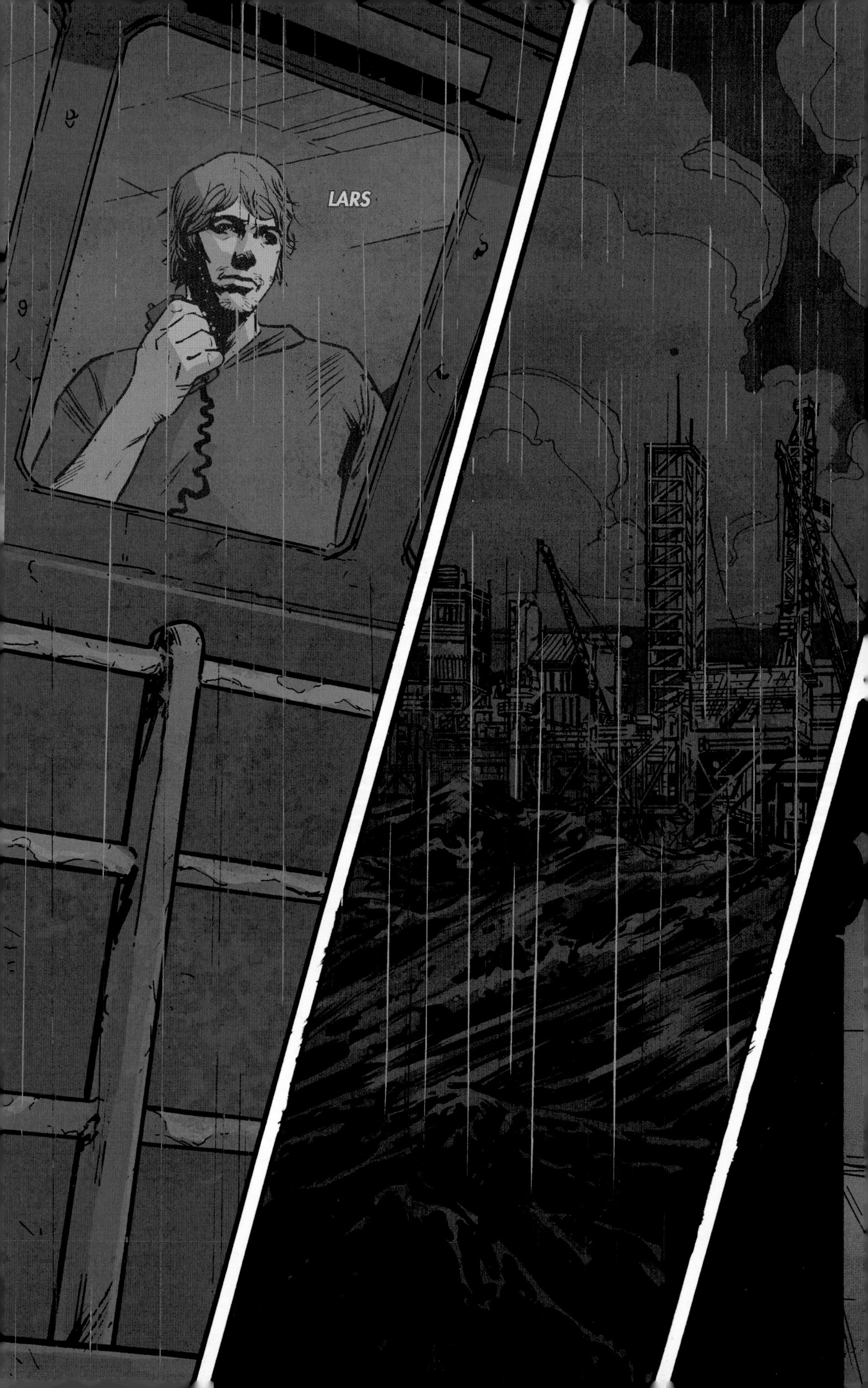
LARS

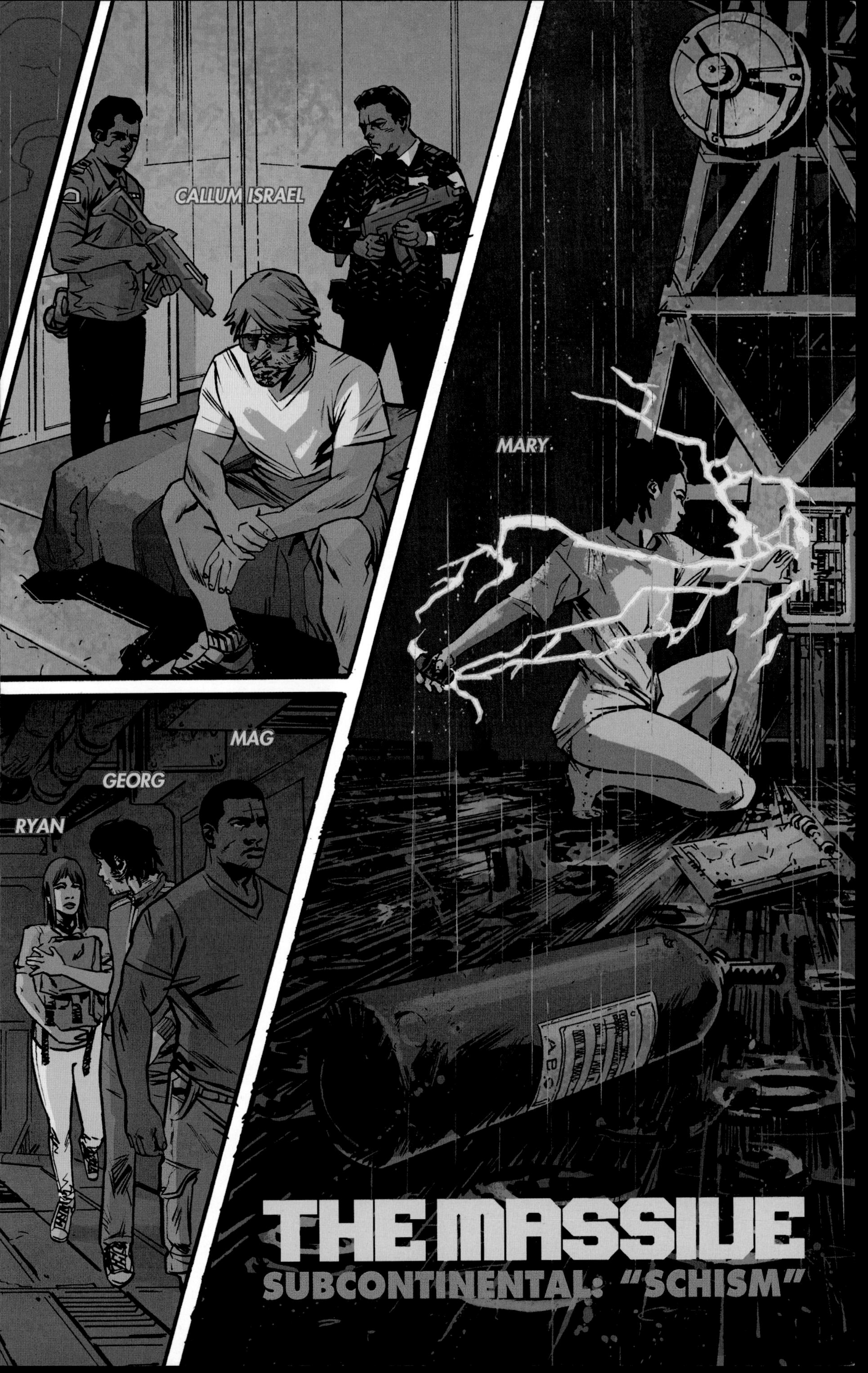
CALLUM ISRAEL
MARY
MAG
GEORG
RYAN
THE MASSIVE
SUBCONTINENTAL: "SCHISM"

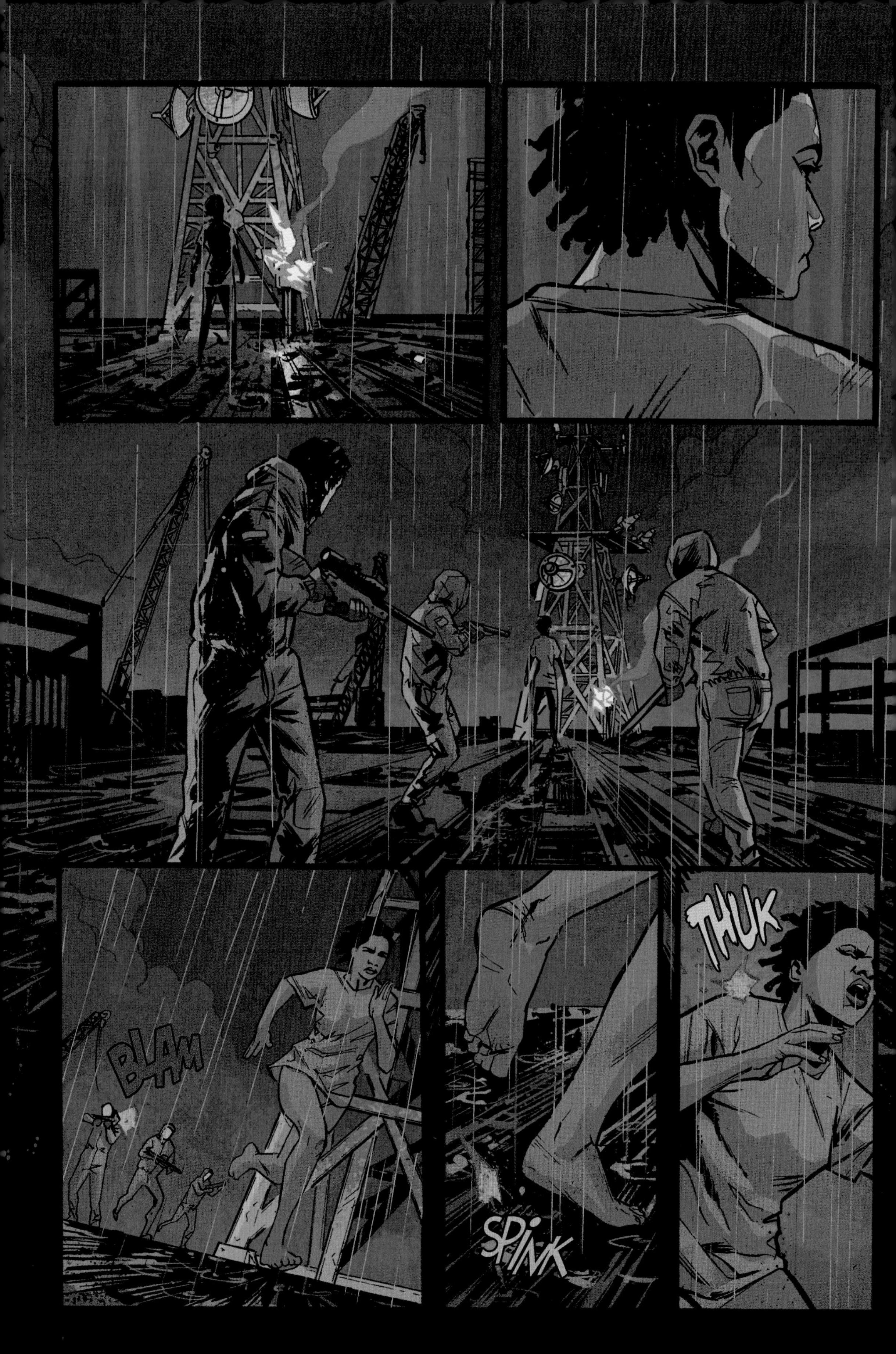
BLAM
SPINK
THUK

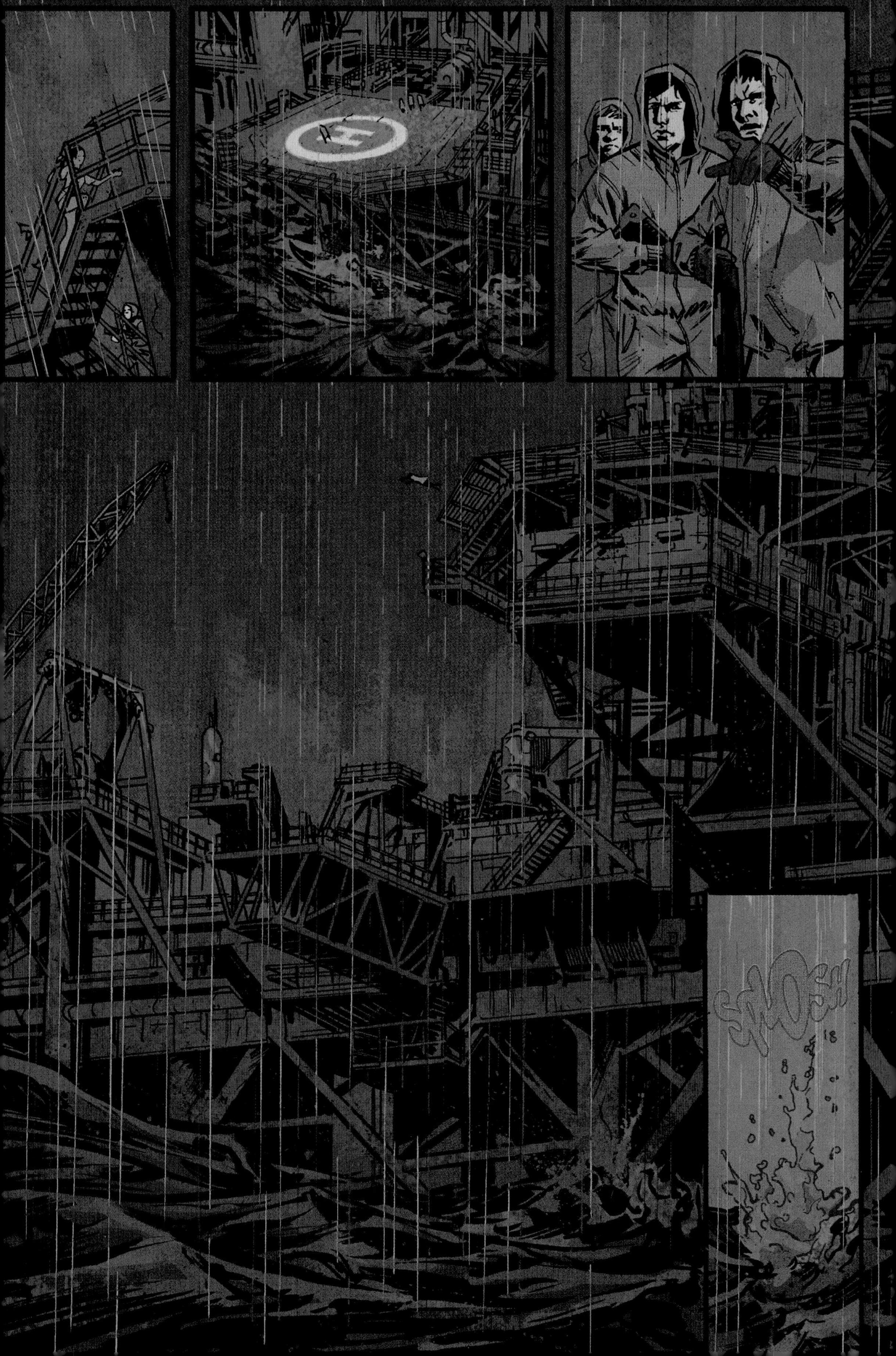

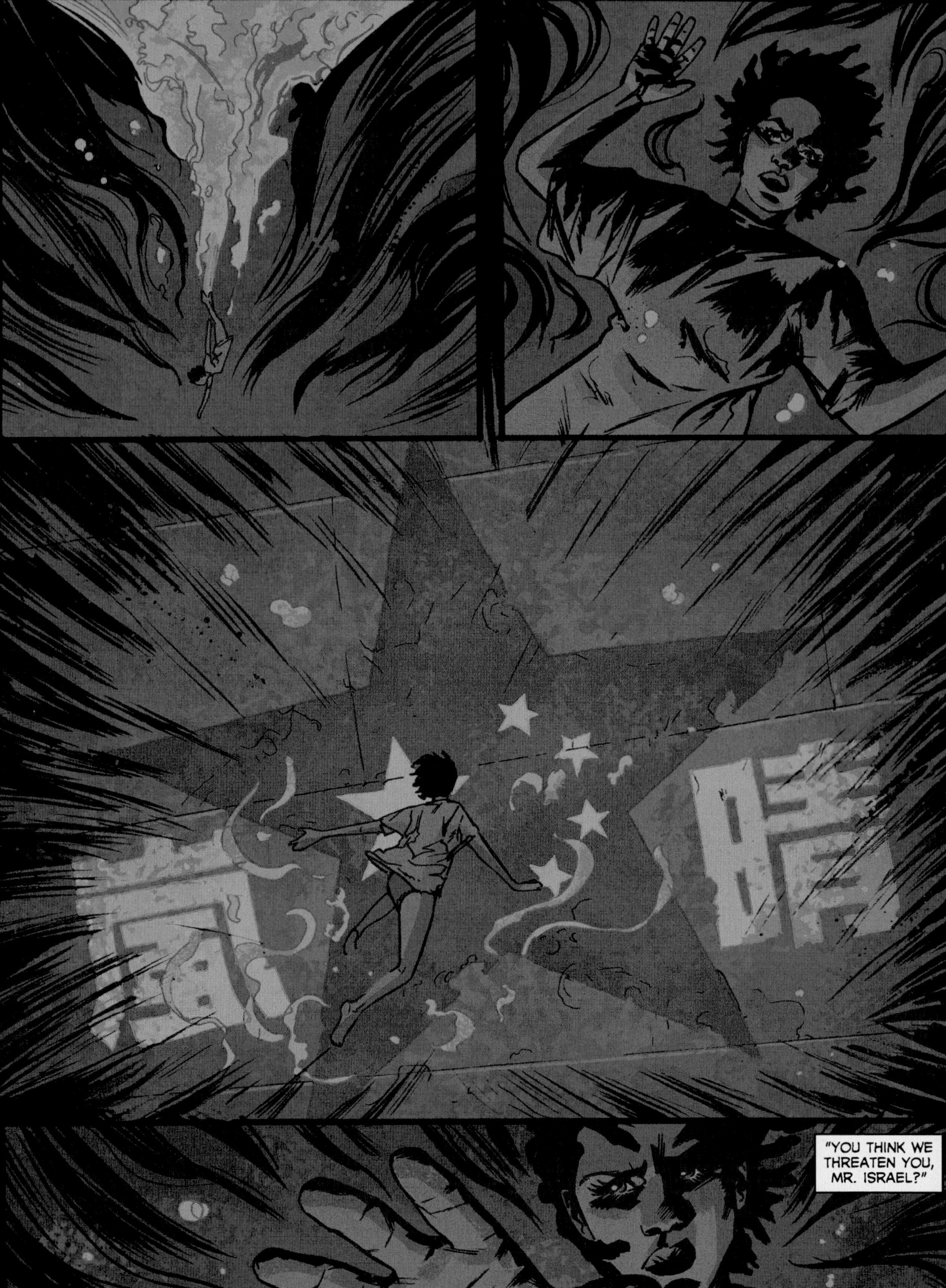
"YOU THINK WE THREATEN YOU, MR. ISRAEL?"

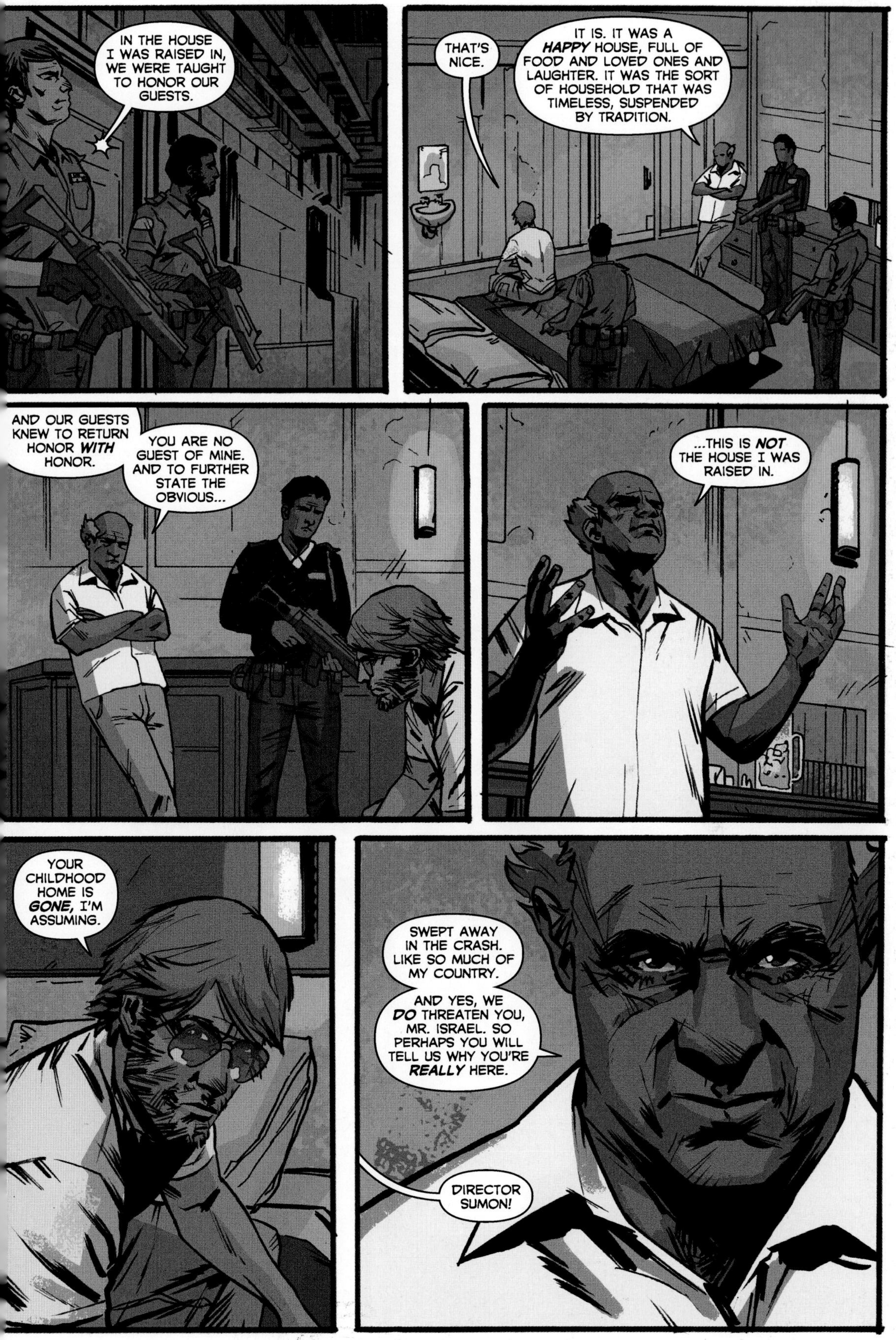
IN THE HOUSE I WAS RAISED IN, WE WERE TAUGHT TO HONOR OUR GUESTS.
THAT'S NICE.
IT IS. IT WAS A HAPPY HOUSE, FULL OF FOOD AND LOVED ONES AND LAUGHTER. IT WAS THE SORT OF HOUSEHOLD THAT WAS TIMELESS, SUSPENDED BY TRADITION.
AND OUR GUESTS KNEW TO RETURN HONOR WITH HONOR.
YOU ARE NO GUEST OF MINE. AND TO FURTHER STATE THE OBVIOUS...
...THIS IS NOT THE HOUSE I WAS RAISED IN.
YOUR CHILDHOOD HOME IS GONE, I'M ASSUMING.
SWEPT AWAY IN THE CRASH. LIKE SO MUCH OF MY COUNTRY.
AND YES, WE DO THREATEN YOU, MR. ISRAEL. SO PERHAPS YOU WILL TELL US WHY YOU'RE REALLY HERE.
DIRECTOR SUMON!

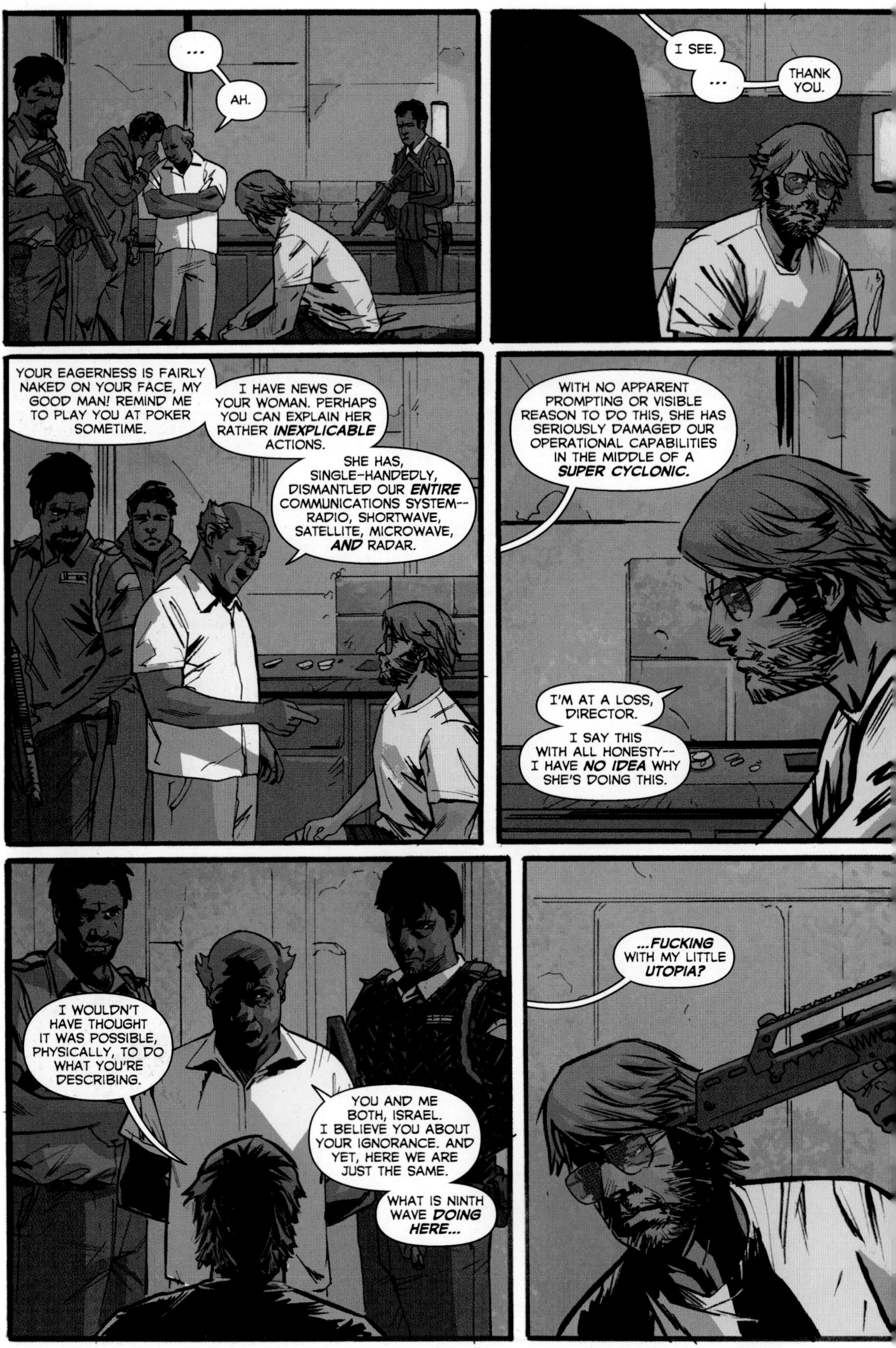
...
AH.
I SEE.
...
THANK YOU.
YOUR EAGERNESS IS FAIRLY NAKED ON YOUR FACE, MY GOOD MAN! REMIND ME TO PLAY YOU AT POKER SOMETIME.
I HAVE NEWS OF YOUR WOMAN. PERHAPS YOU CAN EXPLAIN HER RATHER INEXPLICABLE ACTIONS.
SHE HAS, SINGLE-HANDEDLY, DISMANTLED OUR ENTIRE COMMUNICATIONS SYSTEM-- RADIO, SHORTWAVE, SATELLITE, MICROWAVE, AND RADAR.
WITH NO APPARENT PROMPTING OR VISIBLE REASON TO DO THIS, SHE HAS SERIOUSLY DAMAGED OUR OPERATIONAL CAPABILITIES IN THE MIDDLE OF A SUPER CYCLONIC.
I'M AT A LOSS, DIRECTOR.
I SAY THIS WITH ALL HONESTY-- I HAVE NO IDEA WHY SHE'S DOING THIS.
I WOULDN'T HAVE THOUGHT IT WAS POSSIBLE, PHYSICALLY, TO DO WHAT YOU'RE DESCRIBING.
YOU AND ME BOTH, ISRAEL. I BELIEVE YOU ABOUT YOUR IGNORANCE. AND YET, HERE WE ARE JUST THE SAME.
WHAT IS NINTH WAVE DOING HERE...
...FUCKING WITH MY LITTLE UTOPIA?

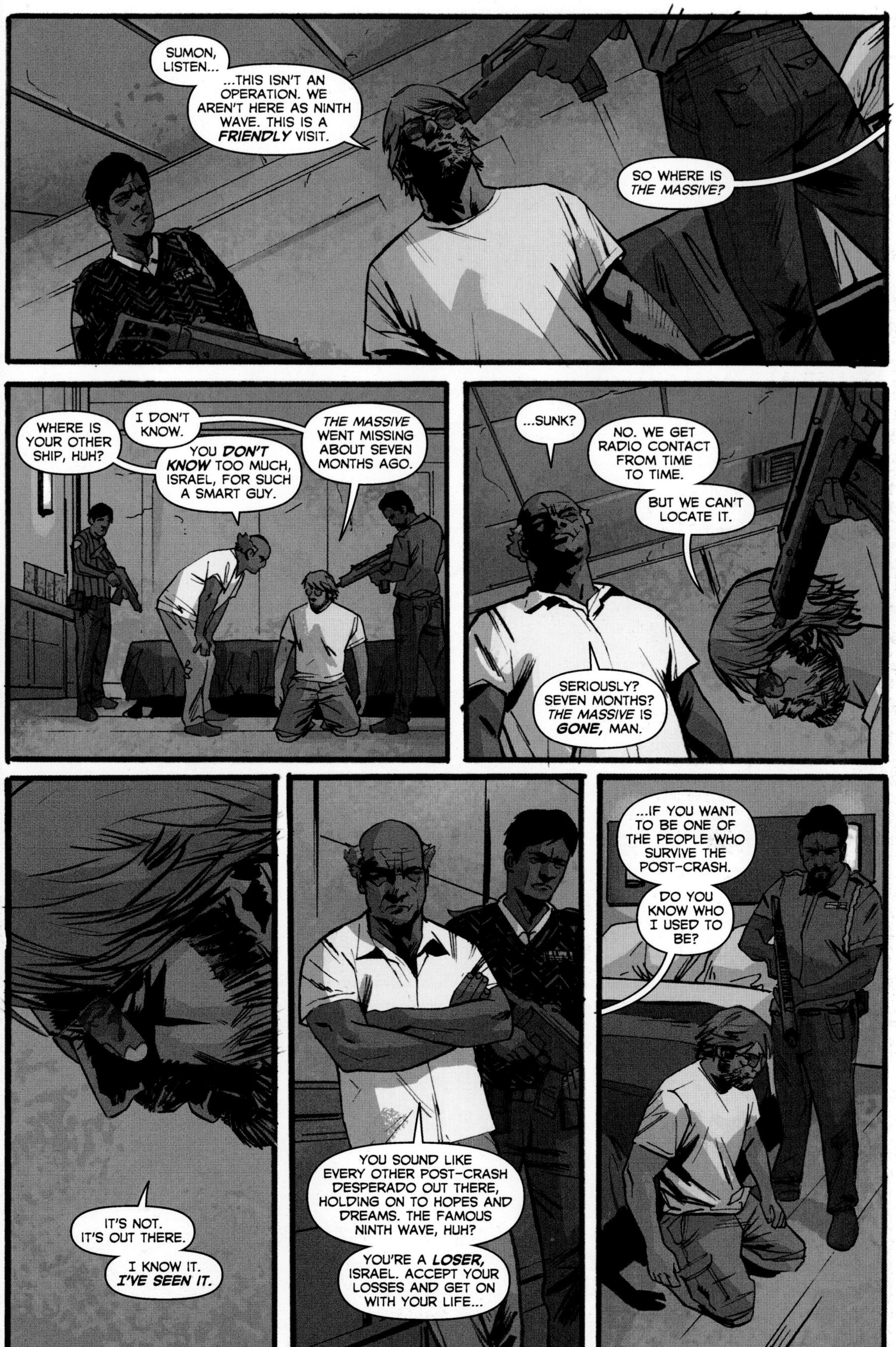
SUMON, LISTEN...
...THIS ISN'T AN OPERATION. WE AREN'T HERE AS NINTH WAVE. THIS IS A FRIENDLY VISIT.
SO WHERE IS THE MASSIVE?
WHERE IS YOUR OTHER SHIP, HUH?
I DON'T KNOW.
YOU DON'T KNOW TOO MUCH, ISRAEL, FOR SUCH A SMART GUY.
THE MASSIVE WENT MISSING ABOUT SEVEN MONTHS AGO.
...SUNK?
NO. WE GET RADIO CONTACT FROM TIME TO TIME.
BUT WE CAN'T LOCATE IT.
SERIOUSLY? SEVEN MONTHS? THE MASSIVE IS GONE, MAN.
IT'S NOT. IT'S OUT THERE.
I KNOW IT. I'VE SEEN IT.
YOU SOUND LIKE EVERY OTHER POST-CRASH DESPERADO OUT THERE, HOLDING ON TO HOPES AND DREAMS. THE FAMOUS NINTH WAVE, HUH?
YOU'RE A LOSER, ISRAEL. ACCEPT YOUR LOSSES AND GET ON WITH YOUR LIFE...
...IF YOU WANT TO BE ONE OF THE PEOPLE WHO SURVIVE THE POST-CRASH.
DO YOU KNOW WHO I USED TO BE?

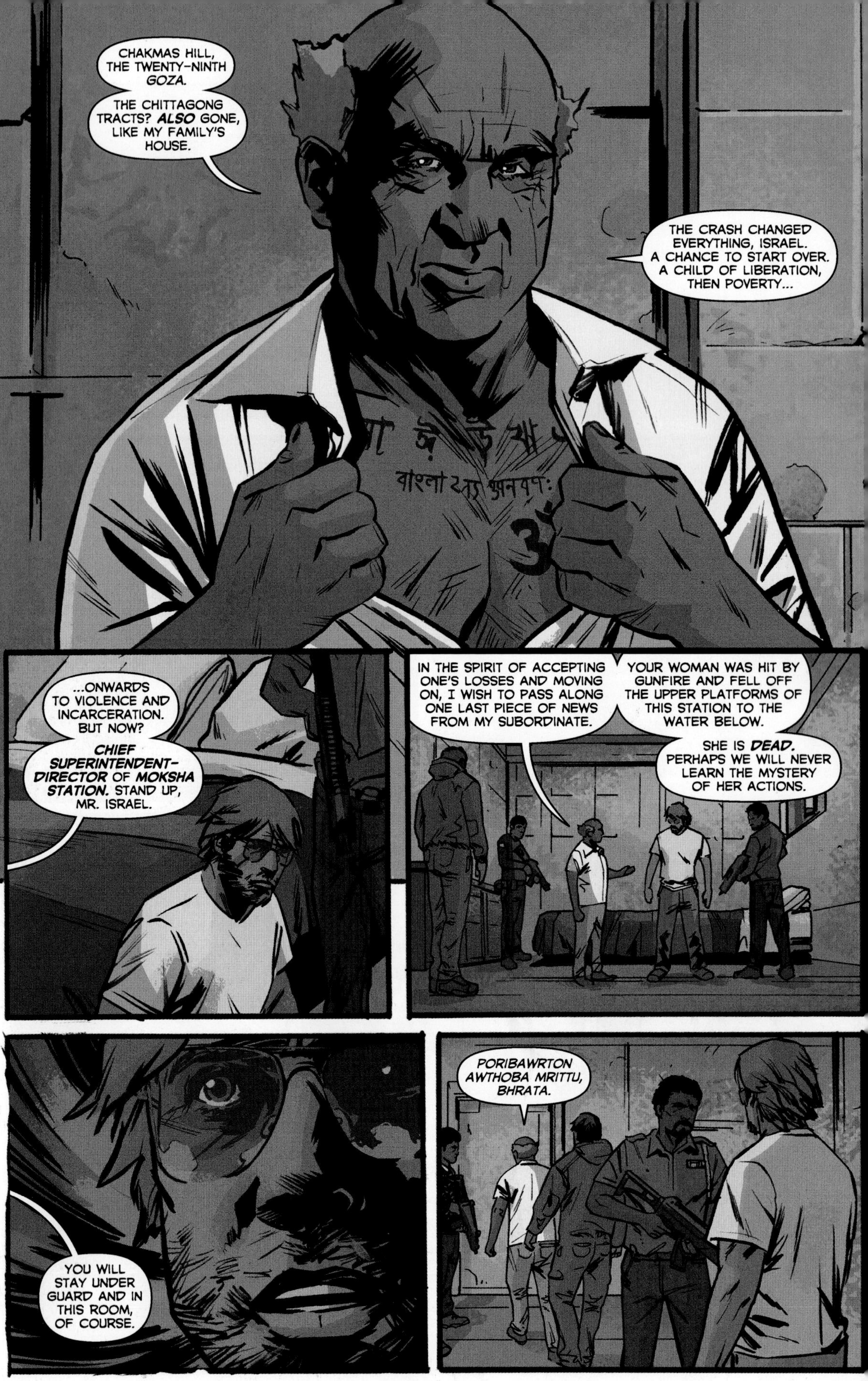
CHAKMAS HILL, THE TWENTY-NINTH *GOZA.*
THE CHITTAGONG TRACTS? ***ALSO*** GONE, LIKE MY FAMILY'S HOUSE.
THE CRASH CHANGED EVERYTHING, ISRAEL. A CHANCE TO START OVER. A CHILD OF LIBERATION, THEN POVERTY...
...ONWARDS TO VIOLENCE AND INCARCERATION. BUT NOW?
CHIEF SUPERINTENDENT-DIRECTOR OF ***MOKSHA STATION.*** STAND UP, MR. ISRAEL.
IN THE SPIRIT OF ACCEPTING ONE'S LOSSES AND MOVING ON, I WISH TO PASS ALONG ONE LAST PIECE OF NEWS FROM MY SUBORDINATE.
YOUR WOMAN WAS HIT BY GUNFIRE AND FELL OFF THE UPPER PLATFORMS OF THIS STATION TO THE WATER BELOW.
SHE IS ***DEAD.*** PERHAPS WE WILL NEVER LEARN THE MYSTERY OF HER ACTIONS.
YOU WILL STAY UNDER GUARD AND IN THIS ROOM, OF COURSE.
PORIBAWRTON AWTHOBA MRITTU, BHRATA.

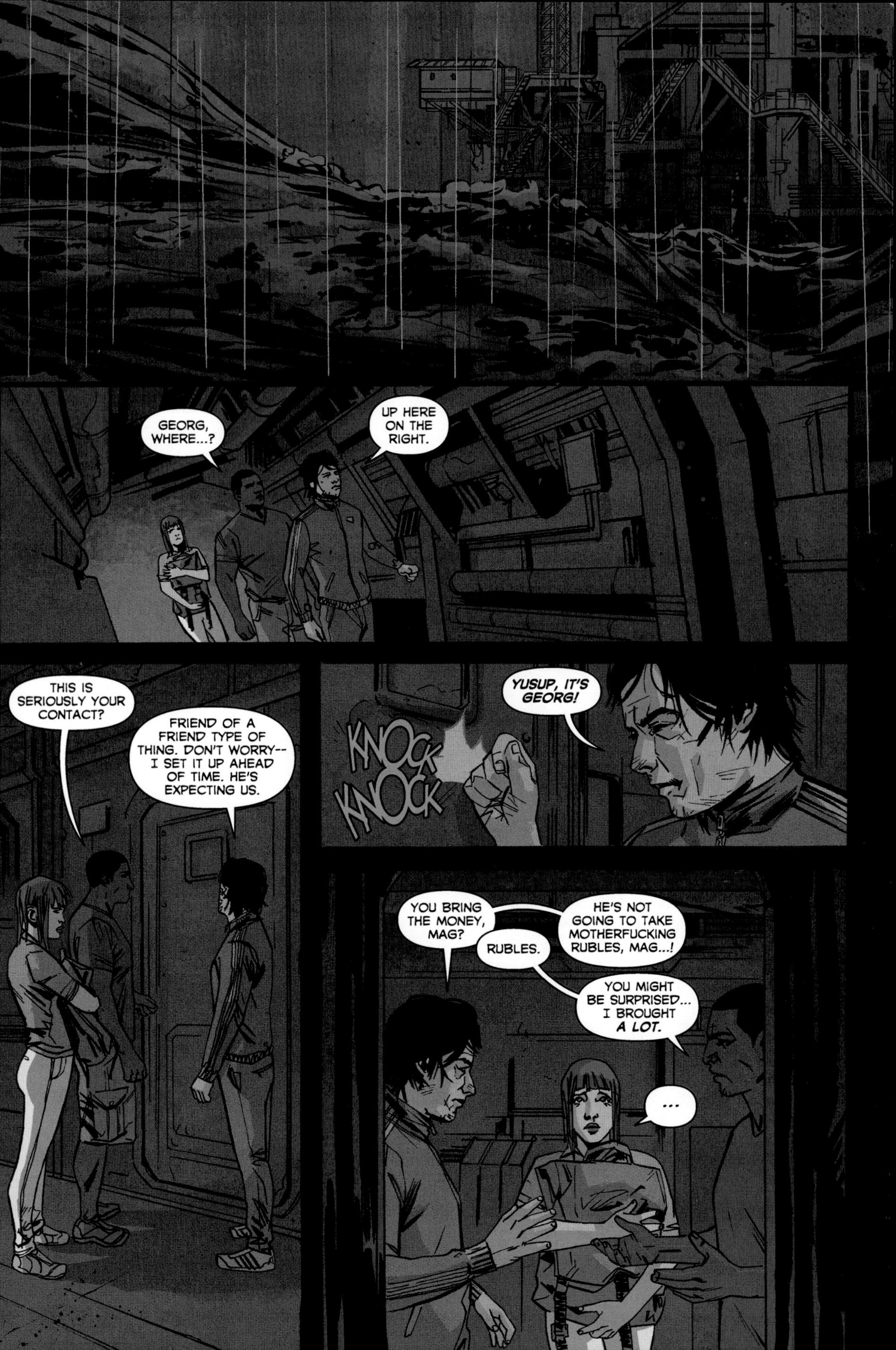
GEORG, WHERE...?
UP HERE ON THE RIGHT.
THIS IS SERIOUSLY YOUR CONTACT?
FRIEND OF A FRIEND TYPE OF THING. DON'T WORRY-- I SET IT UP AHEAD OF TIME. HE'S EXPECTING US.
KNOCK KNOCK
YUSUP, IT'S GEORG!
YOU BRING THE MONEY, MAG?
RUBLES.
HE'S NOT GOING TO TAKE MOTHERFUCKING RUBLES, MAG...!
YOU MIGHT BE SURPRISED... I BROUGHT A LOT.
...

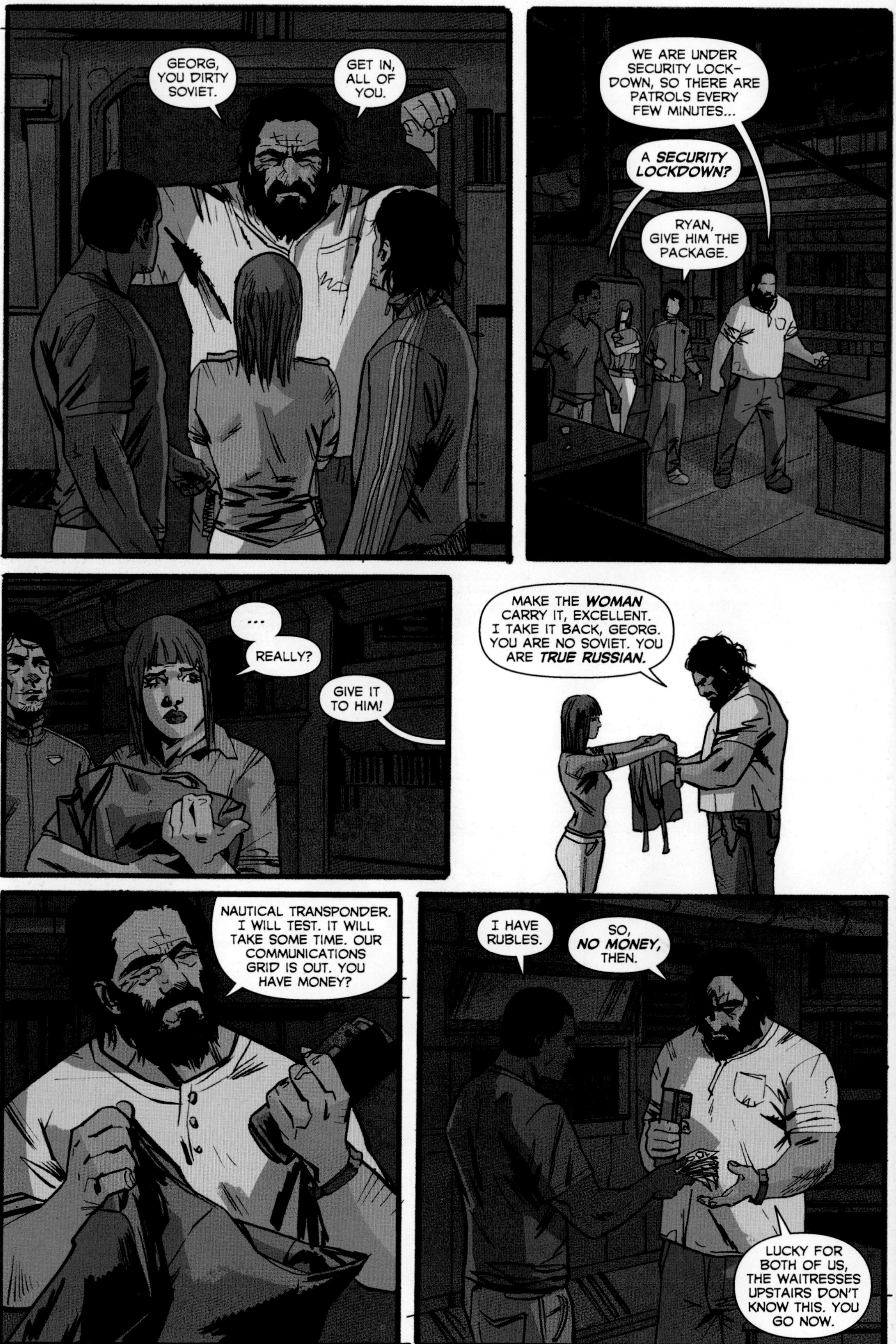
GEORG, YOU DIRTY SOVIET.
GET IN, ALL OF YOU.
WE ARE UNDER SECURITY LOCK-DOWN, SO THERE ARE PATROLS EVERY FEW MINUTES...
A *SECURITY LOCKDOWN?*
RYAN, GIVE HIM THE PACKAGE.
...
REALLY?
GIVE IT TO HIM!
MAKE THE *WOMAN* CARRY IT, EXCELLENT. I TAKE IT BACK, GEORG. YOU ARE NO SOVIET. YOU ARE *TRUE RUSSIAN.*
NAUTICAL TRANSPONDER. I WILL TEST. IT WILL TAKE SOME TIME. OUR COMMUNICATIONS GRID IS OUT. YOU HAVE MONEY?
I HAVE RUBLES.
SO, *NO MONEY,* THEN.
LUCKY FOR BOTH OF US, THE WAITRESSES UPSTAIRS DON'T KNOW THIS. YOU GO NOW.

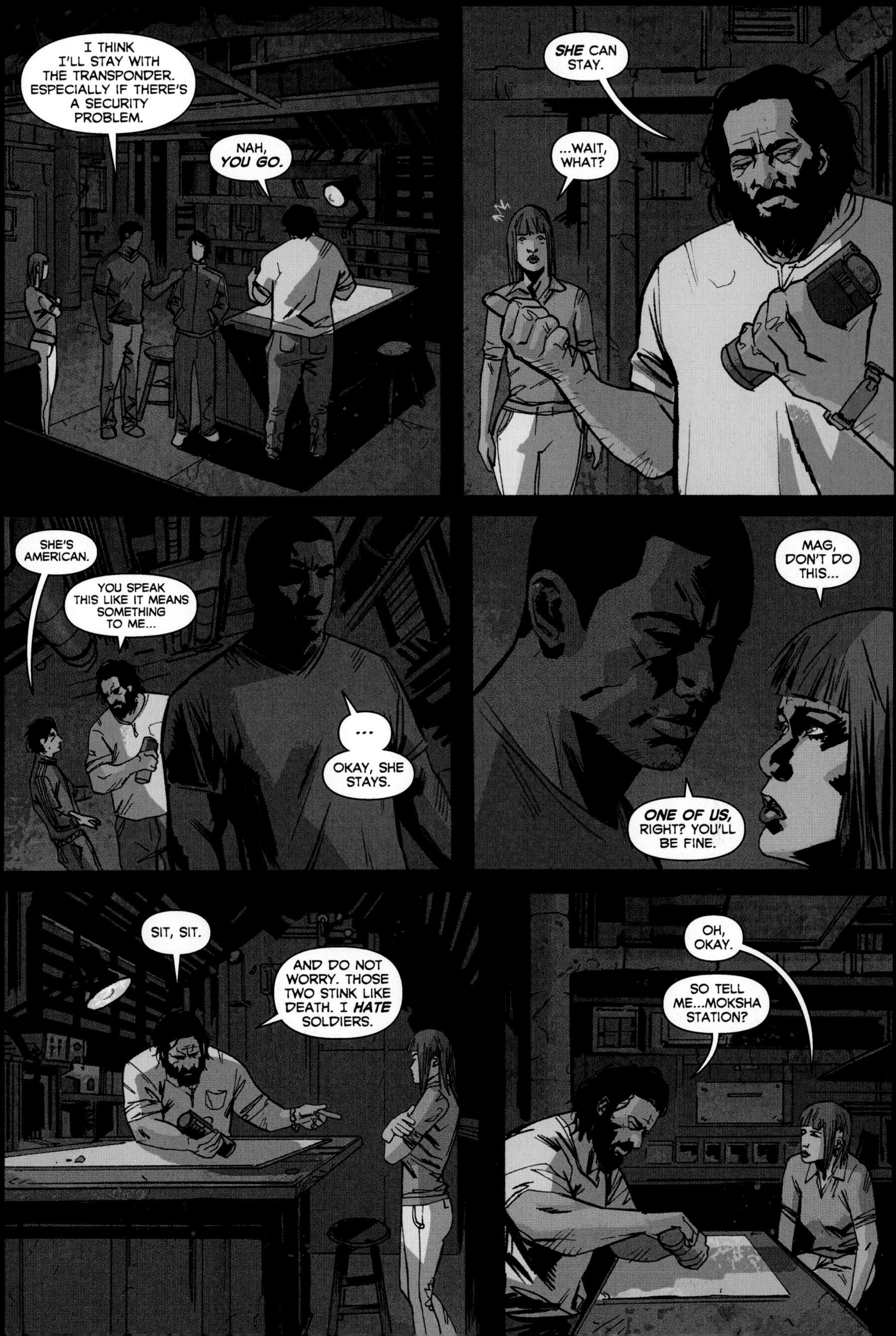
I THINK I'LL STAY WITH THE TRANSPONDER. ESPECIALLY IF THERE'S A SECURITY PROBLEM.
NAH, *YOU GO.*
SHE CAN STAY.
...WAIT, WHAT?
SHE'S AMERICAN.
YOU SPEAK THIS LIKE IT MEANS SOMETHING TO ME...
...
OKAY, SHE STAYS.
MAG, DON'T DO THIS...
ONE OF US, RIGHT? YOU'LL BE FINE.
SIT, SIT.
AND DO NOT WORRY. THOSE TWO STINK LIKE DEATH. I *HATE* SOLDIERS.
OH, OKAY.
SO TELL ME...MOKSHA STATION?

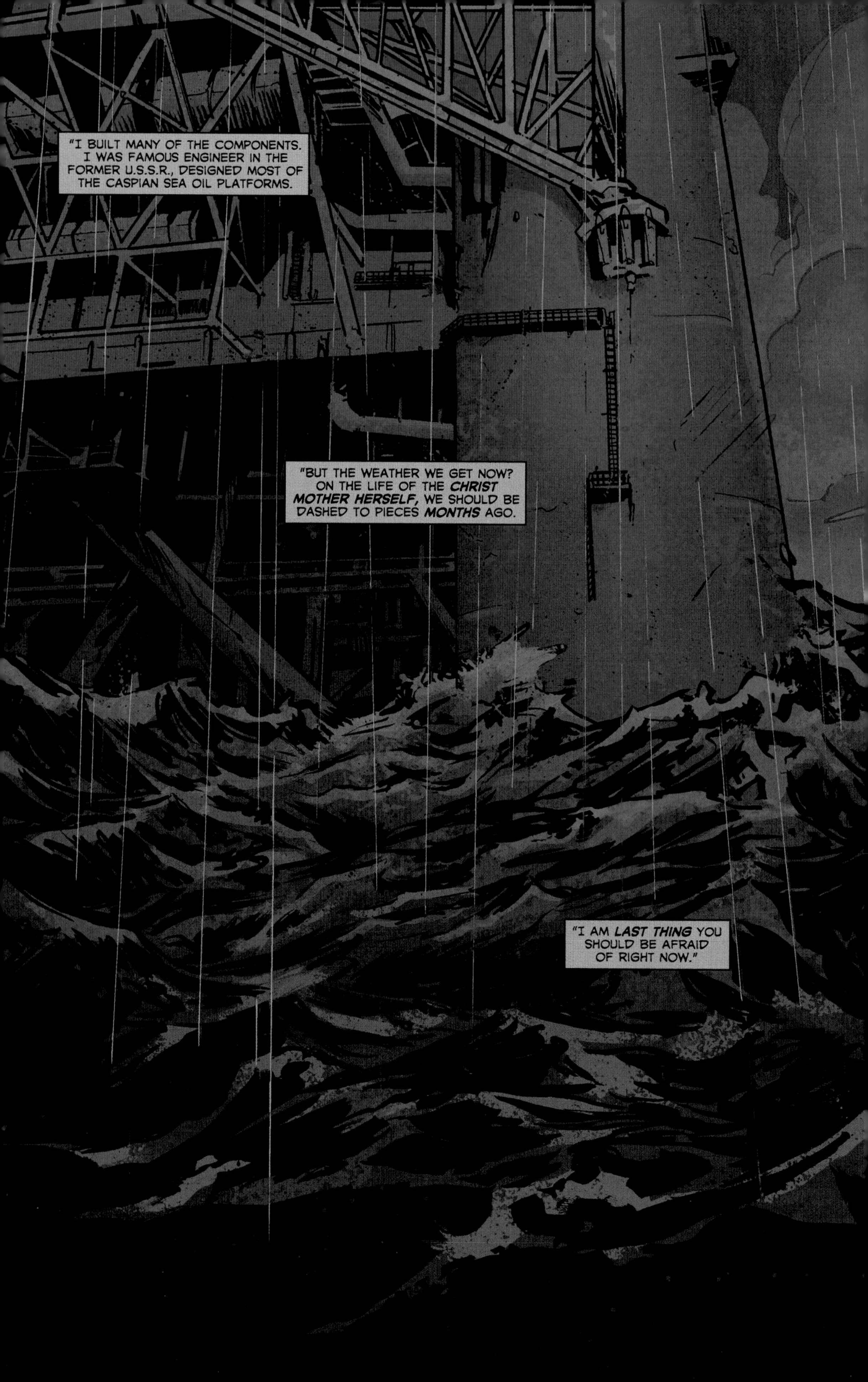
"I BUILT MANY OF THE COMPONENTS. I WAS FAMOUS ENGINEER IN THE FORMER U.S.S.R., DESIGNED MOST OF THE CASPIAN SEA OIL PLATFORMS.
"BUT THE WEATHER WE GET NOW? ON THE LIFE OF THE CHRIST MOTHER HERSELF, WE SHOULD BE DASHED TO PIECES MONTHS AGO.
"I AM LAST THING YOU SHOULD BE AFRAID OF RIGHT NOW."

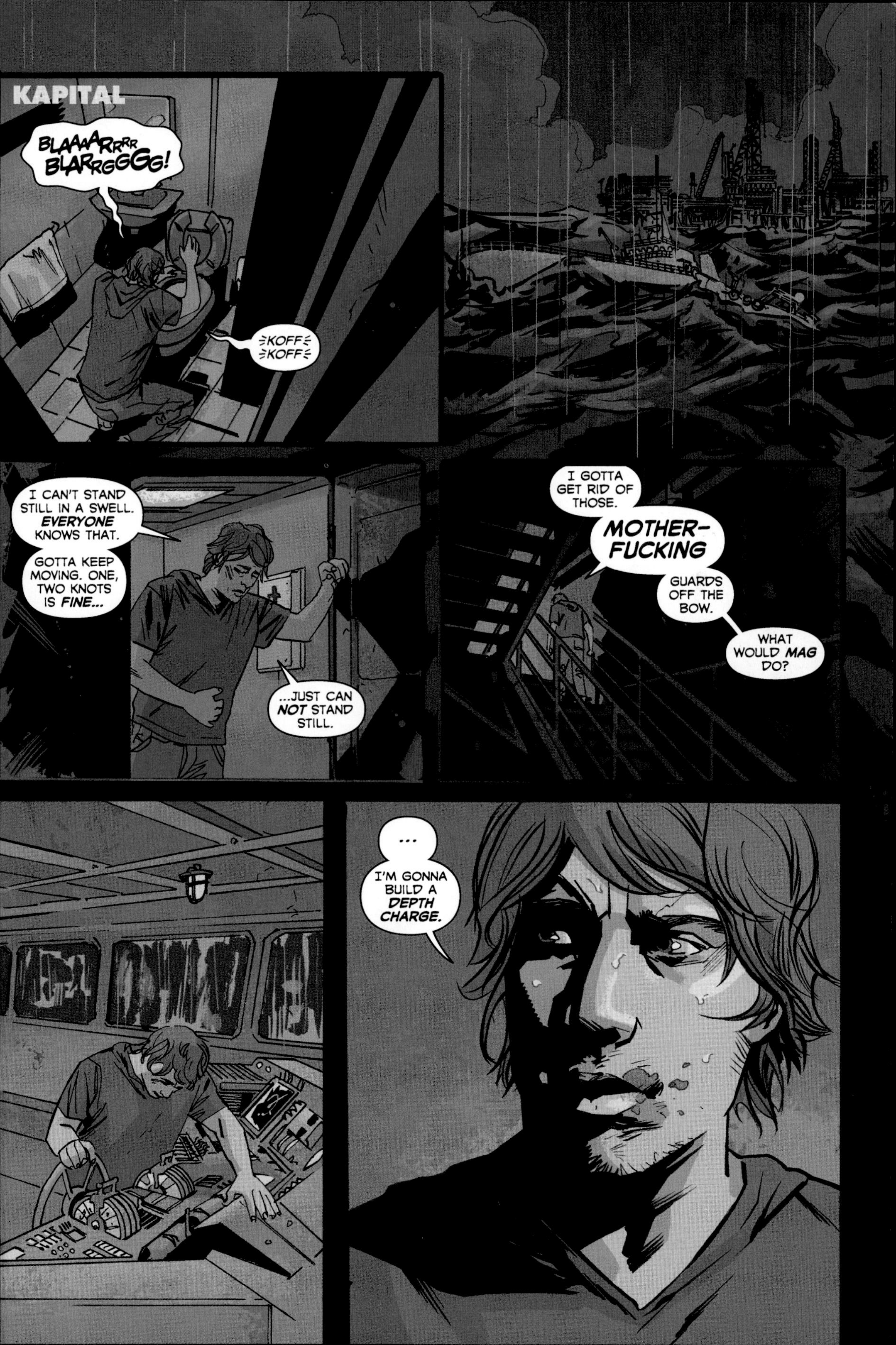
KAPITAL
BLAAAARRRR BLARRGGGG!
KOFF KOFF
I CAN'T STAND STILL IN A SWELL. EVERYONE KNOWS THAT.
GOTTA KEEP MOVING. ONE, TWO KNOTS IS FINE...
...JUST CAN NOT STAND STILL.
I GOTTA GET RID OF THOSE.
MOTHER-FUCKING
GUARDS OFF THE BOW.
WHAT WOULD MAG DO?
...
I'M GONNA BUILD A DEPTH CHARGE.

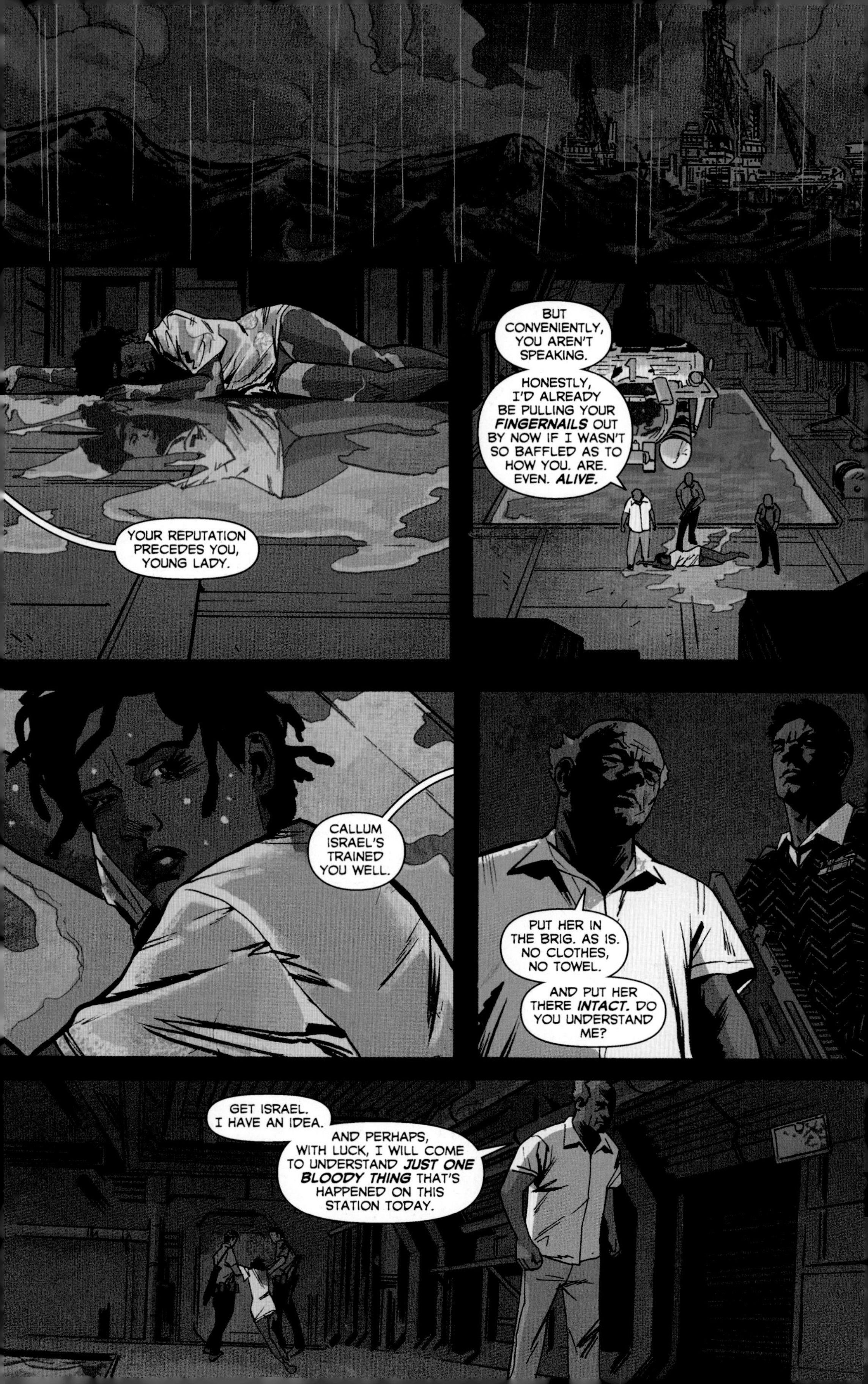
YOUR REPUTATION PRECEDES YOU, YOUNG LADY.
BUT CONVENIENTLY, YOU AREN'T SPEAKING.
HONESTLY, I'D ALREADY BE PULLING YOUR **FINGERNAILS** OUT BY NOW IF I WASN'T SO BAFFLED AS TO HOW YOU. ARE. EVEN. **ALIVE.**
CALLUM ISRAEL'S TRAINED YOU WELL.
PUT HER IN THE BRIG. AS IS. NO CLOTHES, NO TOWEL.
AND PUT HER THERE **INTACT.** DO YOU UNDERSTAND ME?
GET ISRAEL. I HAVE AN IDEA.
AND PERHAPS, WITH LUCK, I WILL COME TO UNDERSTAND **JUST ONE BLOODY THING** THAT'S HAPPENED ON THIS STATION TODAY.

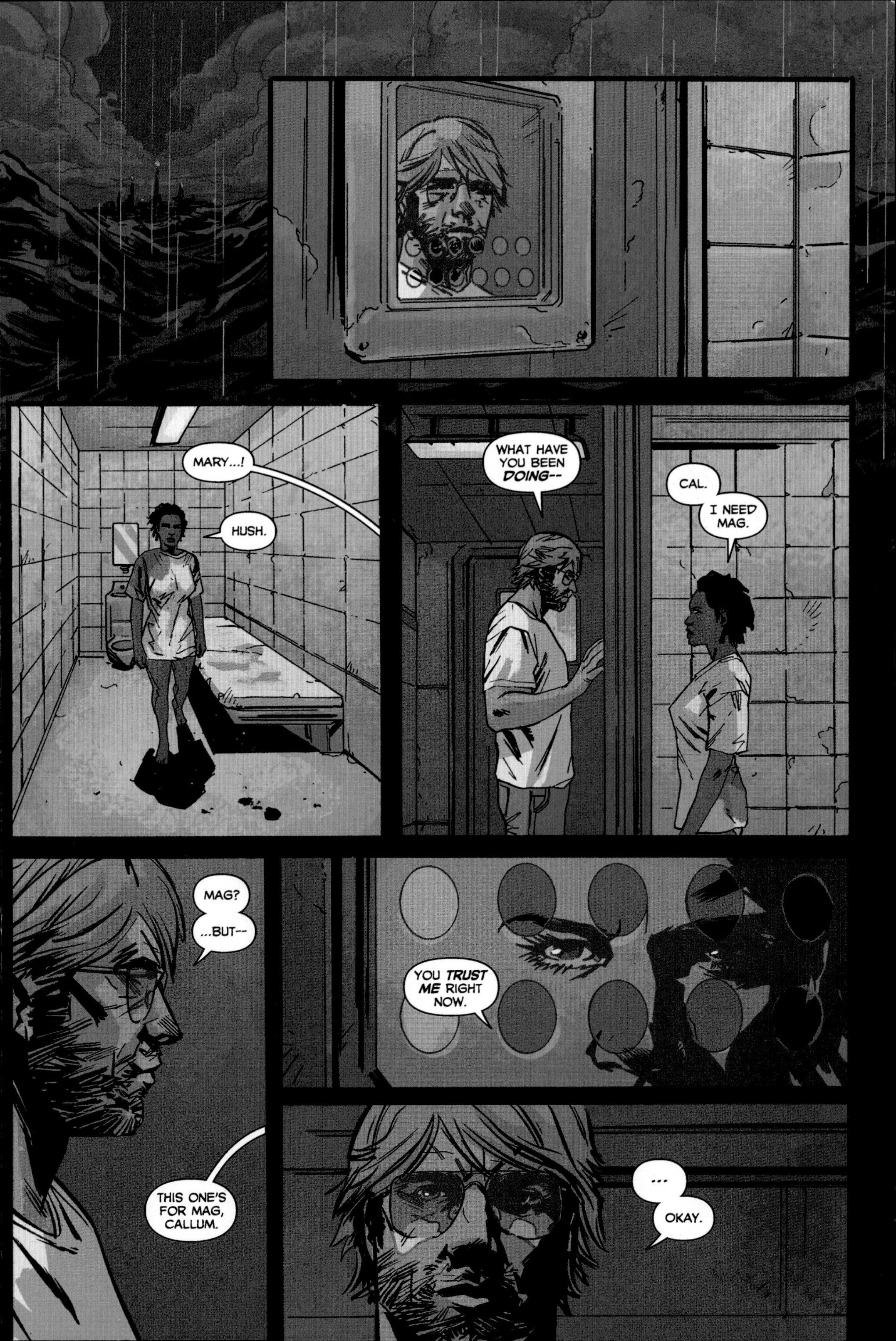
MARY...!
HUSH.
WHAT HAVE YOU BEEN DOING--
CAL.
I NEED MAG.
MAG?
...BUT--
YOU TRUST ME RIGHT NOW.
THIS ONE'S FOR MAG, CALLUM.
...
OKAY.

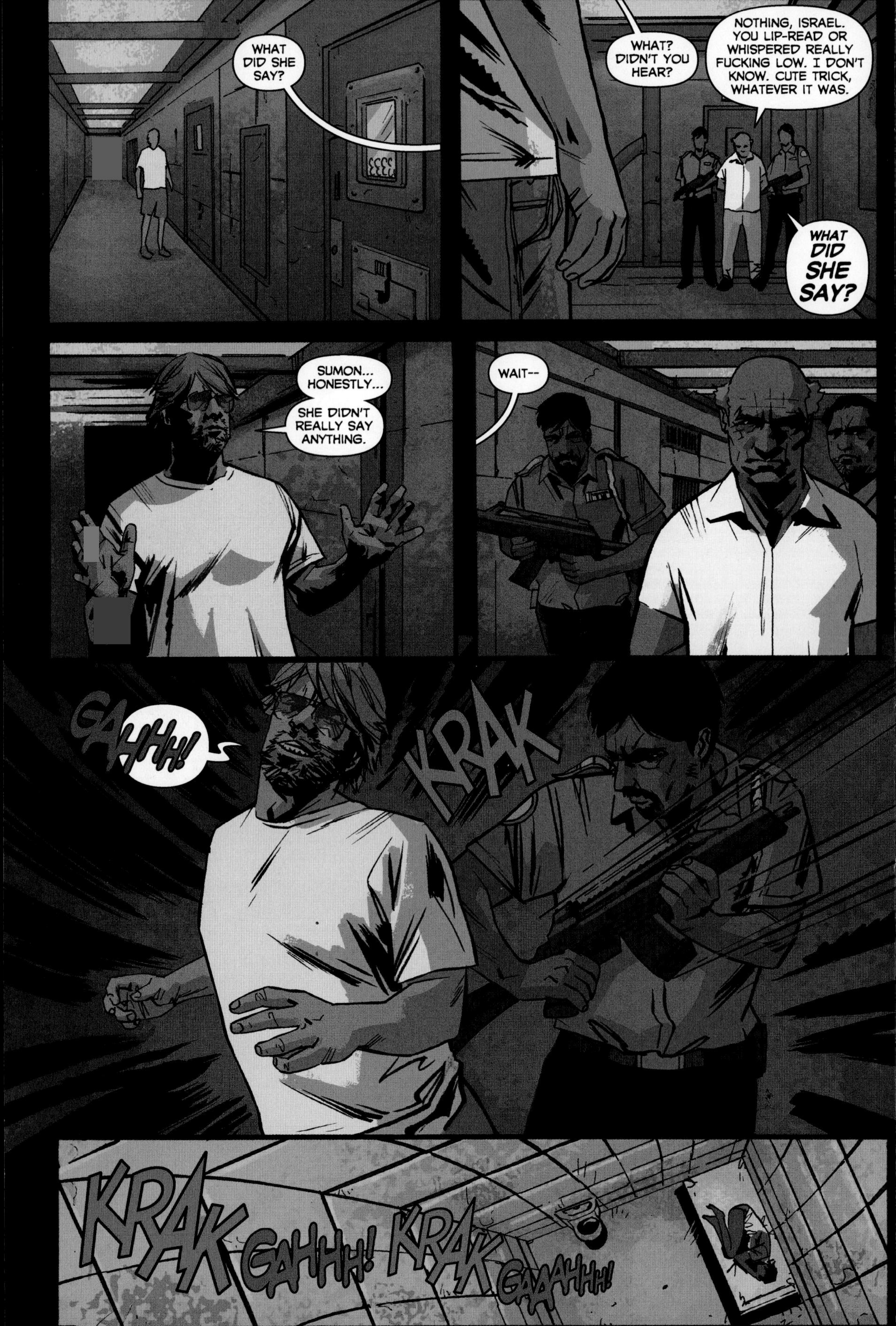
WHAT DID SHE SAY?
WHAT? DIDN'T YOU HEAR?
NOTHING, ISRAEL. YOU LIP-READ OR WHISPERED REALLY FUCKING LOW. I DON'T KNOW. CUTE TRICK, WHATEVER IT WAS.
WHAT DID SHE SAY?
SUMON... HONESTLY...
SHE DIDN'T REALLY SAY ANYTHING.
WAIT--
GAHHH!
KRAK
KRAK
GAHHH!
KRAK
GAAAHHH!

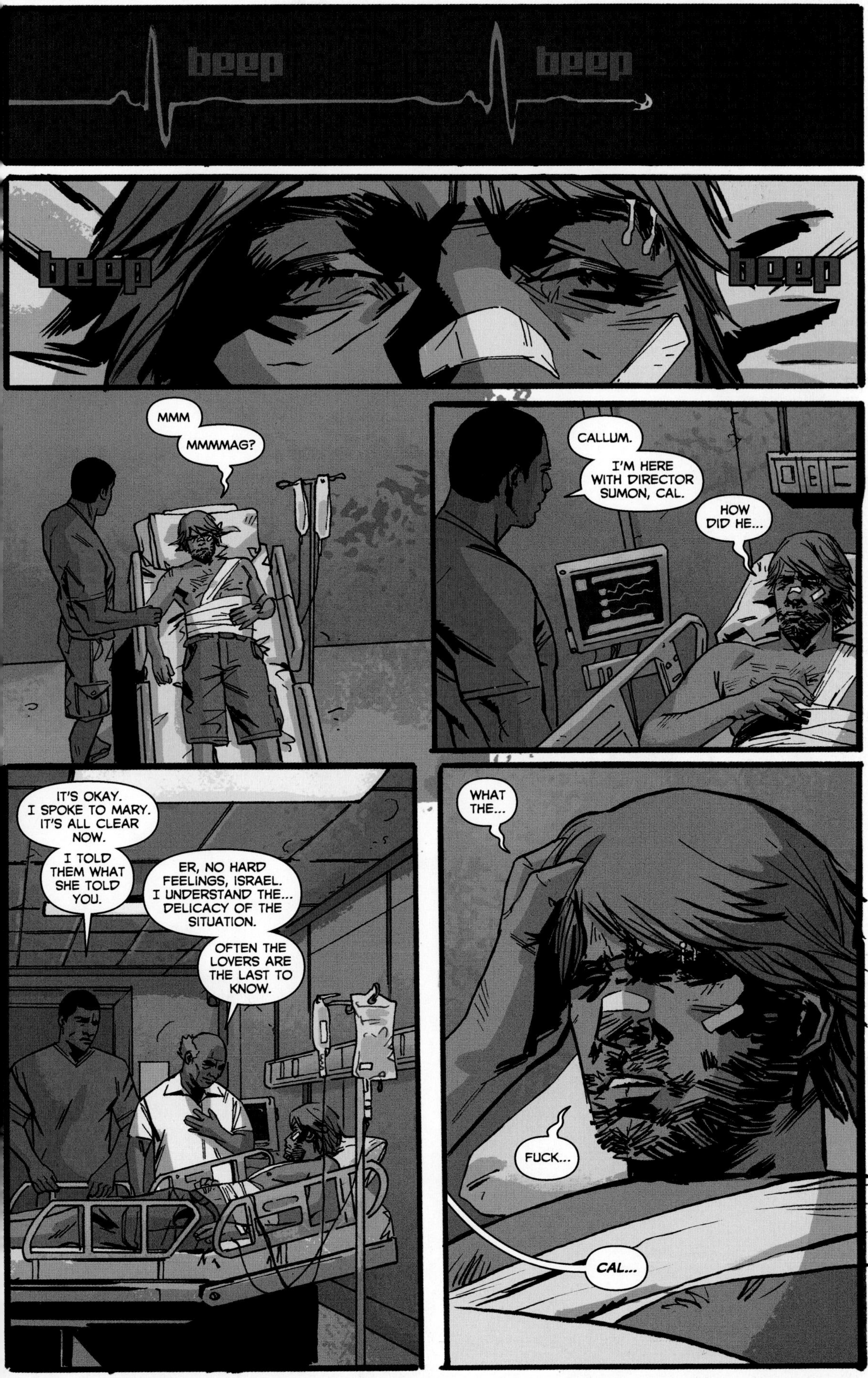
beep
beep
beep
beep
MMM
MMMMAG?
CALLUM.
I'M HERE WITH DIRECTOR SUMON, CAL.
HOW DID HE...
IT'S OKAY. I SPOKE TO MARY. IT'S ALL CLEAR NOW.
I TOLD THEM WHAT SHE TOLD YOU.
ER, NO HARD FEELINGS, ISRAEL. I UNDERSTAND THE... DELICACY OF THE SITUATION.
OFTEN THE LOVERS ARE THE LAST TO KNOW.
WHAT THE...
FUCK...
CAL...

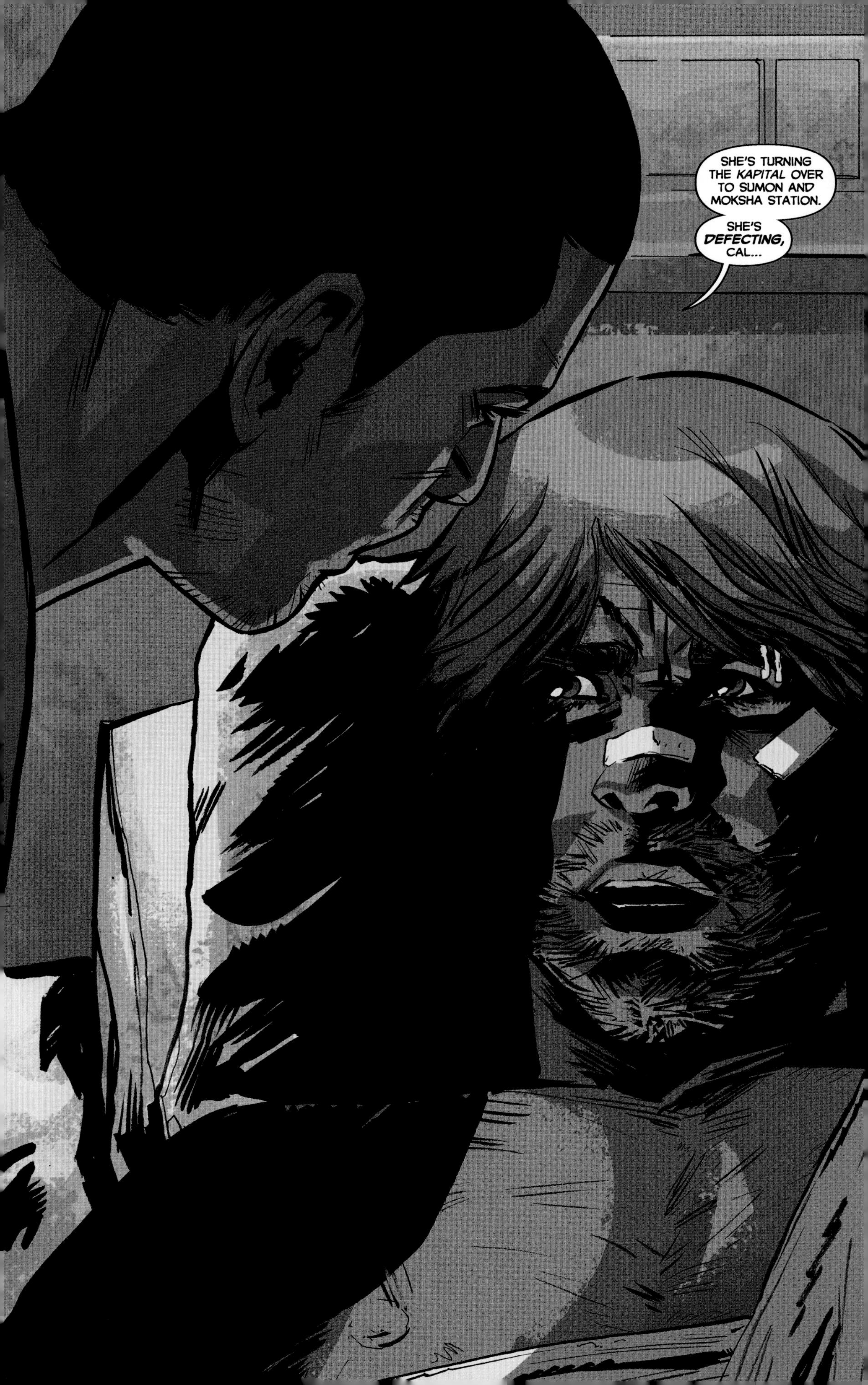
SHE'S TURNING THE *KAPITAL* OVER TO SUMON AND MOKSHA STATION.
SHE'S ***DEFECTING,*** CAL...

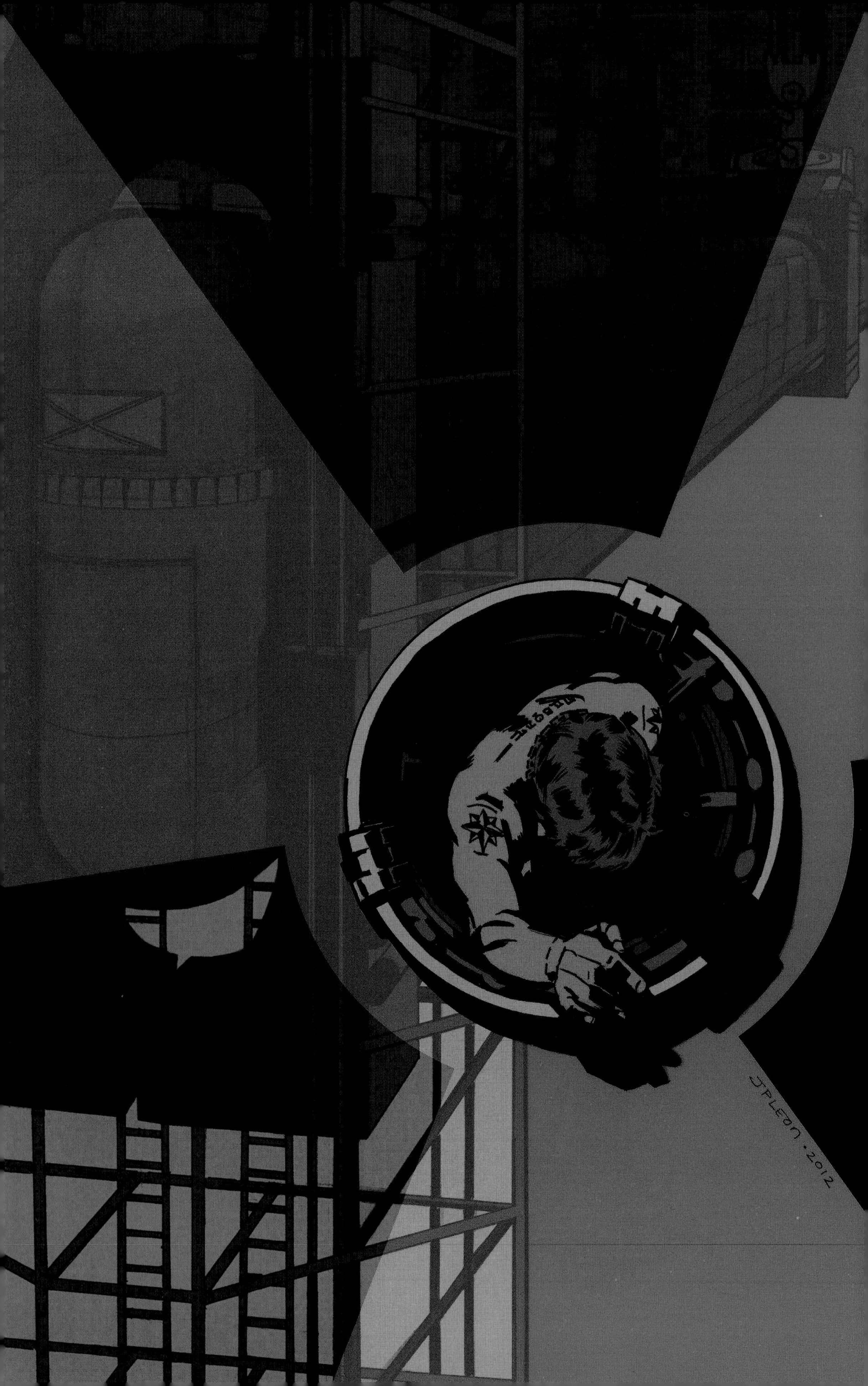
JPLEON • 2012

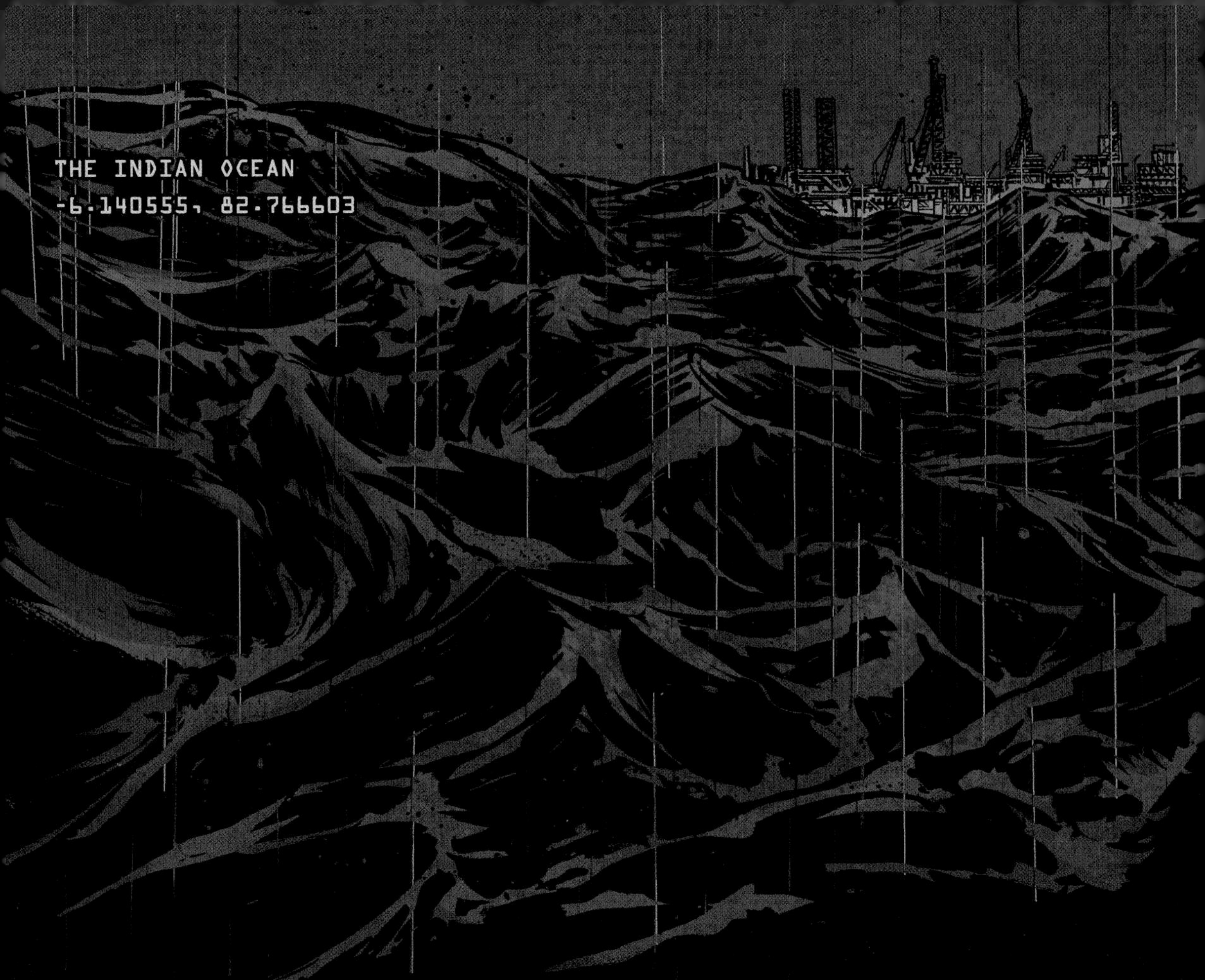
THE INDIAN OCEAN
-6.140555, 82.766603

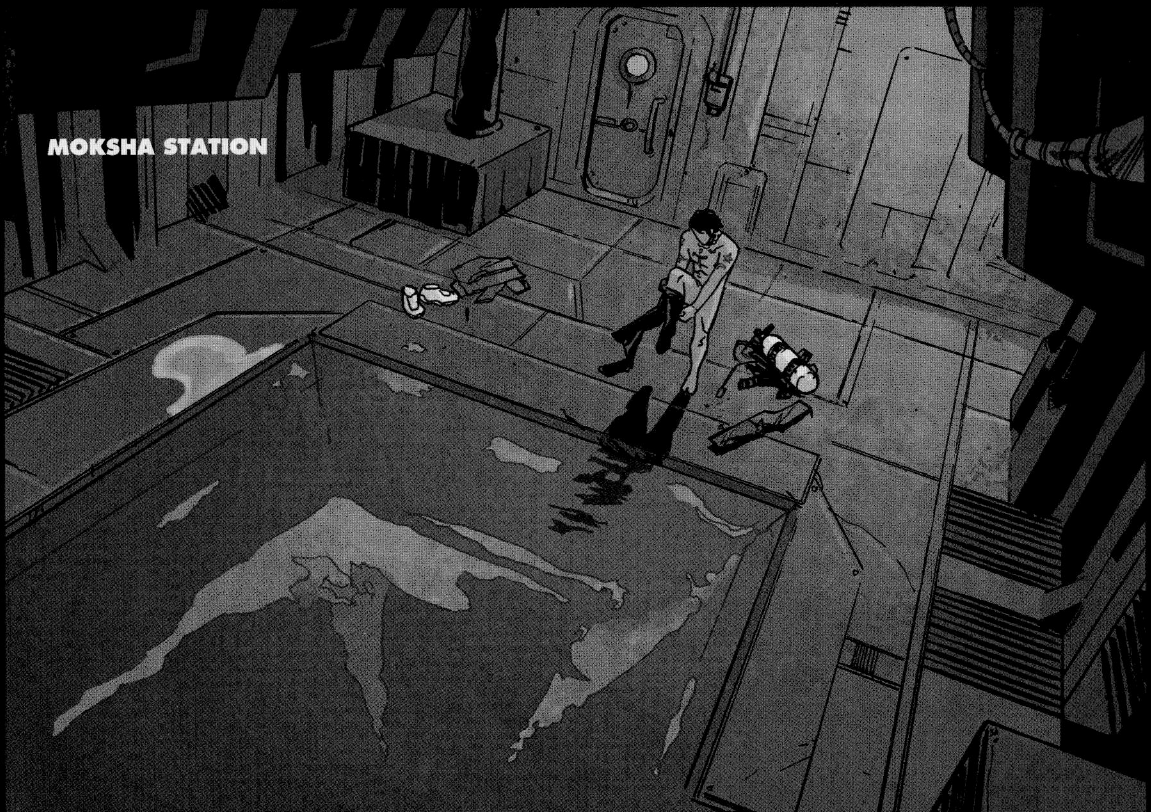
MOKSHA STATION

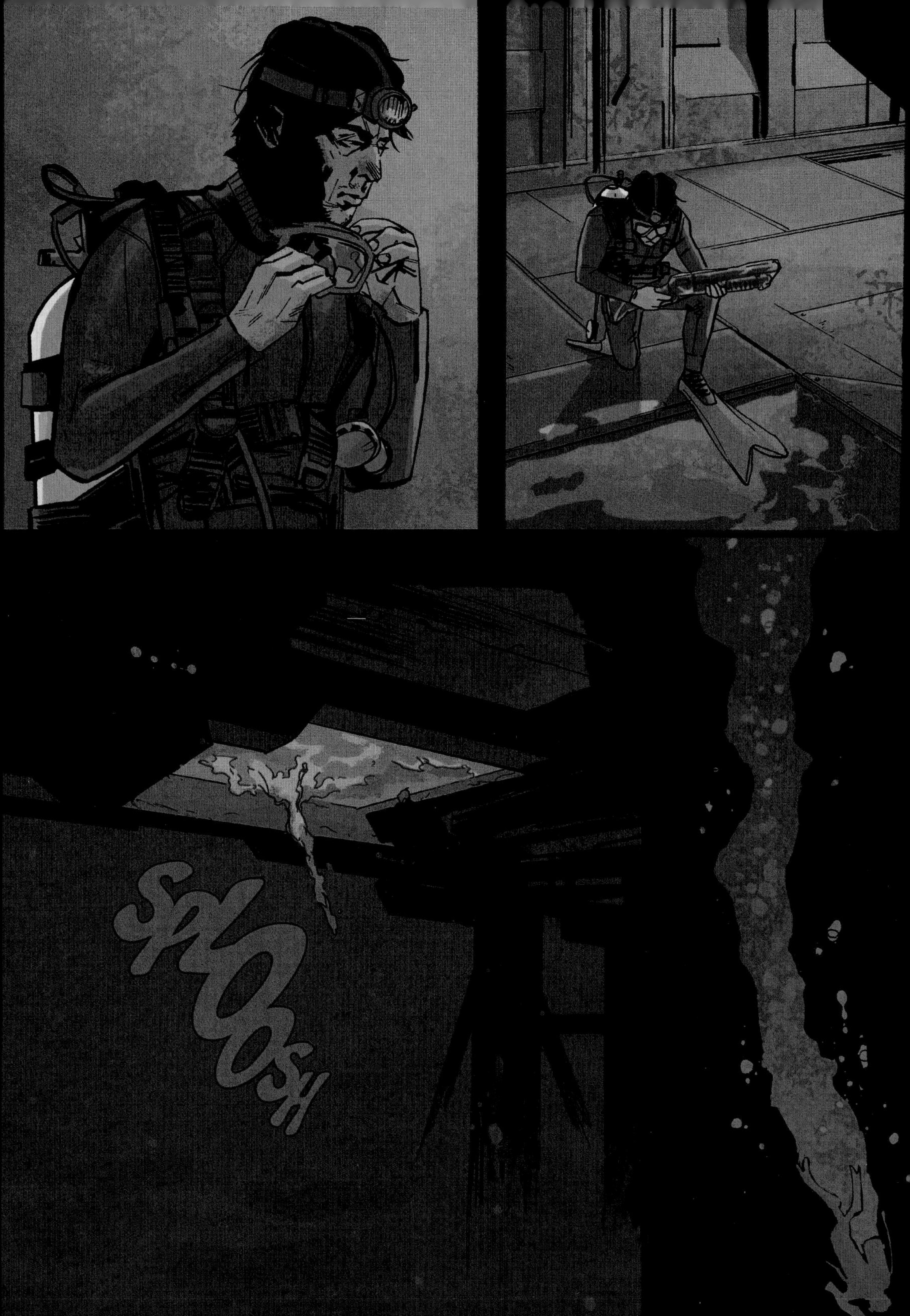
SPLOOSH

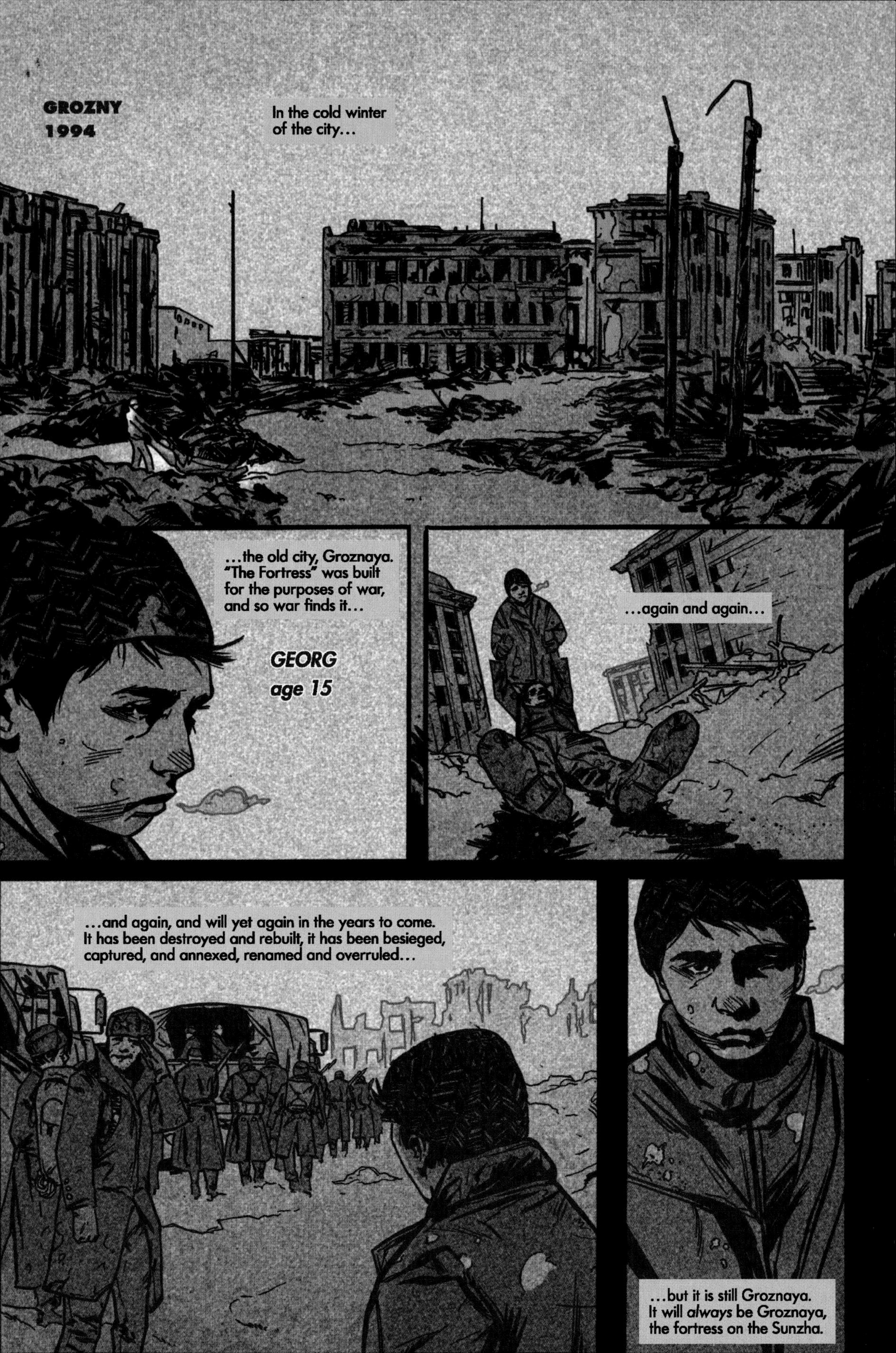
GROZNY
1994
In the cold winter of the city...
...the old city, Groznaya. "The Fortress" was built for the purposes of war, and so war finds it...
GEORG
age 15
...again and again...
...and again, and will yet again in the years to come. It has been destroyed and rebuilt, it has been besieged, captured, and annexed, renamed and overruled...
...but it is still Groznaya. It will *always* be Groznaya, the fortress on the Sunzha.

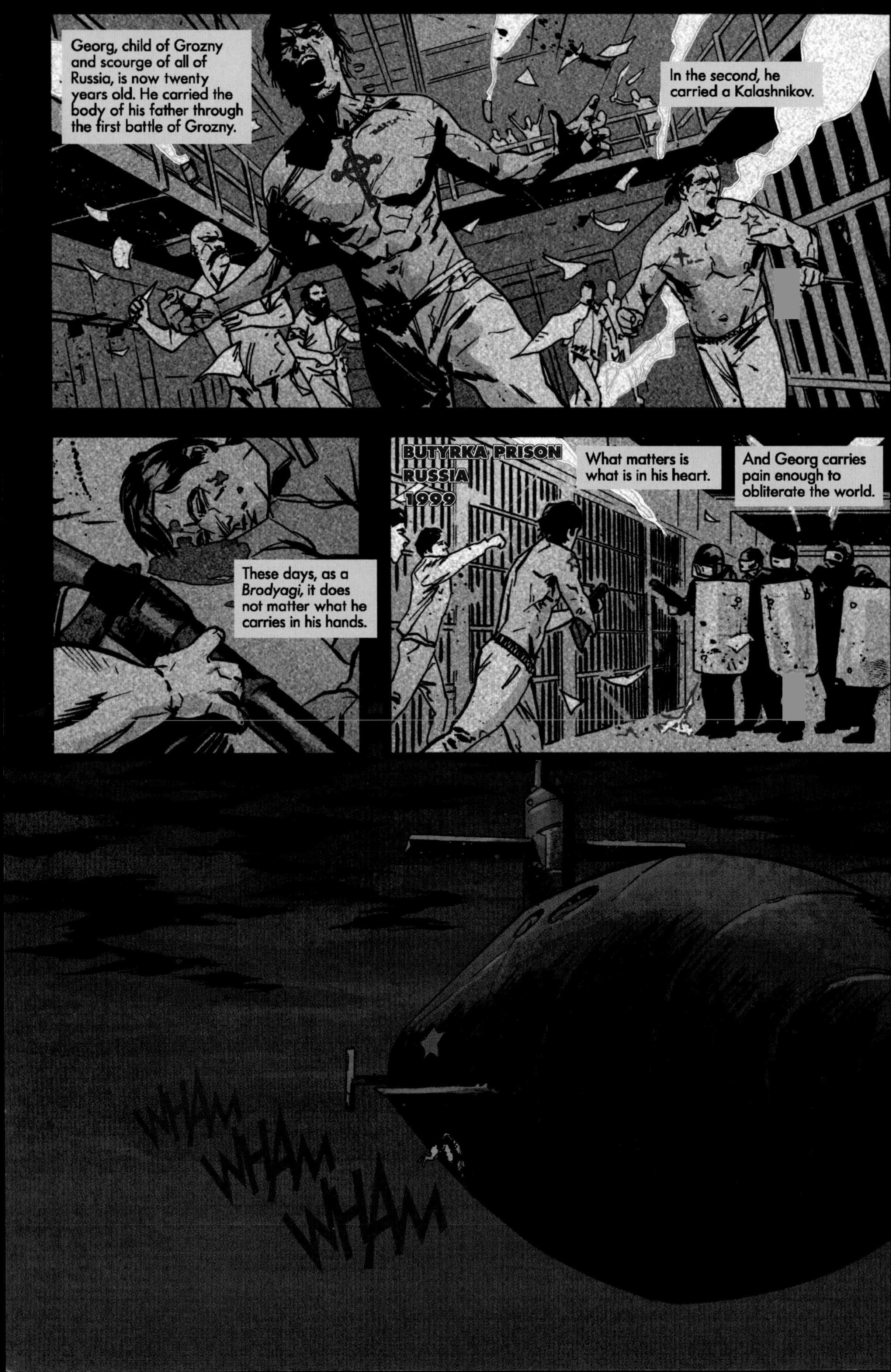
Georg, child of Grozny and scourge of all of Russia, is now twenty years old. He carried the body of his father through the first battle of Grozny.
In the *second,* he carried a Kalashnikov.
These days, as a *Brodyagi,* it does not matter what he carries in his hands.
BUTYRKA PRISON
RUSSIA
1999
What matters is what is in his heart.
And Georg carries pain enough to obliterate the world.
WHAM
WHAM
WHAM

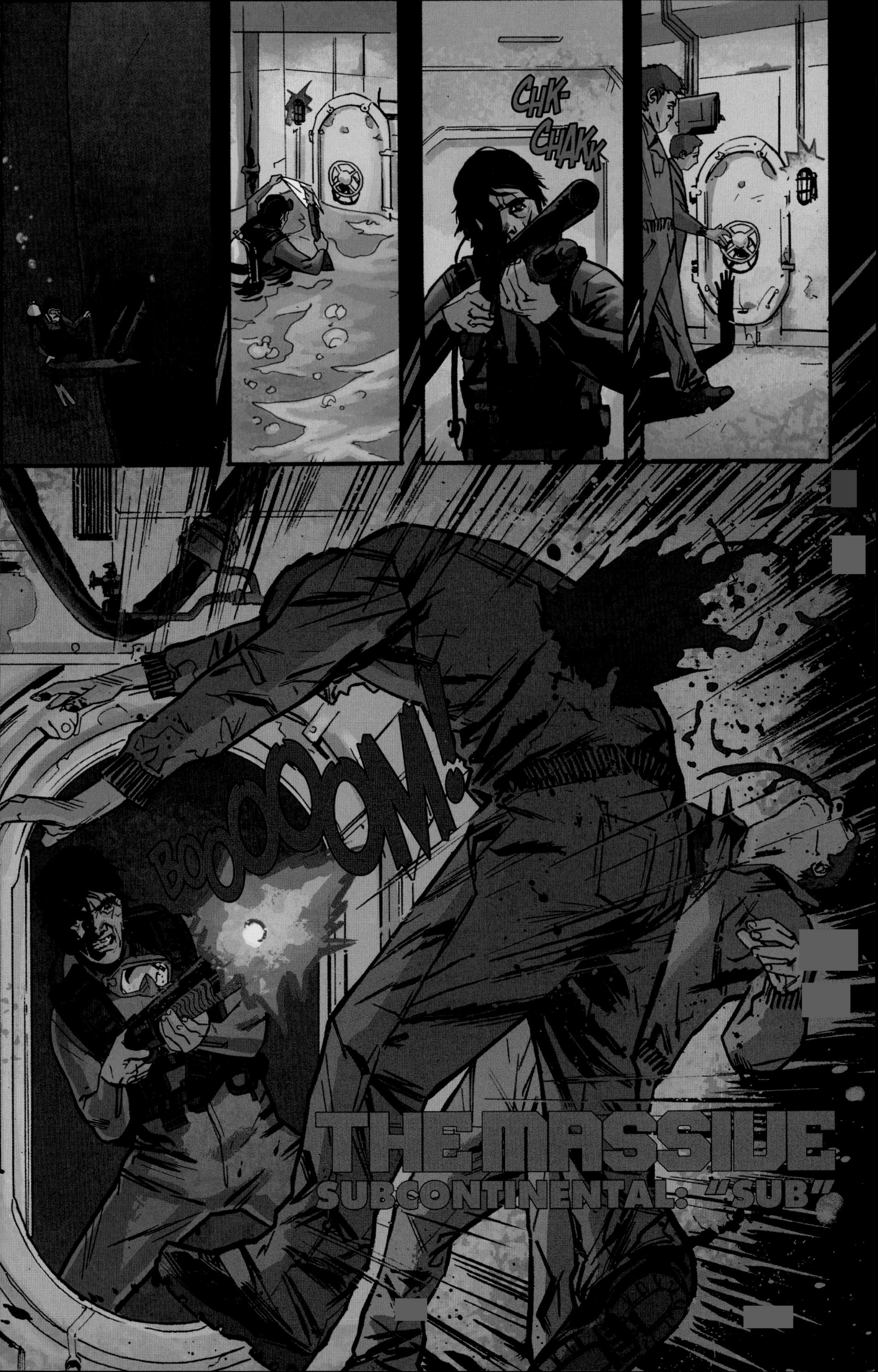
CHK-
CHAKK
BOOOOOM!
THE MASSIVE
SUBCONTINENTAL: "SUB"

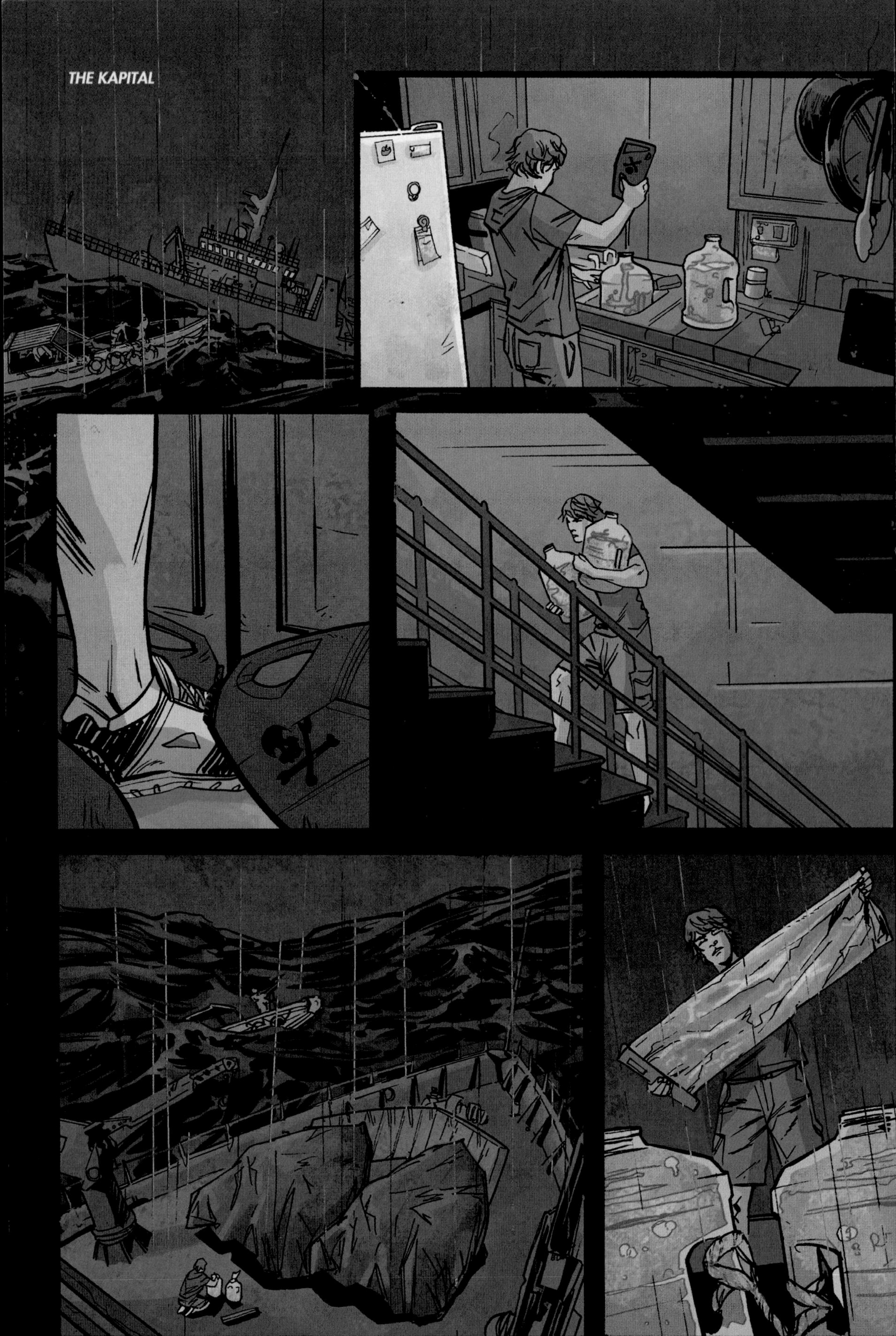
THE KAPITAL

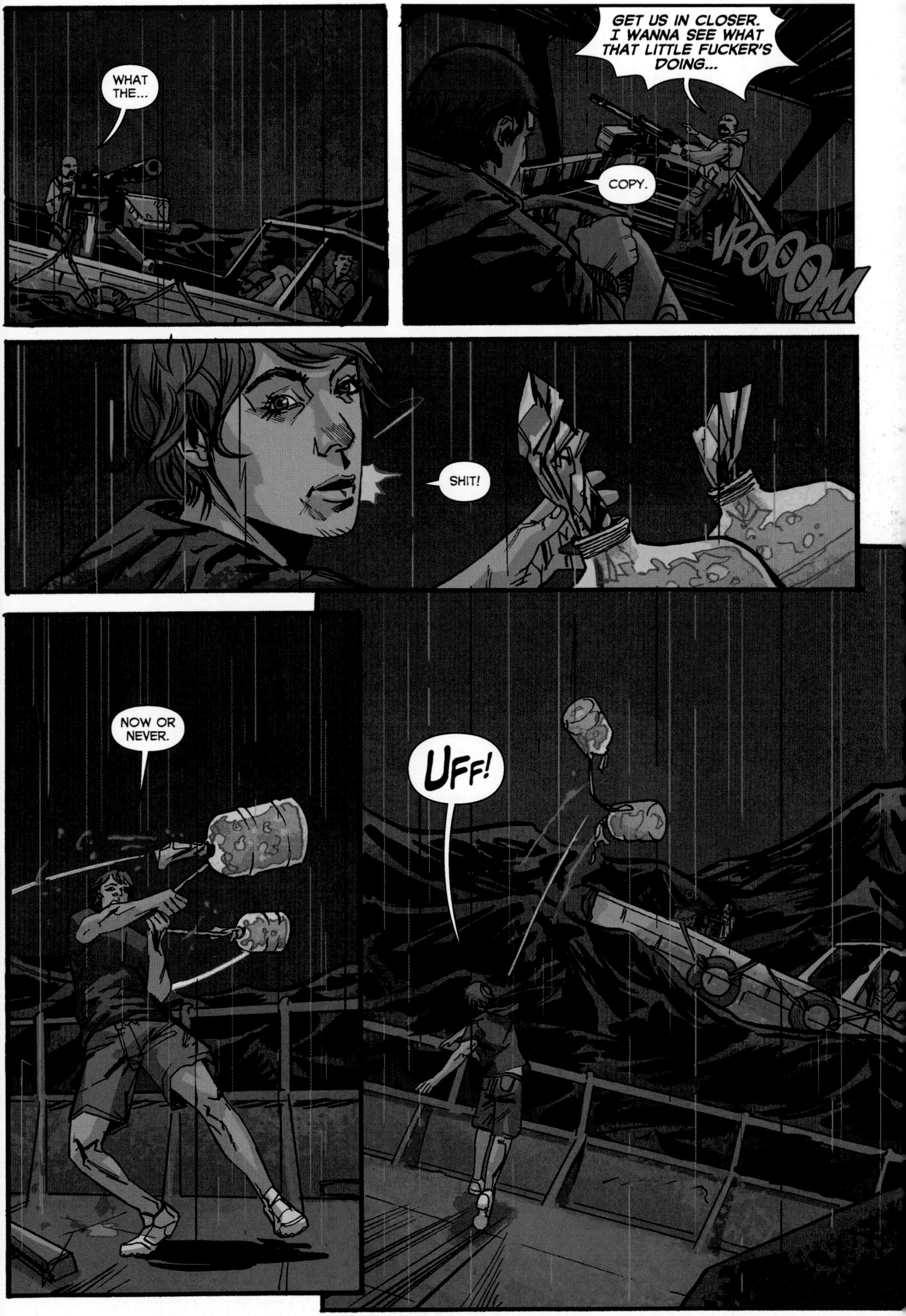
WHAT THE...
GET US IN CLOSER. I WANNA SEE WHAT THAT LITTLE FUCKER'S DOING...
COPY.
VROOOM
SHIT!
NOW OR NEVER.
UFF!

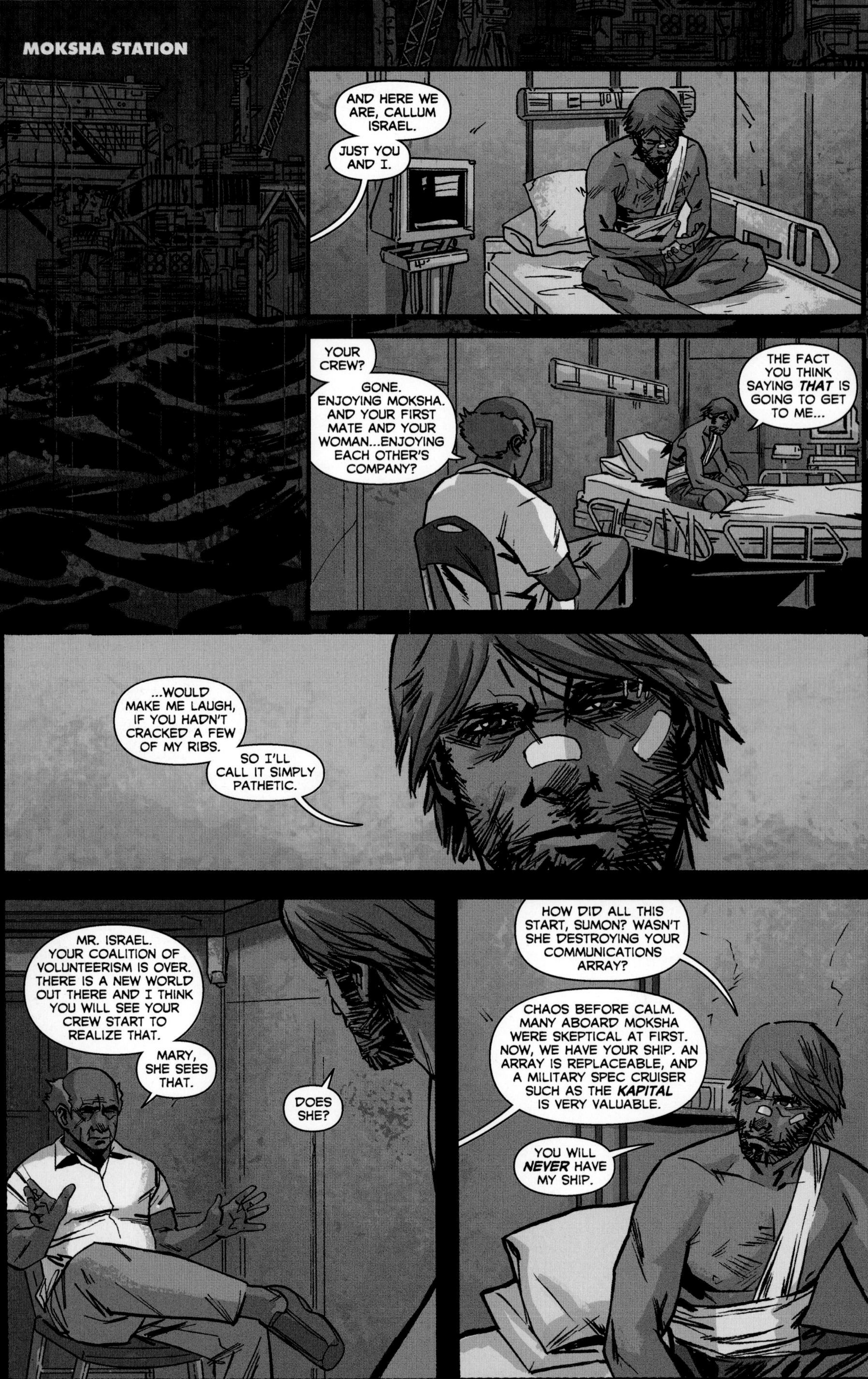
MOKSHA STATION
AND HERE WE ARE, CALLUM ISRAEL.
JUST YOU AND I.
YOUR CREW?
GONE. ENJOYING MOKSHA. AND YOUR FIRST MATE AND YOUR WOMAN...ENJOYING EACH OTHER'S COMPANY?
THE FACT YOU THINK SAYING THAT IS GOING TO GET TO ME...
...WOULD MAKE ME LAUGH, IF YOU HADN'T CRACKED A FEW OF MY RIBS.
SO I'LL CALL IT SIMPLY PATHETIC.
MR. ISRAEL. YOUR COALITION OF VOLUNTEERISM IS OVER. THERE IS A NEW WORLD OUT THERE AND I THINK YOU WILL SEE YOUR CREW START TO REALIZE THAT.
MARY, SHE SEES THAT.
DOES SHE?
HOW DID ALL THIS START, SUMON? WASN'T SHE DESTROYING YOUR COMMUNICATIONS ARRAY?
CHAOS BEFORE CALM. MANY ABOARD MOKSHA WERE SKEPTICAL AT FIRST. NOW, WE HAVE YOUR SHIP. AN ARRAY IS REPLACEABLE, AND A MILITARY SPEC CRUISER SUCH AS THE KAPITAL IS VERY VALUABLE.
YOU WILL NEVER HAVE MY SHIP.

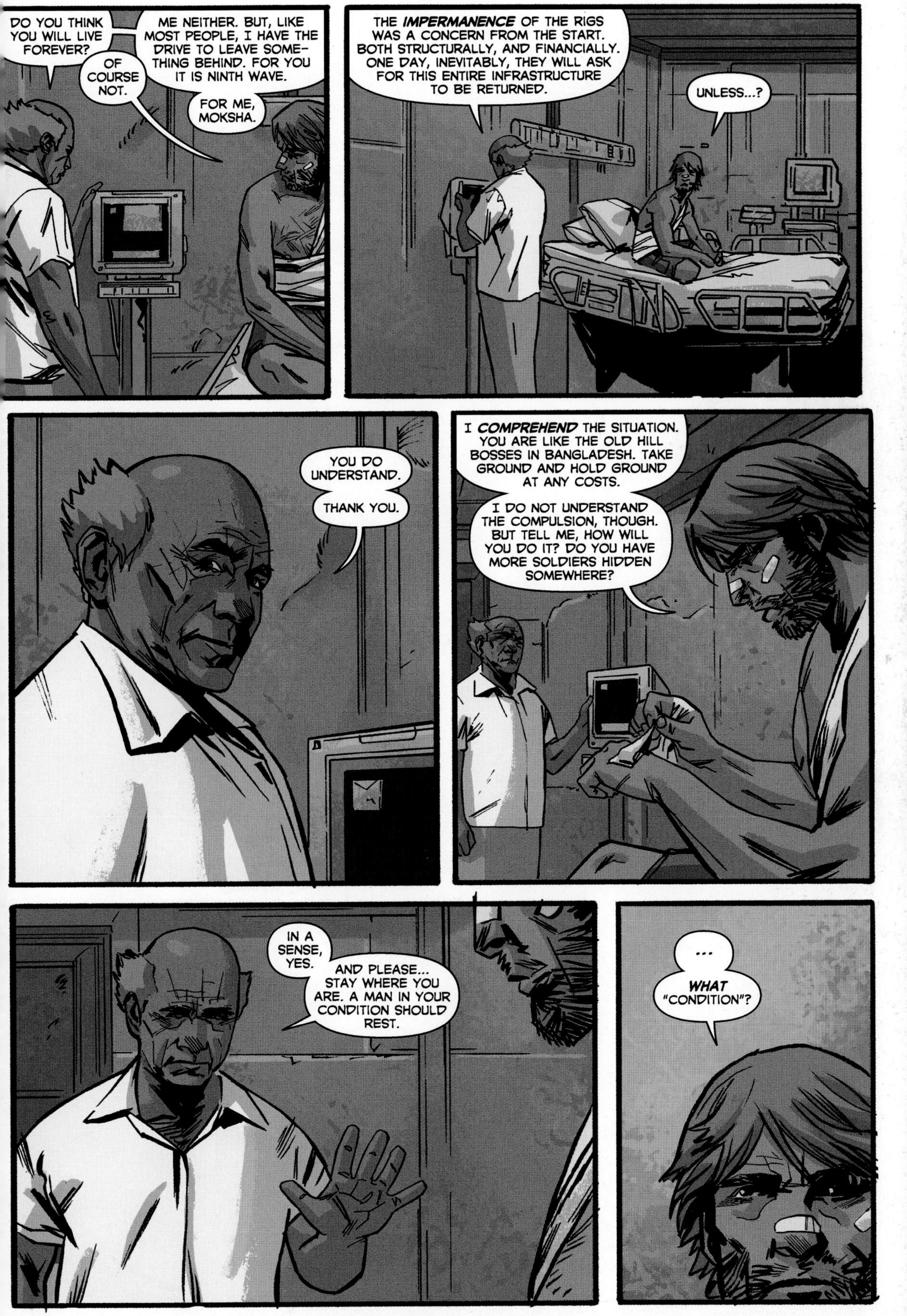
DO YOU THINK YOU WILL LIVE FOREVER?
OF COURSE NOT.
ME NEITHER. BUT, LIKE MOST PEOPLE, I HAVE THE DRIVE TO LEAVE SOMETHING BEHIND. FOR YOU IT IS NINTH WAVE.
FOR ME, MOKSHA.
THE IMPERMANENCE OF THE RIGS WAS A CONCERN FROM THE START. BOTH STRUCTURALLY, AND FINANCIALLY. ONE DAY, INEVITABLY, THEY WILL ASK FOR THIS ENTIRE INFRASTRUCTURE TO BE RETURNED.
UNLESS...?
I COMPREHEND THE SITUATION. YOU ARE LIKE THE OLD HILL BOSSES IN BANGLADESH. TAKE GROUND AND HOLD GROUND AT ANY COSTS.
I DO NOT UNDERSTAND THE COMPULSION, THOUGH. BUT TELL ME, HOW WILL YOU DO IT? DO YOU HAVE MORE SOLDIERS HIDDEN SOMEWHERE?
YOU DO UNDERSTAND.
THANK YOU.
IN A SENSE, YES.
AND PLEASE... STAY WHERE YOU ARE. A MAN IN YOUR CONDITION SHOULD REST.
...
WHAT "CONDITION"?

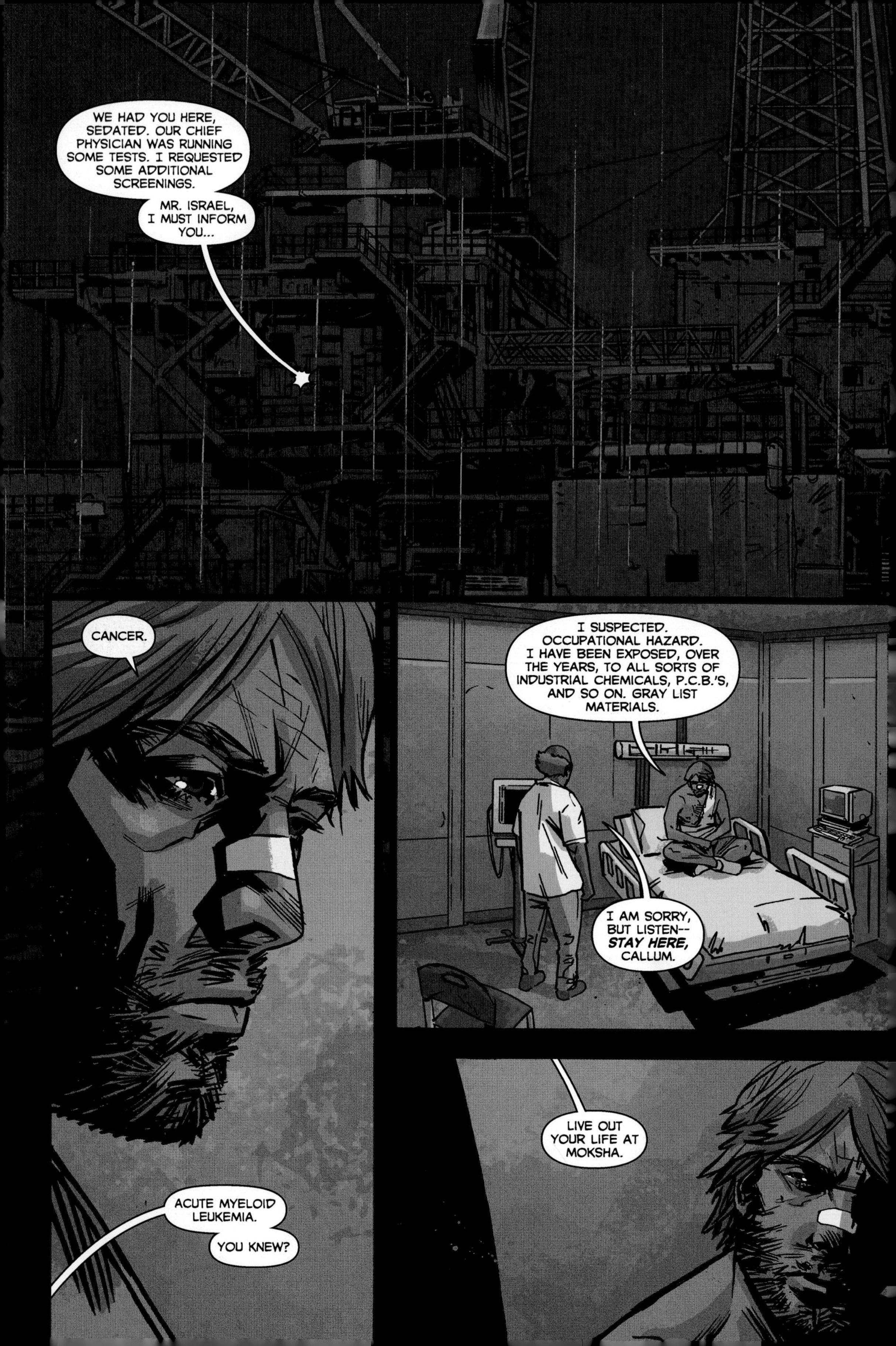
WE HAD YOU HERE, SEDATED. OUR CHIEF PHYSICIAN WAS RUNNING SOME TESTS. I REQUESTED SOME ADDITIONAL SCREENINGS.
MR. ISRAEL, I MUST INFORM YOU...
CANCER.
ACUTE MYELOID LEUKEMIA.
YOU KNEW?
I SUSPECTED. OCCUPATIONAL HAZARD. I HAVE BEEN EXPOSED, OVER THE YEARS, TO ALL SORTS OF INDUSTRIAL CHEMICALS, P.C.B.'S, AND SO ON. GRAY LIST MATERIALS.
I AM SORRY, BUT LISTEN-- *STAY HERE,* CALLUM.
LIVE OUT YOUR LIFE AT MOKSHA.

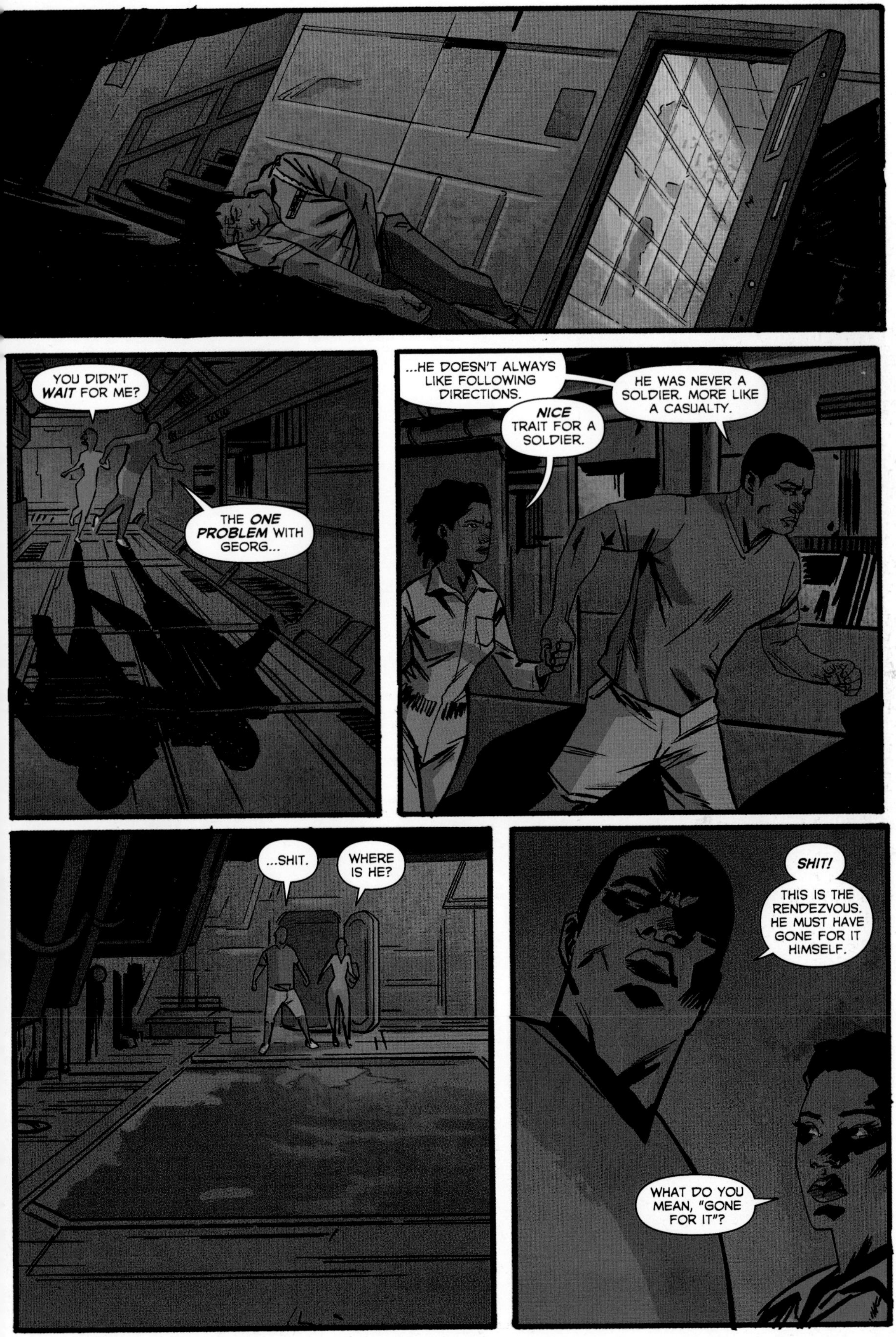
YOU DIDN'T WAIT FOR ME?
THE ONE PROBLEM WITH GEORG...
...HE DOESN'T ALWAYS LIKE FOLLOWING DIRECTIONS.
NICE TRAIT FOR A SOLDIER.
HE WAS NEVER A SOLDIER. MORE LIKE A CASUALTY.
...SHIT.
WHERE IS HE?
SHIT!
THIS IS THE RENDEZVOUS. HE MUST HAVE GONE FOR IT HIMSELF.
WHAT DO YOU MEAN, "GONE FOR IT"?

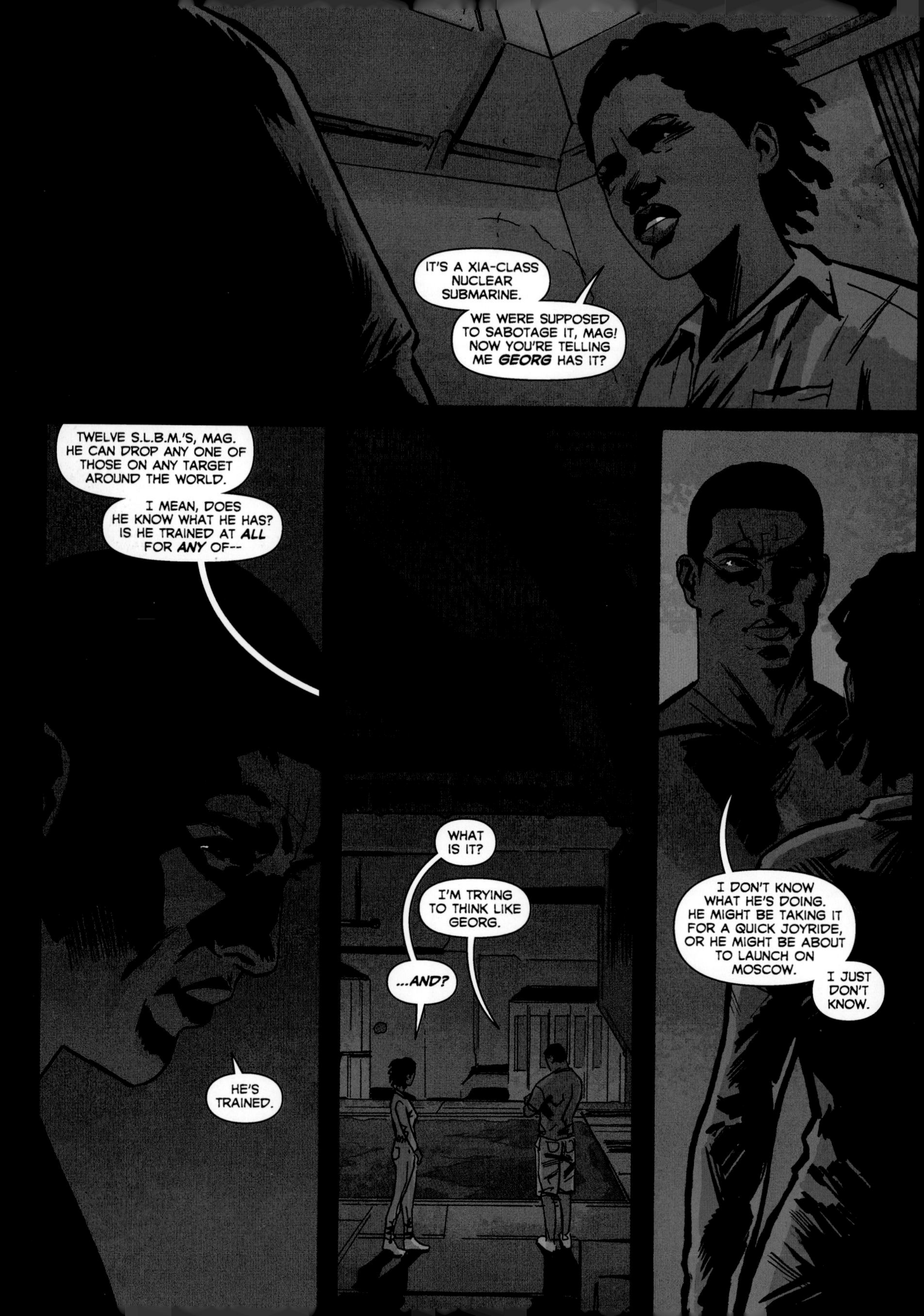
IT'S A XIA-CLASS NUCLEAR SUBMARINE.
WE WERE SUPPOSED TO SABOTAGE IT, MAG! NOW YOU'RE TELLING ME GEORG HAS IT?
TWELVE S.L.B.M.'S, MAG. HE CAN DROP ANY ONE OF THOSE ON ANY TARGET AROUND THE WORLD.
I MEAN, DOES HE KNOW WHAT HE HAS? IS HE TRAINED AT ALL FOR ANY OF--
HE'S TRAINED.
WHAT IS IT?
I'M TRYING TO THINK LIKE GEORG.
...AND?
I DON'T KNOW WHAT HE'S DOING. HE MIGHT BE TAKING IT FOR A QUICK JOYRIDE, OR HE MIGHT BE ABOUT TO LAUNCH ON MOSCOW.
I JUST DON'T KNOW.

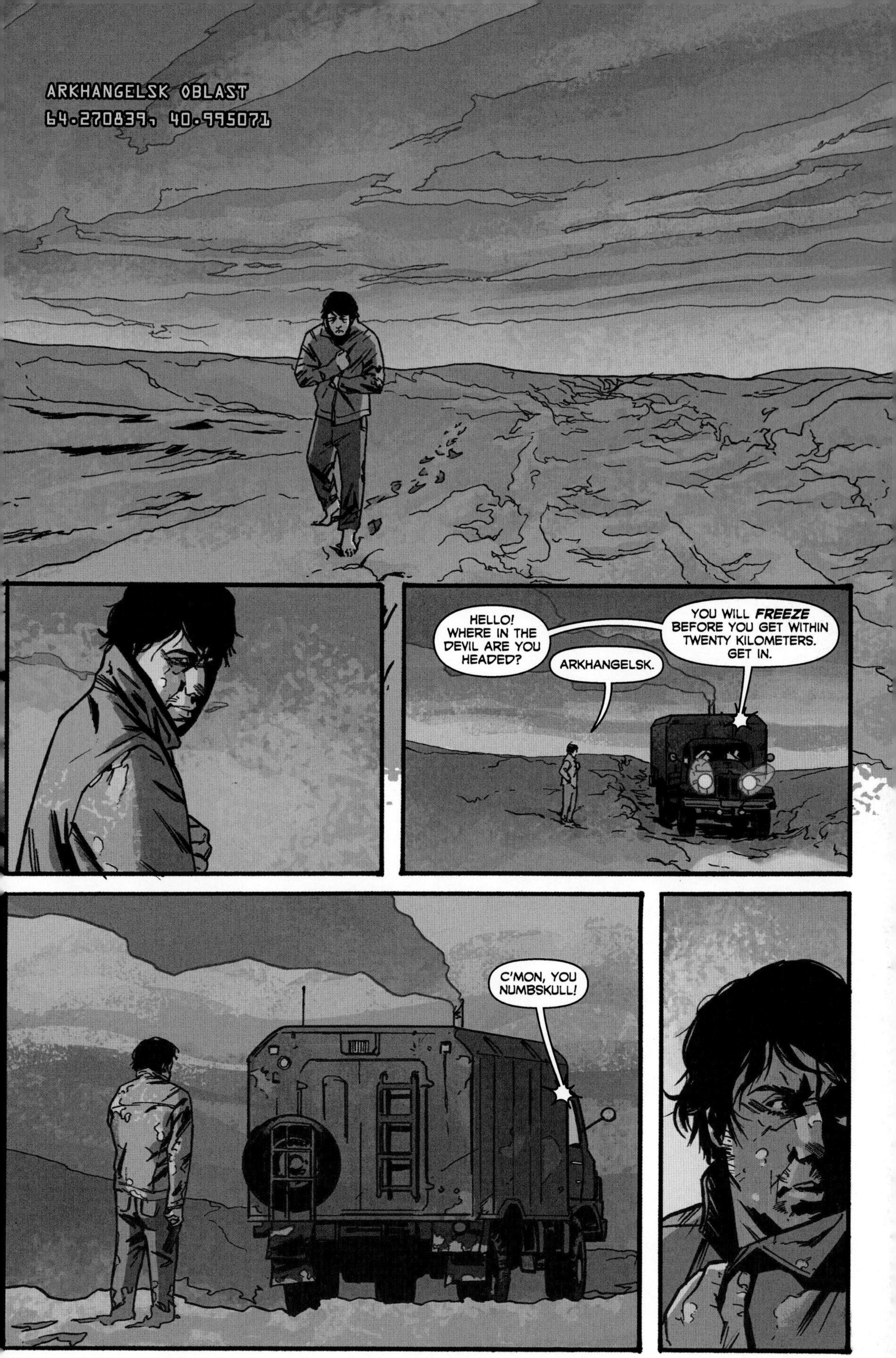
ARKHANGELSK OBLAST
64.270839, 40.995071
HELLO! WHERE IN THE DEVIL ARE YOU HEADED?
ARKHANGELSK.
YOU WILL *FREEZE* BEFORE YOU GET WITHIN TWENTY KILOMETERS. GET IN.
C'MON, YOU NUMBSKULL!

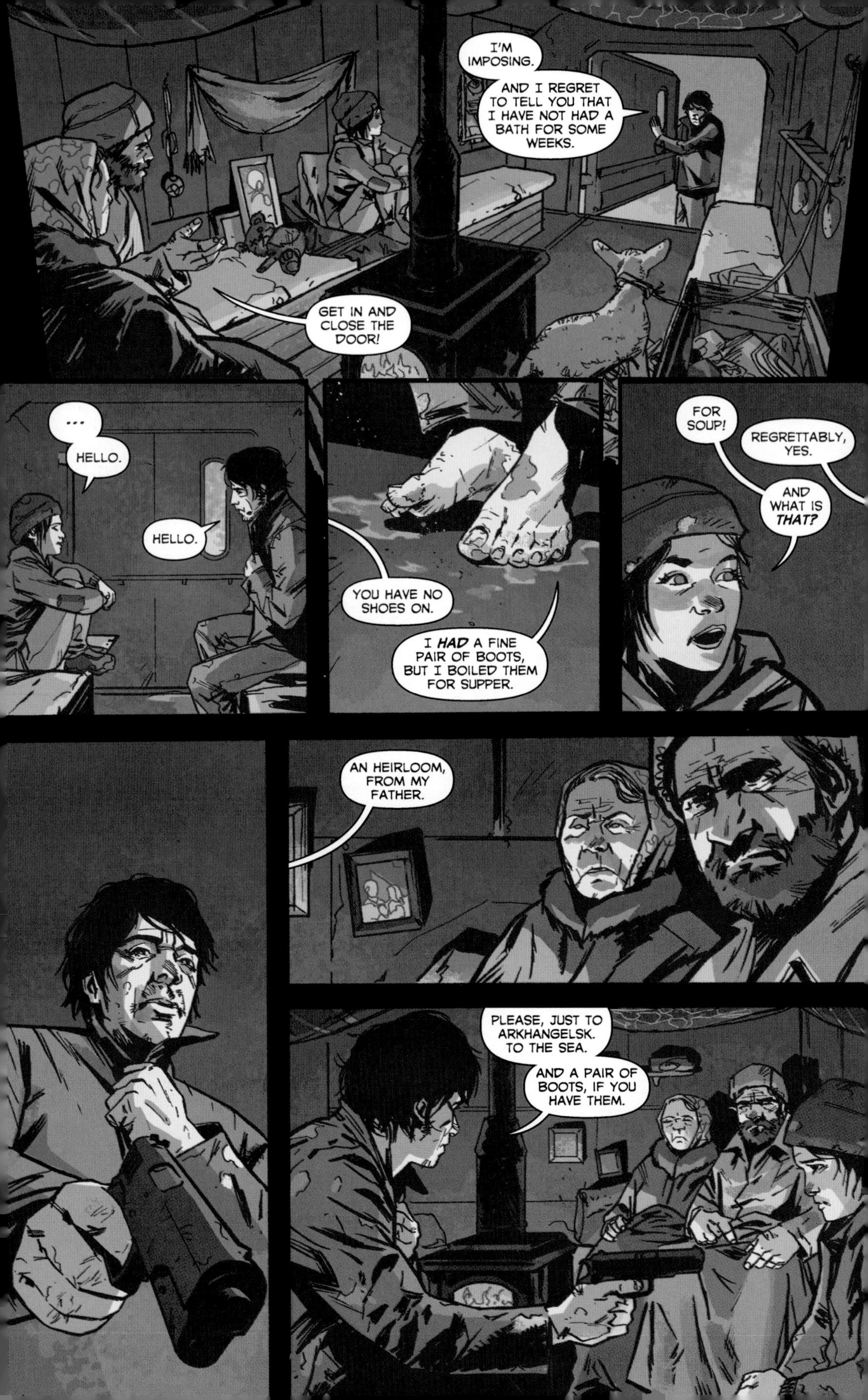
I'M IMPOSING.
AND I REGRET TO TELL YOU THAT I HAVE NOT HAD A BATH FOR SOME WEEKS.
GET IN AND CLOSE THE DOOR!
...
HELLO.
HELLO.
YOU HAVE NO SHOES ON.
I HAD A FINE PAIR OF BOOTS, BUT I BOILED THEM FOR SUPPER.
FOR SOUP!
REGRETTABLY, YES.
AND WHAT IS THAT?
AN HEIRLOOM, FROM MY FATHER.
PLEASE, JUST TO ARKHANGELSK. TO THE SEA.
AND A PAIR OF BOOTS, IF YOU HAVE THEM.

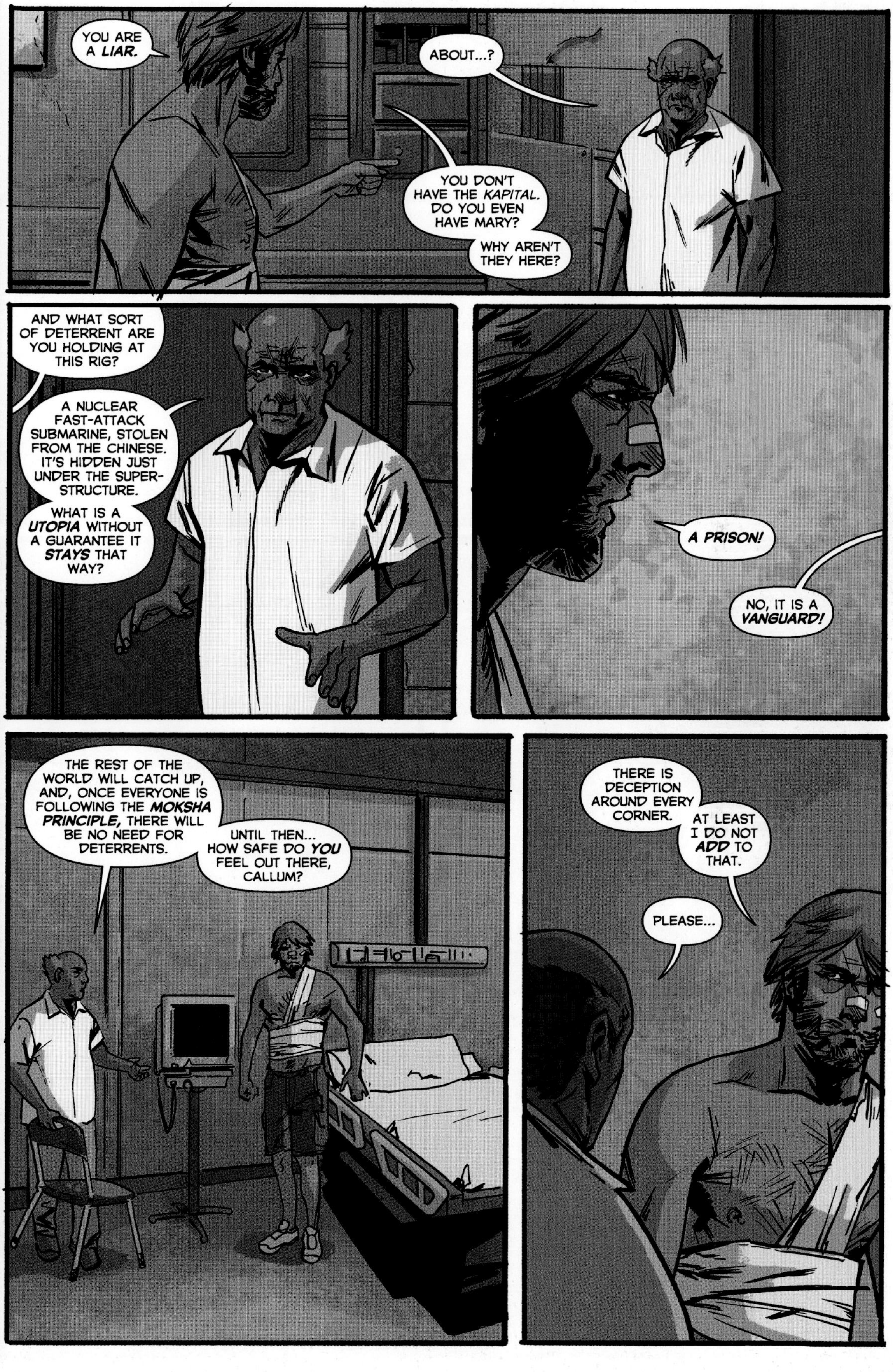
YOU ARE A LIAR.
ABOUT...?
YOU DON'T HAVE THE KAPITAL. DO YOU EVEN HAVE MARY?
WHY AREN'T THEY HERE?
AND WHAT SORT OF DETERRENT ARE YOU HOLDING AT THIS RIG?
A NUCLEAR FAST-ATTACK SUBMARINE, STOLEN FROM THE CHINESE. IT'S HIDDEN JUST UNDER THE SUPER-STRUCTURE.
WHAT IS A UTOPIA WITHOUT A GUARANTEE IT STAYS THAT WAY?
A PRISON!
NO, IT IS A VANGUARD!
THE REST OF THE WORLD WILL CATCH UP, AND, ONCE EVERYONE IS FOLLOWING THE MOKSHA PRINCIPLE, THERE WILL BE NO NEED FOR DETERRENTS.
UNTIL THEN... HOW SAFE DO YOU FEEL OUT THERE, CALLUM?
THERE IS DECEPTION AROUND EVERY CORNER.
AT LEAST I DO NOT ADD TO THAT.
PLEASE...

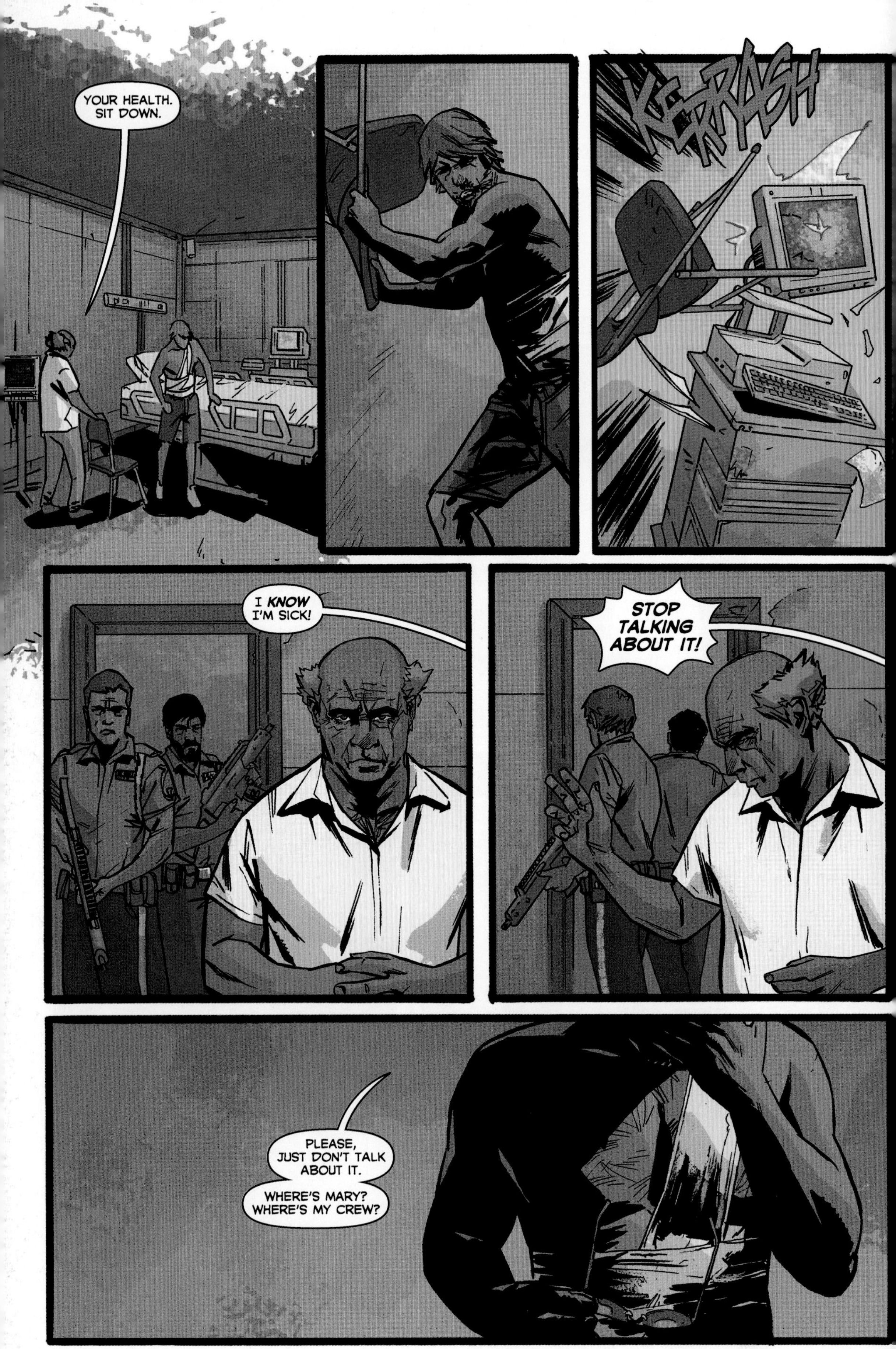
YOUR HEALTH. SIT DOWN.
KERRASH
I KNOW I'M SICK!
STOP TALKING ABOUT IT!
PLEASE, JUST DON'T TALK ABOUT IT.
WHERE'S MARY? WHERE'S MY CREW?

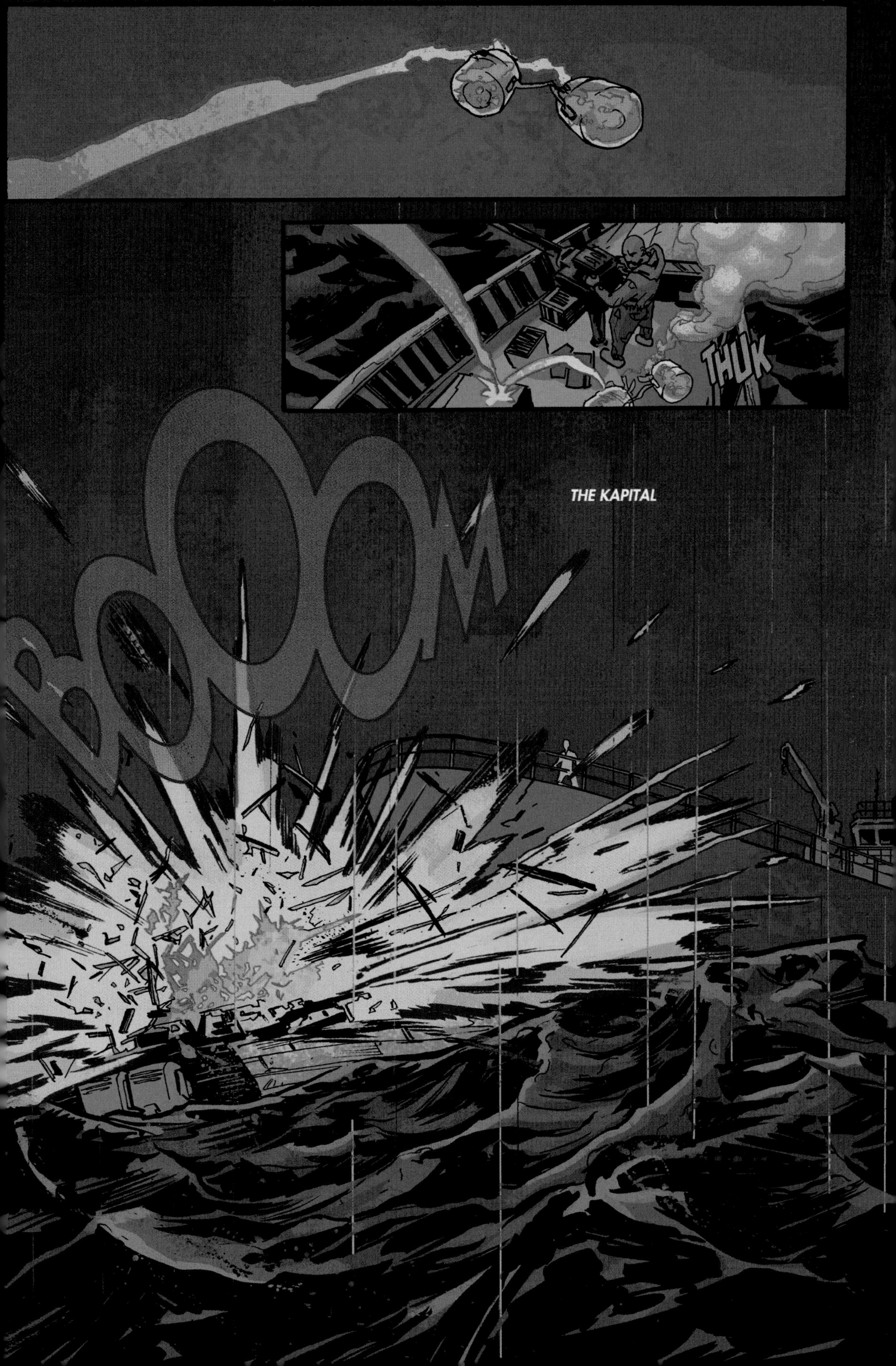
THUK
THE KAPITAL
BOOOOM

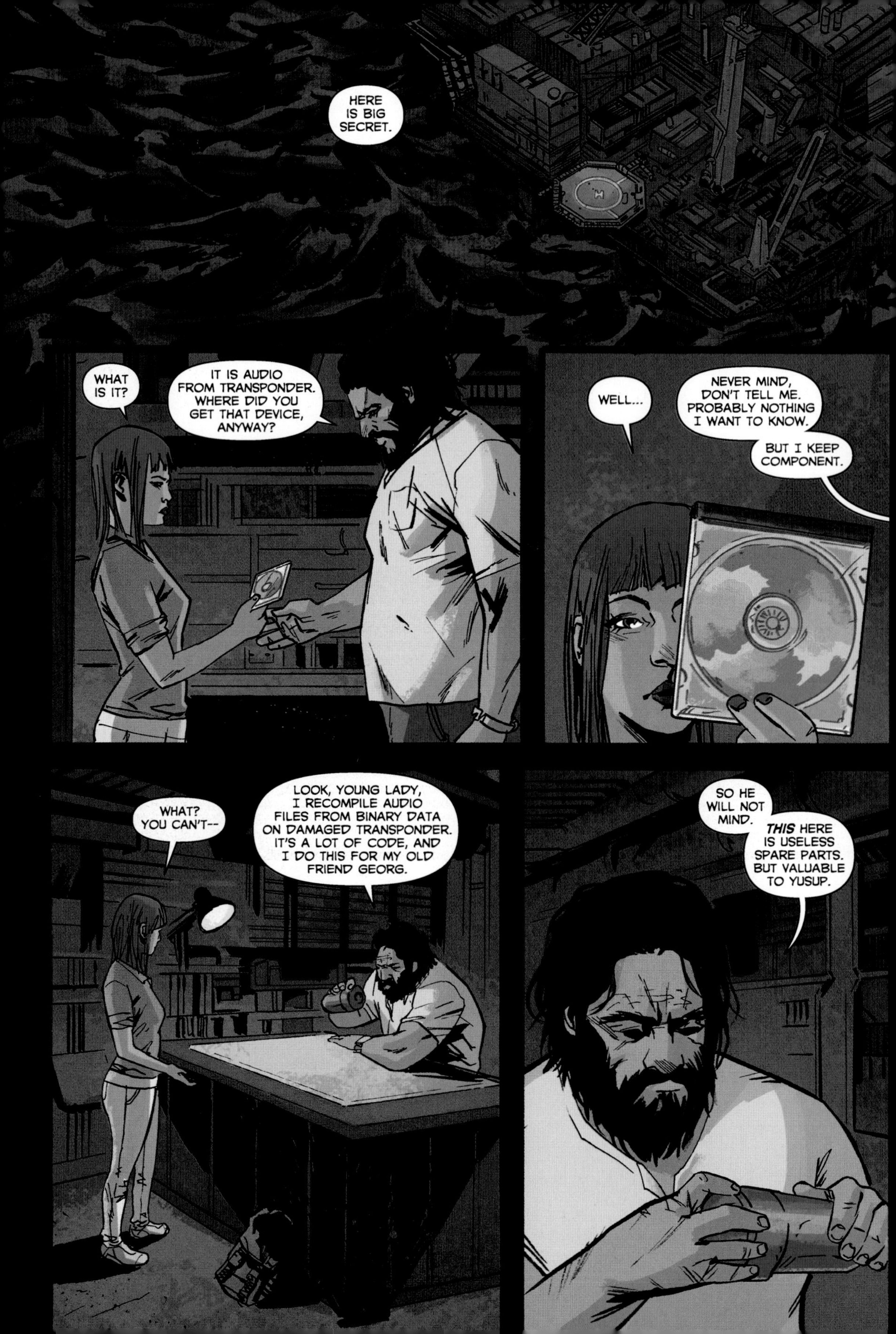
HERE IS BIG SECRET.
WHAT IS IT?
IT IS AUDIO FROM TRANSPONDER. WHERE DID YOU GET THAT DEVICE, ANYWAY?
WELL...
NEVER MIND, DON'T TELL ME. PROBABLY NOTHING I WANT TO KNOW.
BUT I KEEP COMPONENT.
WHAT? YOU CAN'T--
LOOK, YOUNG LADY, I RECOMPILE AUDIO FILES FROM BINARY DATA ON DAMAGED TRANSPONDER. IT'S A LOT OF CODE, AND I DO THIS FOR MY OLD FRIEND GEORG.
SO HE WILL NOT MIND.
THIS HERE IS USELESS SPARE PARTS. BUT VALUABLE TO YUSUP.

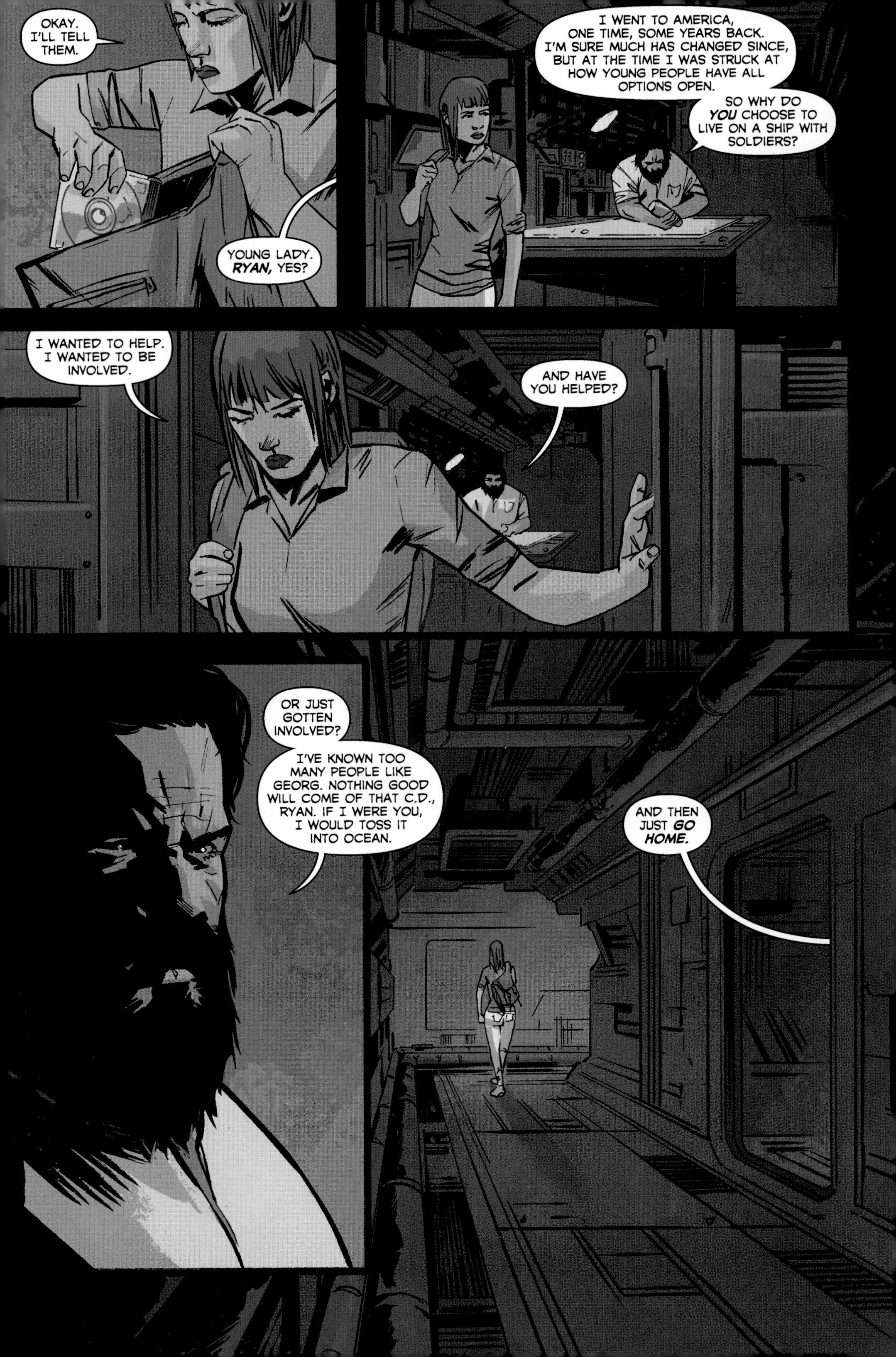
OKAY. I'LL TELL THEM.
YOUNG LADY. ***RYAN,*** YES?
I WENT TO AMERICA, ONE TIME, SOME YEARS BACK. I'M SURE MUCH HAS CHANGED SINCE, BUT AT THE TIME I WAS STRUCK AT HOW YOUNG PEOPLE HAVE ALL OPTIONS OPEN.
SO WHY DO ***YOU*** CHOOSE TO LIVE ON A SHIP WITH SOLDIERS?
I WANTED TO HELP. I WANTED TO BE INVOLVED.
AND HAVE YOU HELPED?
OR JUST GOTTEN INVOLVED?
I'VE KNOWN TOO MANY PEOPLE LIKE GEORG. NOTHING GOOD WILL COME OF THAT C.D., RYAN. IF I WERE YOU, I WOULD TOSS IT INTO OCEAN.
AND THEN JUST ***GO HOME.***

CAL?

CAL, ARE YOU OKAY?

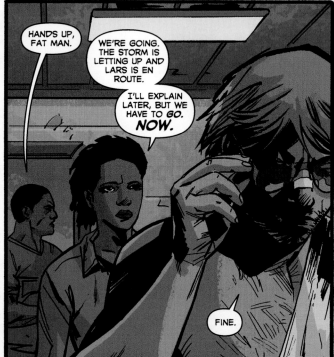

HANDS UP, FAT MAN.

WE'RE GOING. THE STORM IS LETTING UP AND LARS IS EN ROUTE.

I'LL EXPLAIN LATER, BUT WE HAVE TO *GO.* *NOW.*

FINE.

BUT NO ONE STAYS BEHIND. THE WHOLE CREW IS COMING WITH US.

I KNOW. I--

ALL OF THEM, NO EXCEPTIONS.

NO EXCEPTIONS, CAL, YOU GOT IT.

NOW LET'S GO.

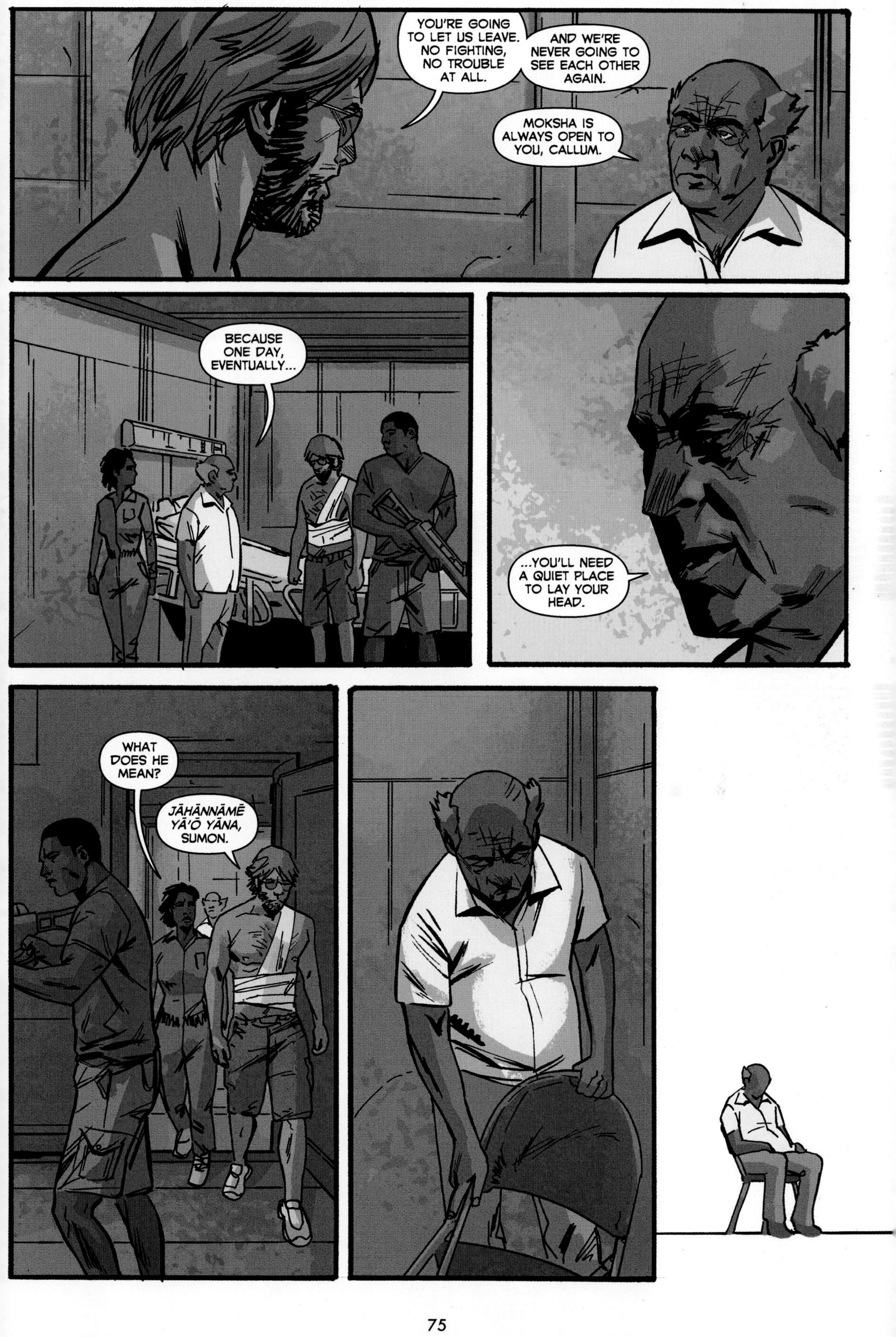
YOU'RE GOING TO LET US LEAVE. NO FIGHTING, NO TROUBLE AT ALL.
AND WE'RE NEVER GOING TO SEE EACH OTHER AGAIN.
MOKSHA IS ALWAYS OPEN TO YOU, CALLUM.
BECAUSE ONE DAY, EVENTUALLY...
...YOU'LL NEED A QUIET PLACE TO LAY YOUR HEAD.
WHAT DOES HE MEAN?
JĀHĀNNĀMĒ YĀ'Ō YĀNA, SUMON.

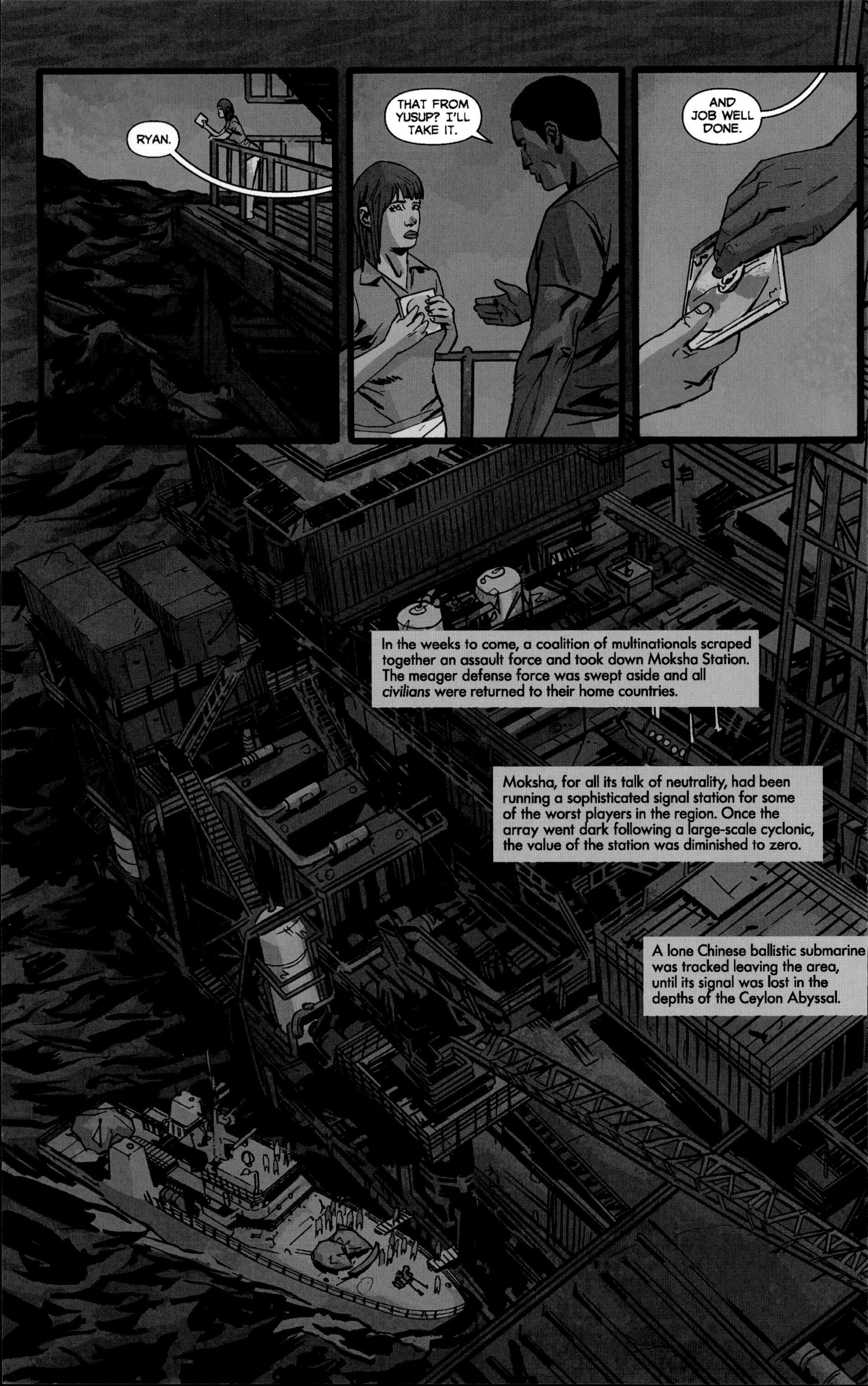
RYAN.
THAT FROM YUSUP? I'LL TAKE IT.
AND JOB WELL DONE.
In the weeks to come, a coalition of multinationals scraped together an assault force and took down Moksha Station. The meager defense force was swept aside and all *civilians* were returned to their home countries.
Moksha, for all its talk of neutrality, had been running a sophisticated signal station for some of the worst players in the region. Once the array went dark following a large-scale cyclonic, the value of the station was diminished to zero.
A lone Chinese ballistic submarine was tracked leaving the area, until its signal was lost in the depths of the Ceylon Abyssal.

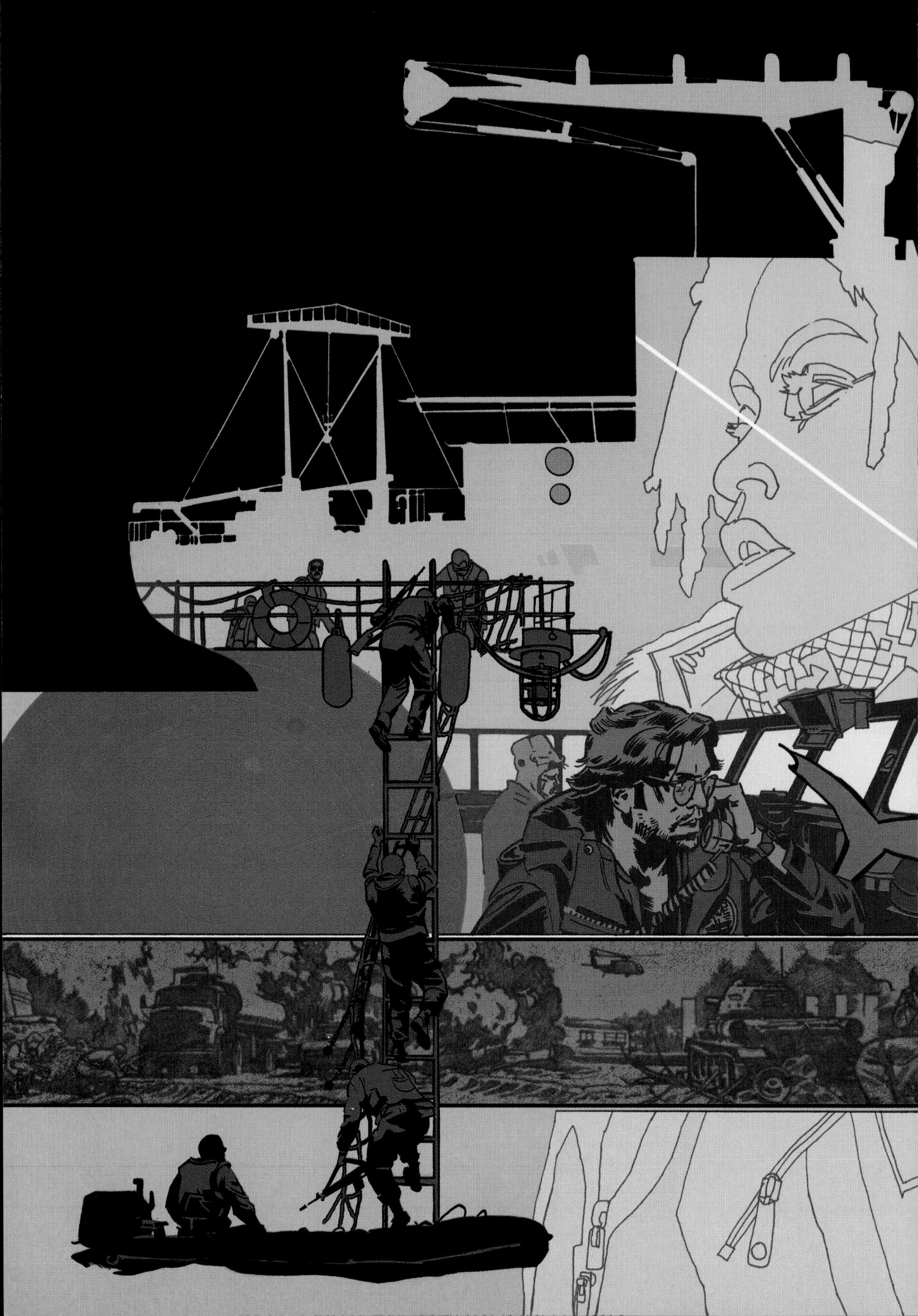

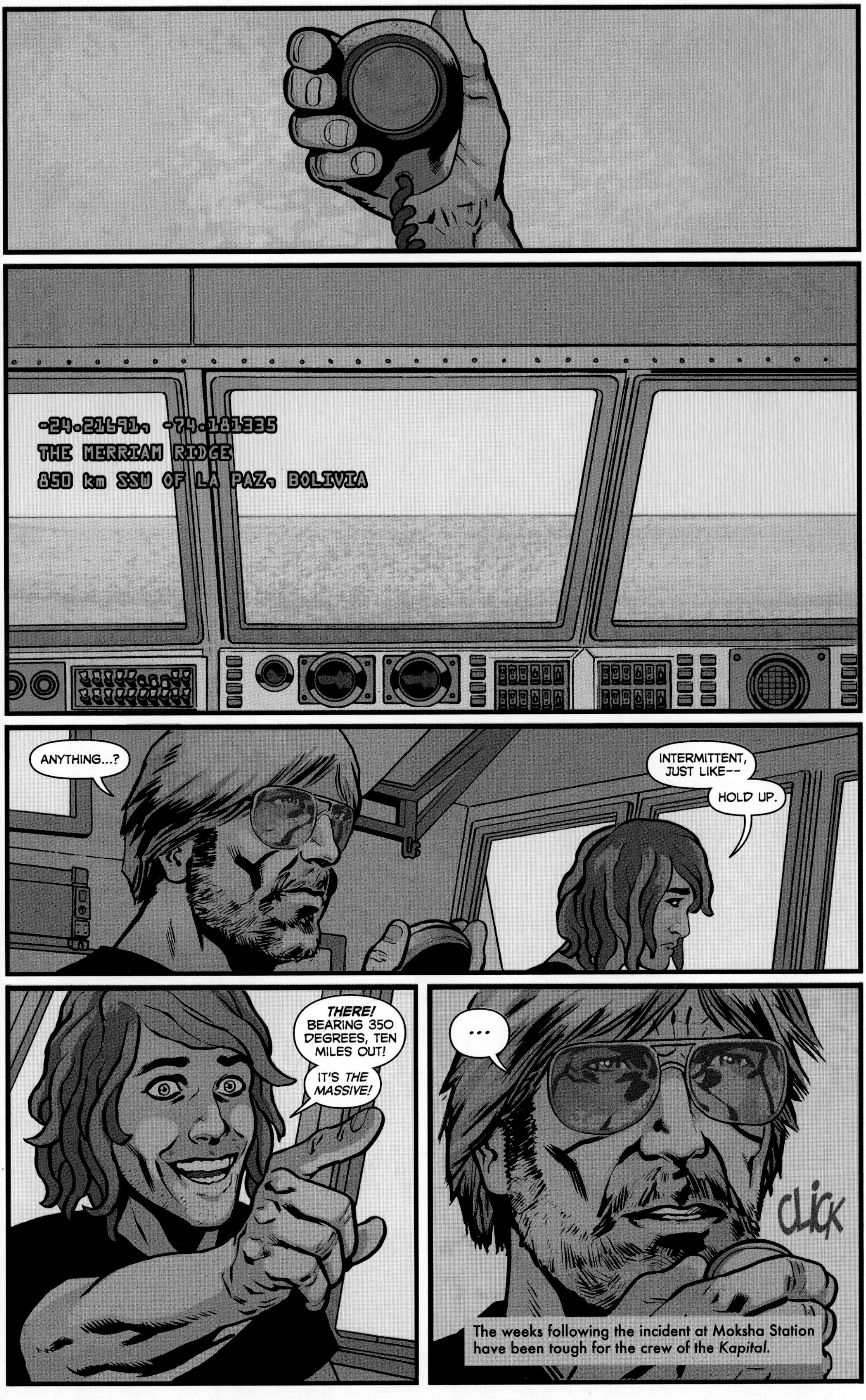
-24.21691, -74.181335
THE MERRIAM RIDGE
850 km SSW OF LA PAZ, BOLIVIA
ANYTHING...?
INTERMITTENT, JUST LIKE--
HOLD UP.
THERE! BEARING 350 DEGREES, TEN MILES OUT!
IT'S THE MASSIVE!
...
CLICK
The weeks following the incident at Moksha Station have been tough for the crew of the Kapital.

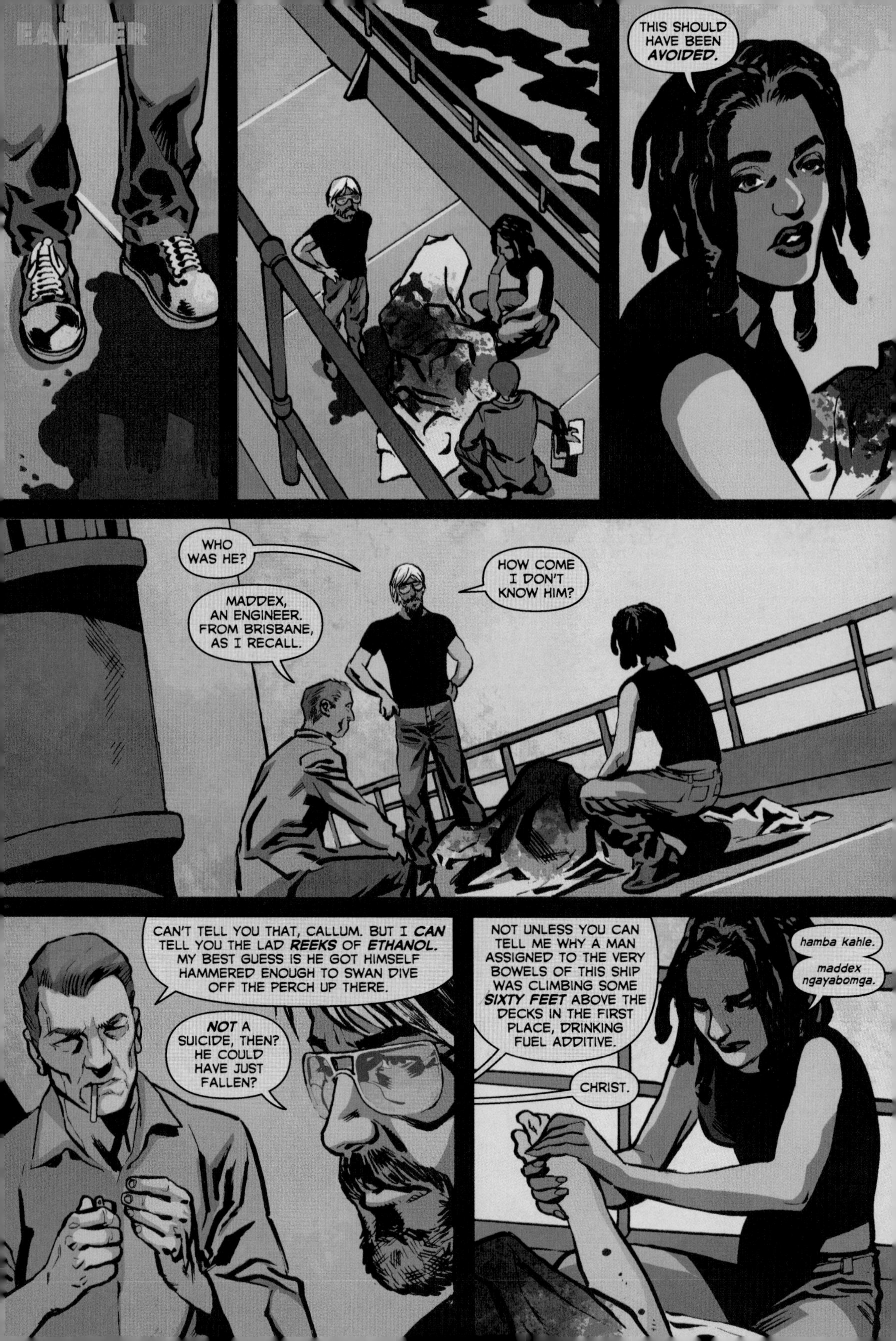
EARLIER
THIS SHOULD HAVE BEEN AVOIDED.
WHO WAS HE?
HOW COME I DON'T KNOW HIM?
MADDEX, AN ENGINEER. FROM BRISBANE, AS I RECALL.
CAN'T TELL YOU THAT, CALLUM. BUT I CAN TELL YOU THE LAD REEKS OF ETHANOL. MY BEST GUESS IS HE GOT HIMSELF HAMMERED ENOUGH TO SWAN DIVE OFF THE PERCH UP THERE.
NOT A SUICIDE, THEN? HE COULD HAVE JUST FALLEN?
NOT UNLESS YOU CAN TELL ME WHY A MAN ASSIGNED TO THE VERY BOWELS OF THIS SHIP WAS CLIMBING SOME SIXTY FEET ABOVE THE DECKS IN THE FIRST PLACE, DRINKING FUEL ADDITIVE.
CHRIST.
hamba kahle.
maddex ngayabomga.

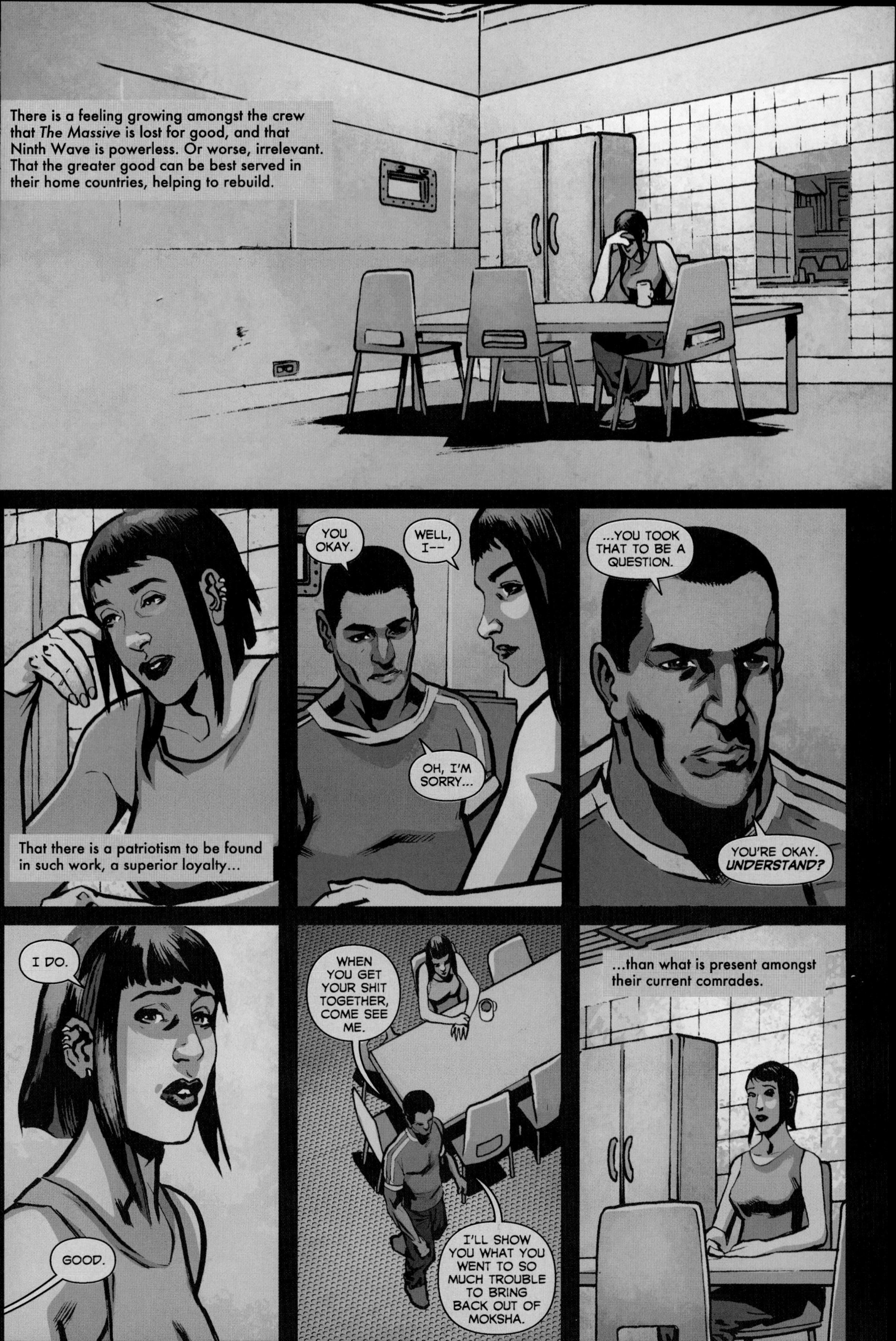
There is a feeling growing amongst the crew that *The Massive* is lost for good, and that Ninth Wave is powerless. Or worse, irrelevant. That the greater good can be best served in their home countries, helping to rebuild.
That there is a patriotism to be found in such work, a superior loyalty...
YOU OKAY.
WELL, I--
OH, I'M SORRY...
...YOU TOOK THAT TO BE A QUESTION.
YOU'RE OKAY. *UNDERSTAND?*
I DO.
GOOD.
WHEN YOU GET YOUR SHIT TOGETHER, COME SEE ME.
I'LL SHOW YOU WHAT YOU WENT TO SO MUCH TROUBLE TO BRING BACK OUT OF MOKSHA.
...than what is present amongst their current comrades.

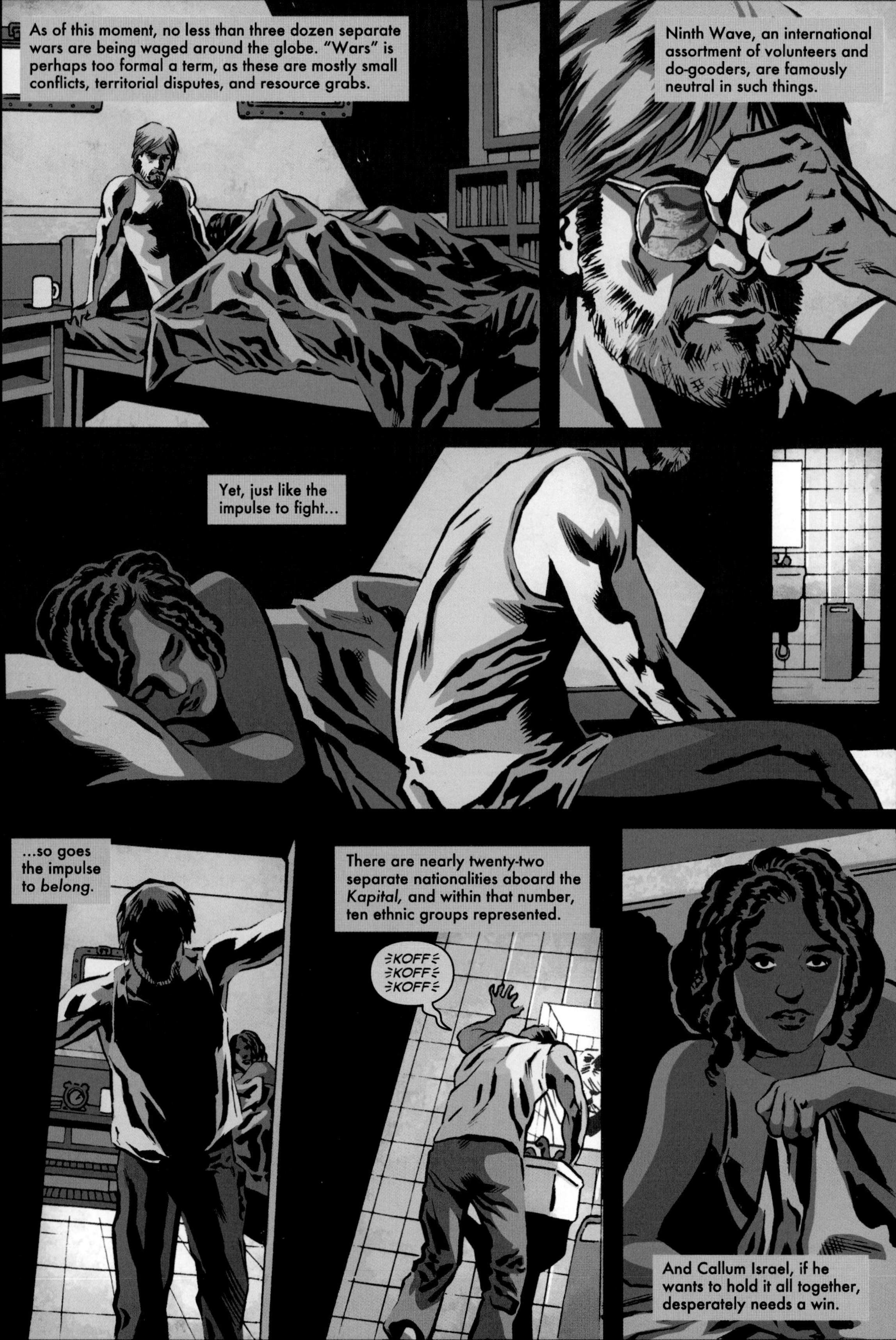
As of this moment, no less than three dozen separate wars are being waged around the globe. "Wars" is perhaps too formal a term, as these are mostly small conflicts, territorial disputes, and resource grabs.
Ninth Wave, an international assortment of volunteers and do-gooders, are famously neutral in such things.
Yet, just like the impulse to fight...
...so goes the impulse to *belong*.
There are nearly twenty-two separate nationalities aboard the *Kapital,* and within that number, ten ethnic groups represented.
KOFF KOFF KOFF
And Callum Israel, if he wants to hold it all together, desperately needs a win.

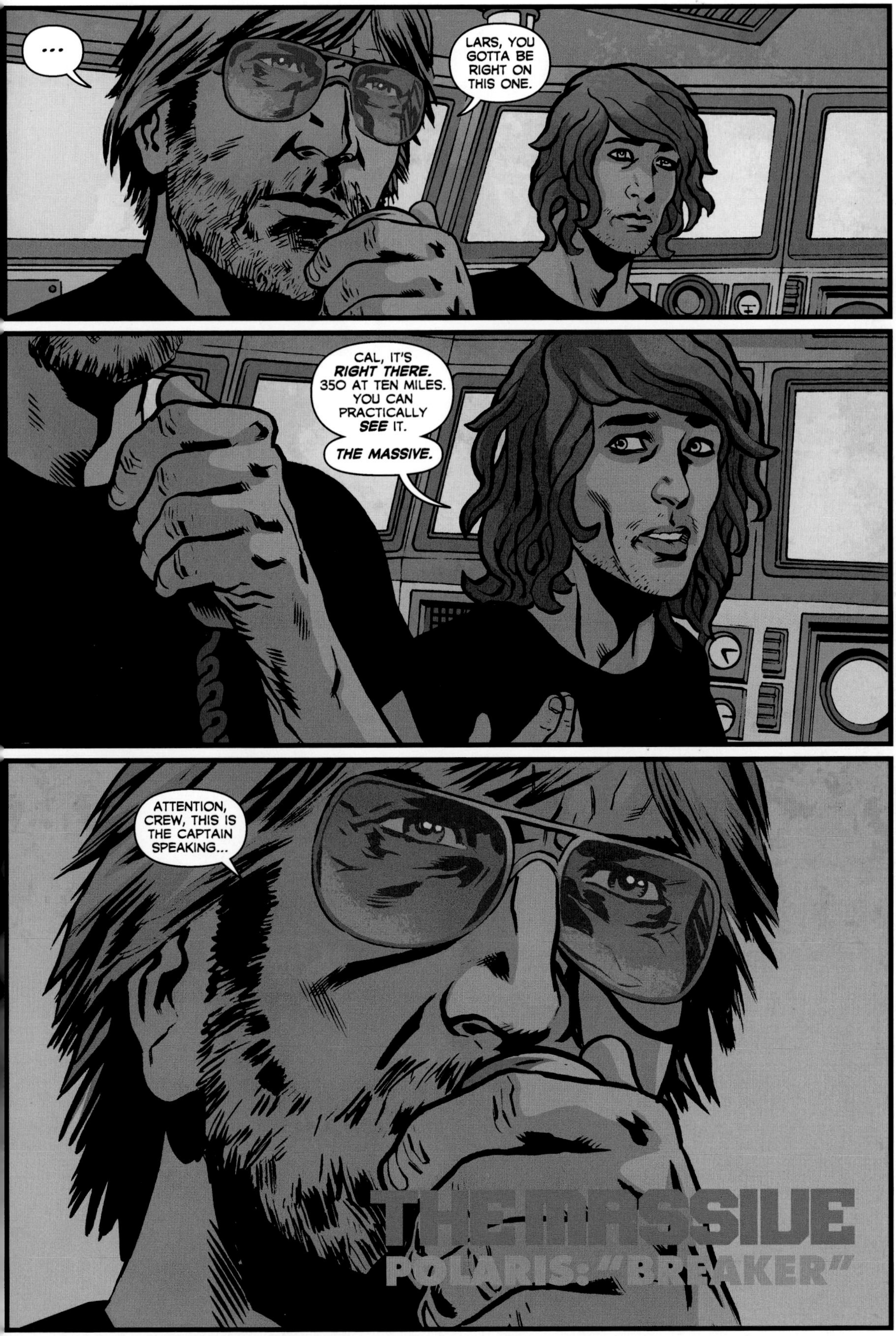
...
LARS, YOU GOTTA BE RIGHT ON THIS ONE.
CAL, IT'S RIGHT THERE. 350 AT TEN MILES. YOU CAN PRACTICALLY SEE IT.
THE MASSIVE.
ATTENTION, CREW, THIS IS THE CAPTAIN SPEAKING...
THE MASSIVE
POLARIS: "BREAKER"

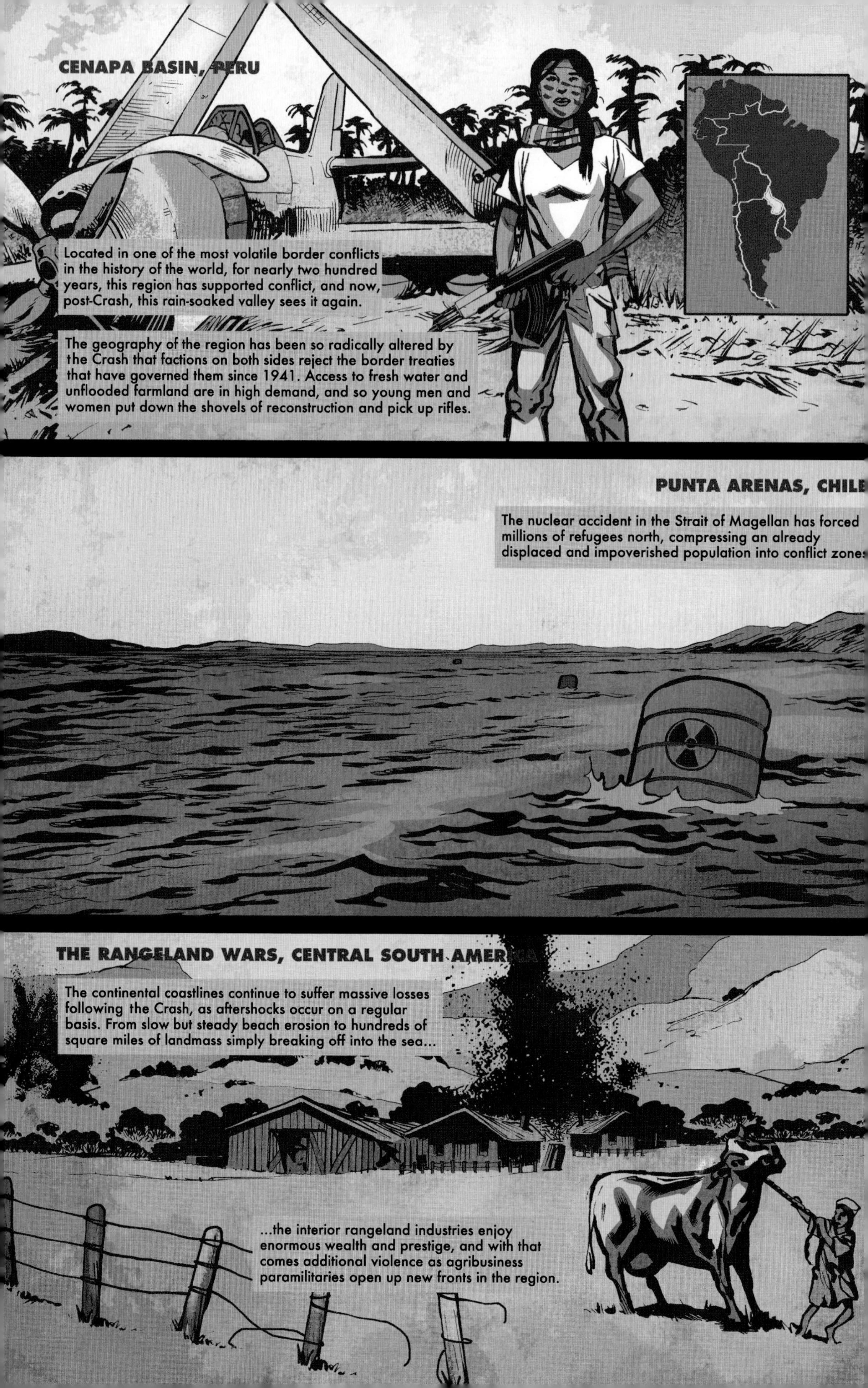

CENAPA BASIN, PERU
Located in one of the most volatile border conflicts in the history of the world, for nearly two hundred years, this region has supported conflict, and now, post-Crash, this rain-soaked valley sees it again.
The geography of the region has been so radically altered by the Crash that factions on both sides reject the border treaties that have governed them since 1941. Access to fresh water and unflooded farmland are in high demand, and so young men and women put down the shovels of reconstruction and pick up rifles.
PUNTA ARENAS, CHILE
The nuclear accident in the Strait of Magellan has forced millions of refugees north, compressing an already displaced and impoverished population into conflict zones
THE RANGELAND WARS, CENTRAL SOUTH AMERICA
The continental coastlines continue to suffer massive losses following the Crash, as aftershocks occur on a regular basis. From slow but steady beach erosion to hundreds of square miles of landmass simply breaking off into the sea...
...the interior rangeland industries enjoy enormous wealth and prestige, and with that comes additional violence as agribusiness paramilitaries open up new fronts in the region.

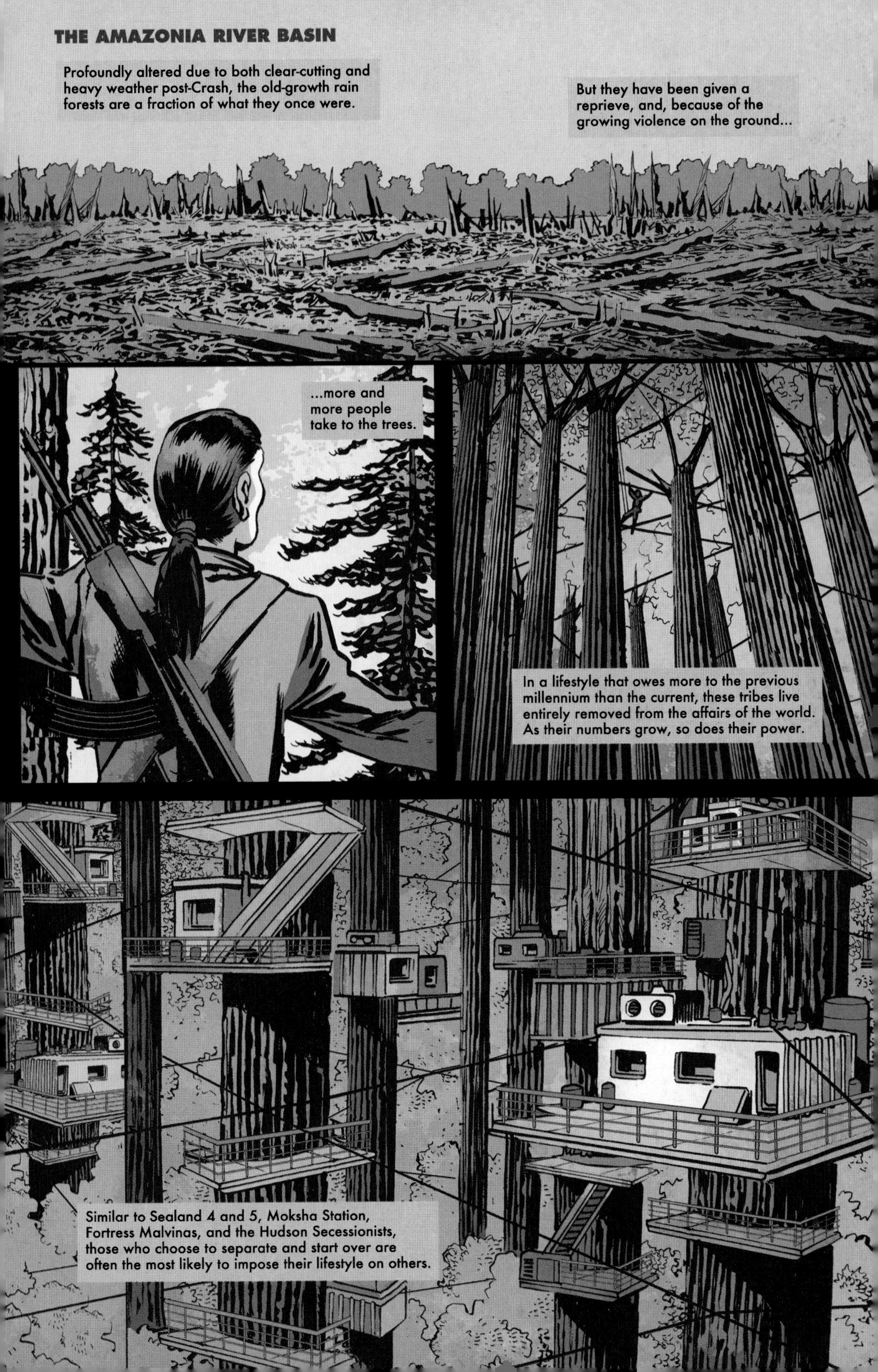
THE AMAZONIA RIVER BASIN
Profoundly altered due to both clear-cutting and heavy weather post-Crash, the old-growth rain forests are a fraction of what they once were.
But they have been given a reprieve, and, because of the growing violence on the ground...
...more and more people take to the trees.
In a lifestyle that owes more to the previous millennium than the current, these tribes live entirely removed from the affairs of the world. As their numbers grow, so does their power.
Similar to Sealand 4 and 5, Moksha Station, Fortress Malvinas, and the Hudson Secessionists, those who choose to separate and start over are often the most likely to impose their lifestyle on others.

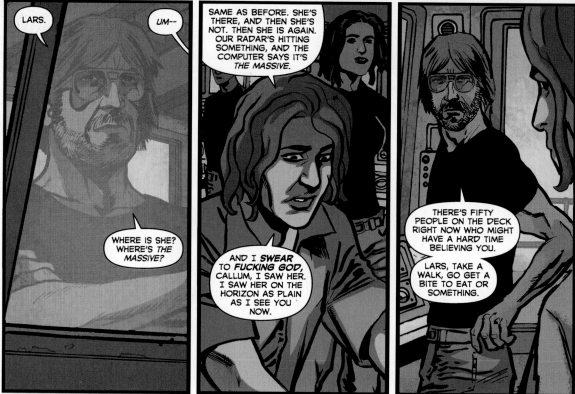

LARS.

UM--

WHERE IS SHE? WHERE'S *THE MASSIVE?*

SAME AS BEFORE. SHE'S THERE, AND THEN SHE'S NOT. THEN SHE IS AGAIN. OUR RADAR'S HITTING SOMETHING, AND THE COMPUTER SAYS IT'S *THE MASSIVE.*

AND I *SWEAR* TO *FUCKING GOD*, CALLUM, I SAW HER. I SAW HER ON THE HORIZON AS PLAIN AS I SEE YOU NOW.

THERE'S FIFTY PEOPLE ON THE DECK RIGHT NOW WHO MIGHT HAVE A HARD TIME BELIEVING YOU.

LARS, TAKE A WALK, GO GET A BITE TO EAT OR SOMETHING.

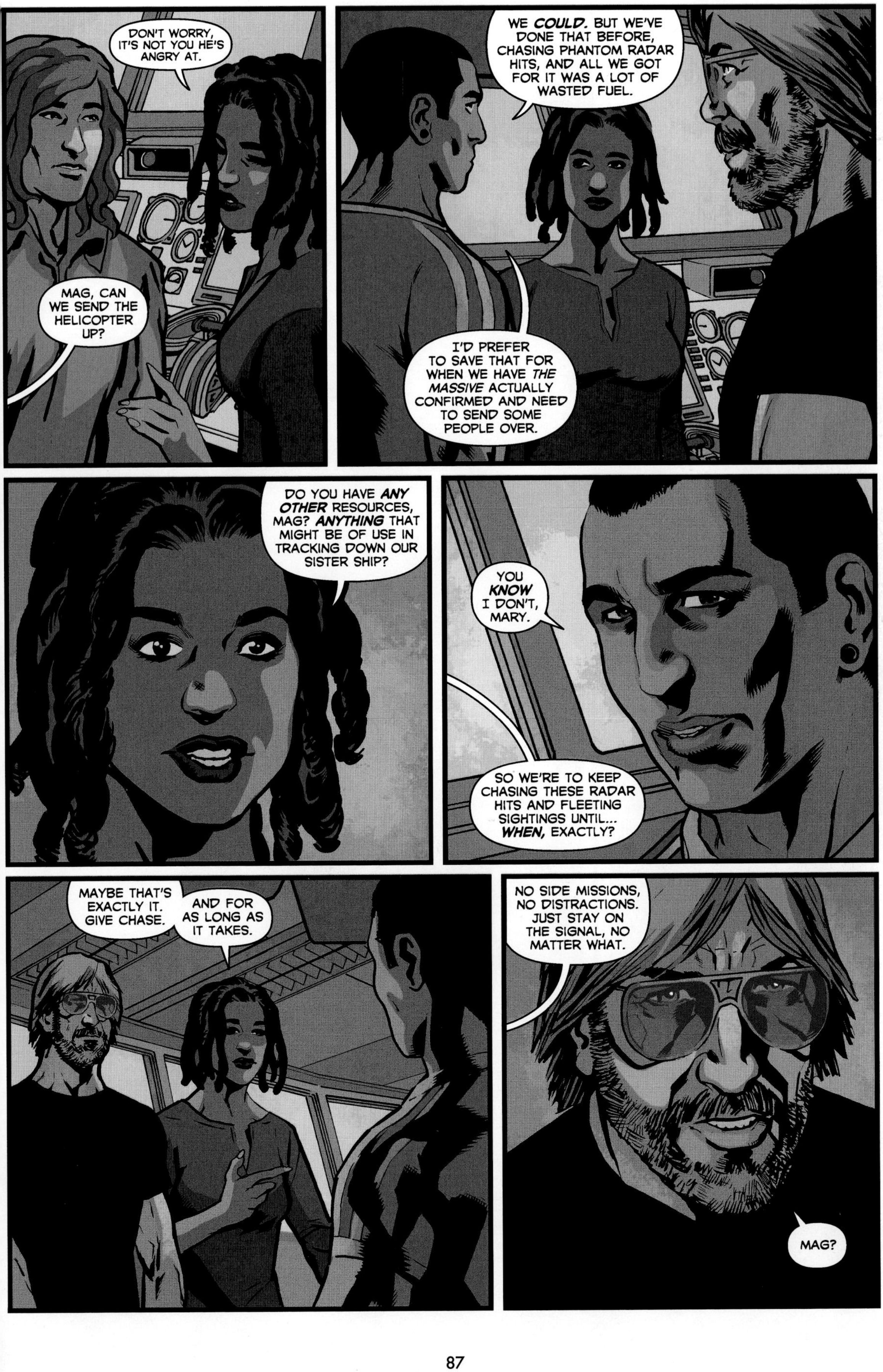
DON'T WORRY, IT'S NOT YOU HE'S ANGRY AT.
MAG, CAN WE SEND THE HELICOPTER UP?
WE *COULD.* BUT WE'VE DONE THAT BEFORE, CHASING PHANTOM RADAR HITS, AND ALL WE GOT FOR IT WAS A LOT OF WASTED FUEL.
I'D PREFER TO SAVE THAT FOR WHEN WE HAVE *THE MASSIVE* ACTUALLY CONFIRMED AND NEED TO SEND SOME PEOPLE OVER.
DO YOU HAVE ***ANY OTHER*** RESOURCES, MAG? ***ANYTHING*** THAT MIGHT BE OF USE IN TRACKING DOWN OUR SISTER SHIP?
YOU ***KNOW*** I DON'T, MARY.
SO WE'RE TO KEEP CHASING THESE RADAR HITS AND FLEETING SIGHTINGS UNTIL... ***WHEN,*** EXACTLY?
MAYBE THAT'S EXACTLY IT. GIVE CHASE.
AND FOR AS LONG AS IT TAKES.
NO SIDE MISSIONS, NO DISTRACTIONS. JUST STAY ON THE SIGNAL, NO MATTER WHAT.
MAG?

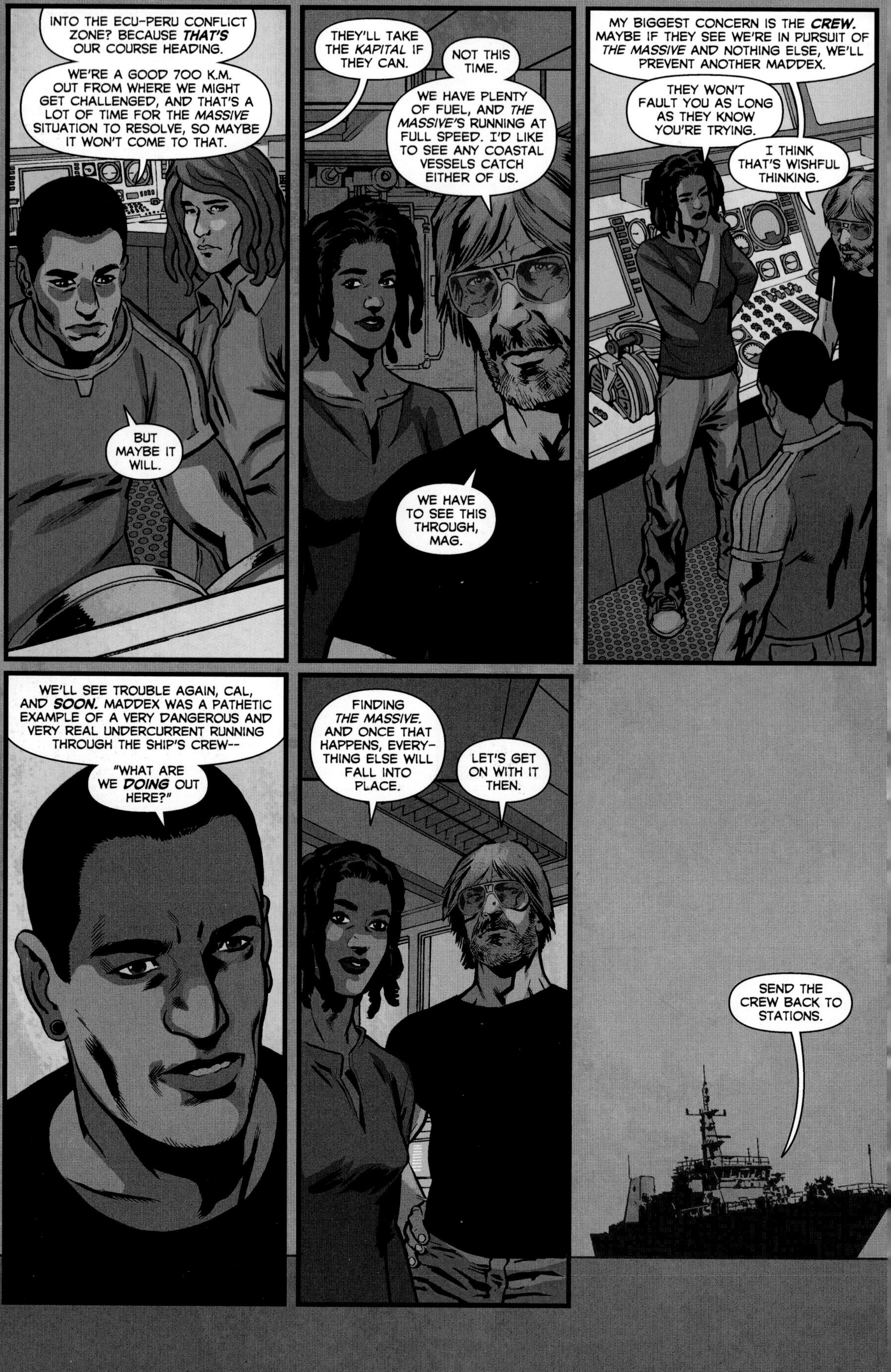
INTO THE ECU-PERU CONFLICT ZONE? BECAUSE *THAT'S* OUR COURSE HEADING.
WE'RE A GOOD 700 K.M. OUT FROM WHERE WE MIGHT GET CHALLENGED, AND THAT'S A LOT OF TIME FOR THE *MASSIVE* SITUATION TO RESOLVE, SO MAYBE IT WON'T COME TO THAT.
BUT MAYBE IT WILL.
THEY'LL TAKE THE *KAPITAL* IF THEY CAN.
NOT THIS TIME.
WE HAVE PLENTY OF FUEL, AND *THE MASSIVE'S* RUNNING AT FULL SPEED. I'D LIKE TO SEE ANY COASTAL VESSELS CATCH EITHER OF US.
WE HAVE TO SEE THIS THROUGH, MAG.
MY BIGGEST CONCERN IS THE ***CREW.*** MAYBE IF THEY SEE WE'RE IN PURSUIT OF *THE MASSIVE* AND NOTHING ELSE, WE'LL PREVENT ANOTHER MADDEX.
THEY WON'T FAULT YOU AS LONG AS THEY KNOW YOU'RE TRYING.
I THINK THAT'S WISHFUL THINKING.
WE'LL SEE TROUBLE AGAIN, CAL, AND ***SOON.*** MADDEX WAS A PATHETIC EXAMPLE OF A VERY DANGEROUS AND VERY REAL UNDERCURRENT RUNNING THROUGH THE SHIP'S CREW--
"WHAT ARE WE ***DOING*** OUT HERE?"
FINDING *THE MASSIVE.* AND ONCE THAT HAPPENS, EVERY-THING ELSE WILL FALL INTO PLACE.
LET'S GET ON WITH IT THEN.
SEND THE CREW BACK TO STATIONS.

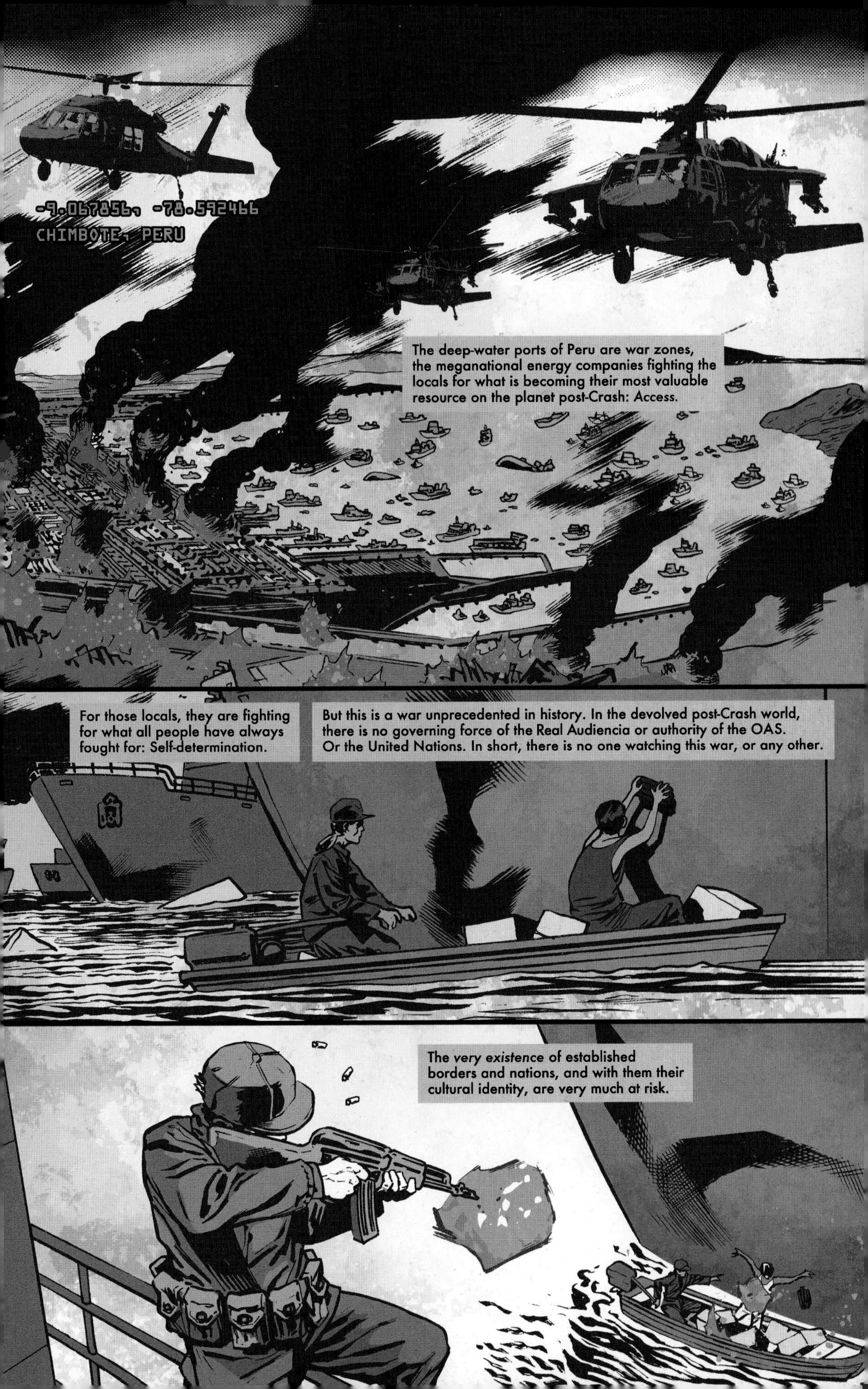
-9.067856, -78.592466
CHIMBOTE, PERU
The deep-water ports of Peru are war zones, the meganational energy companies fighting the locals for what is becoming their most valuable resource on the planet post-Crash: Access.
For those locals, they are fighting for what all people have always fought for: Self-determination.
But this is a war unprecedented in history. In the devolved post-Crash world, there is no governing force of the Real Audiencia or authority of the OAS. Or the United Nations. In short, there is no one watching this war, or any other.
The *very existence* of established borders and nations, and with them their cultural identity, are very much at risk.

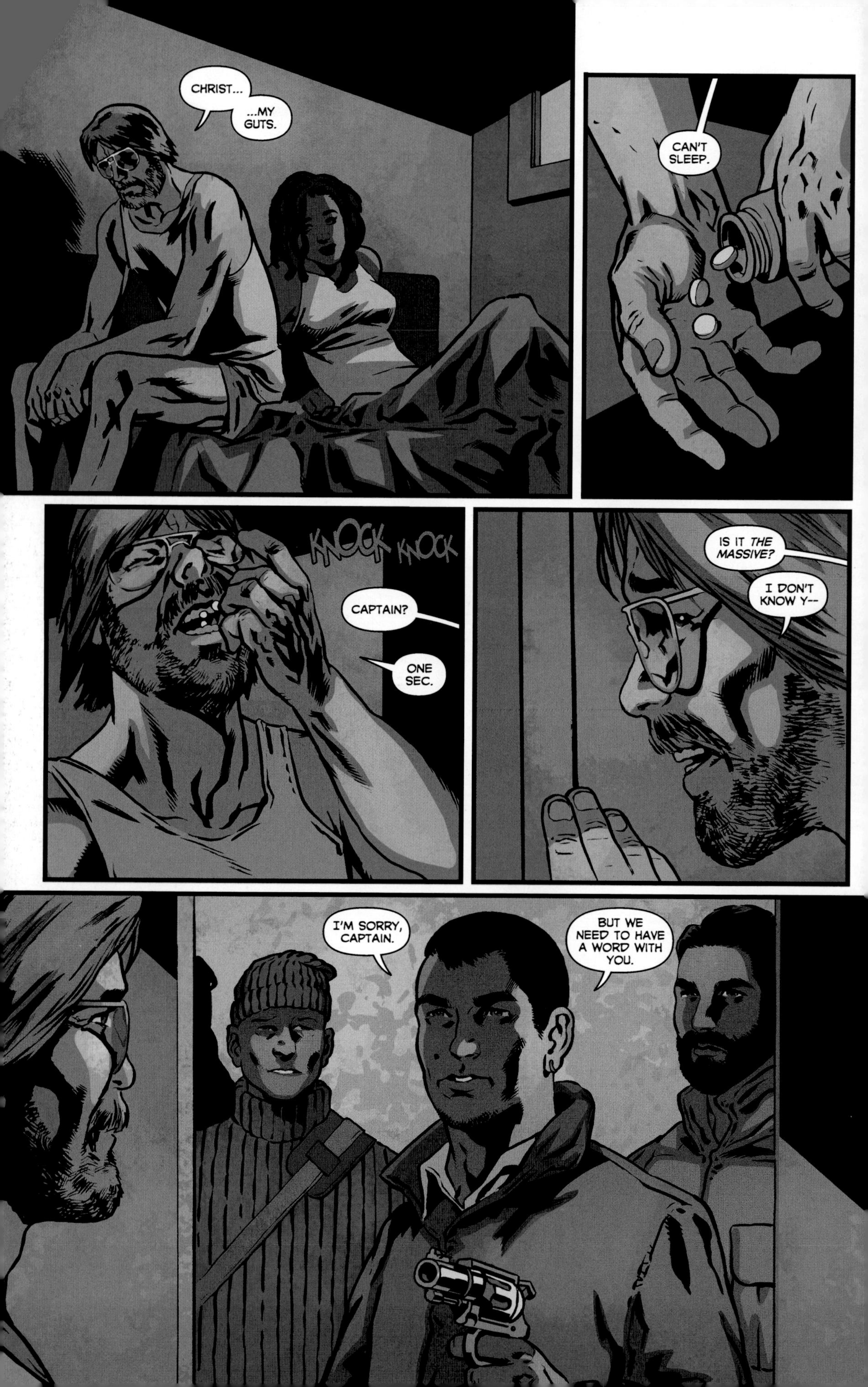
CHRIST...
...MY GUTS.
CAN'T SLEEP.
KNOCK KNOCK
CAPTAIN?
ONE SEC.
IS IT *THE MASSIVE?*
I DON'T KNOW Y--
I'M SORRY, CAPTAIN.
BUT WE NEED TO HAVE A WORD WITH YOU.

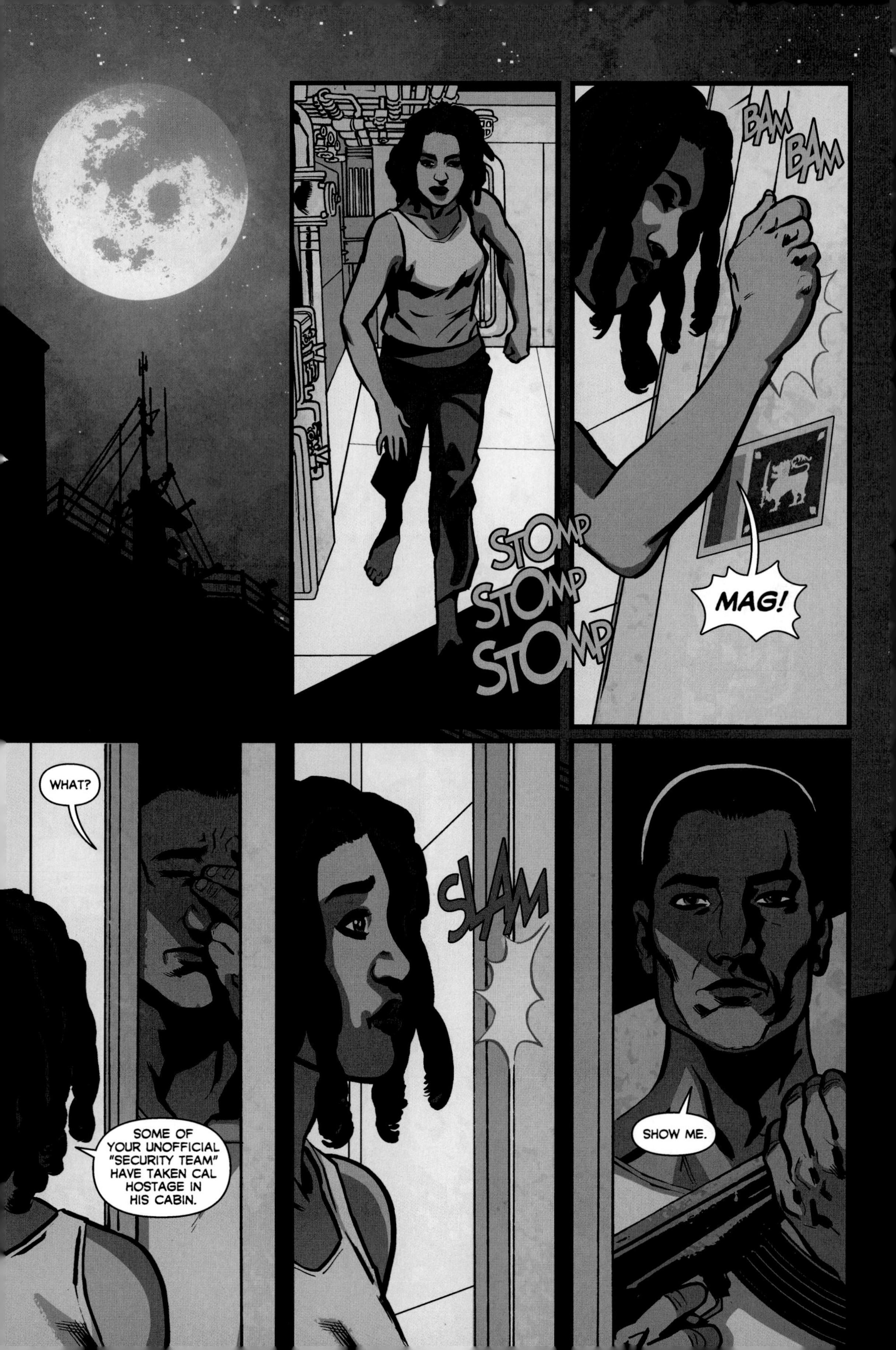
STOMP
STOMP
STOMP
BAM
BAM
MAG!
WHAT?
SOME OF YOUR UNOFFICIAL "SECURITY TEAM" HAVE TAKEN CAL HOSTAGE IN HIS CABIN.
SLAM
SHOW ME.

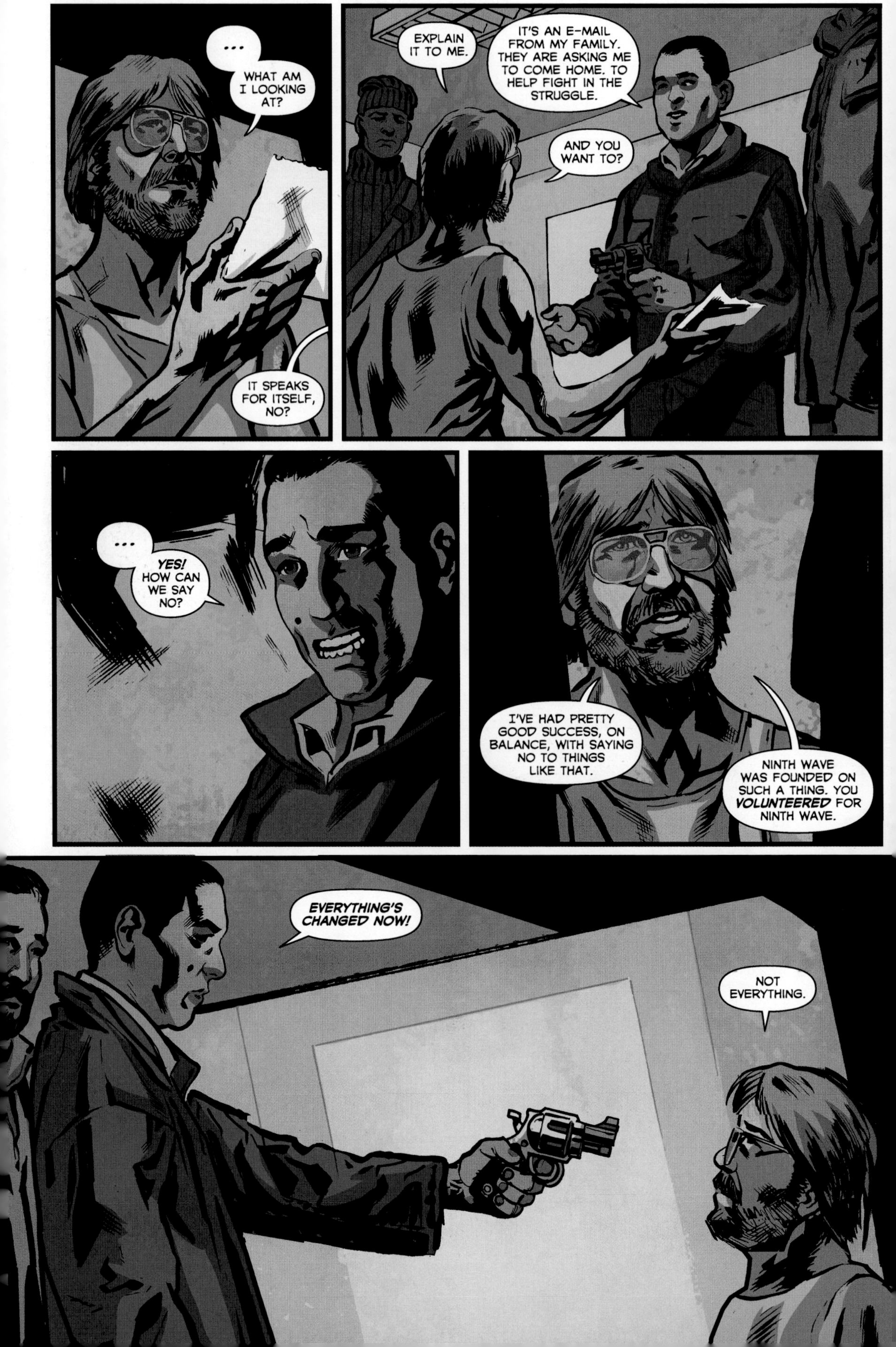
...
WHAT AM I LOOKING AT?
IT SPEAKS FOR ITSELF, NO?
EXPLAIN IT TO ME.
IT'S AN E-MAIL FROM MY FAMILY. THEY ARE ASKING ME TO COME HOME. TO HELP FIGHT IN THE STRUGGLE.
AND YOU WANT TO?
...
YES! HOW CAN WE SAY NO?
I'VE HAD PRETTY GOOD SUCCESS, ON BALANCE, WITH SAYING NO TO THINGS LIKE THAT.
NINTH WAVE WAS FOUNDED ON SUCH A THING. YOU VOLUNTEERED FOR NINTH WAVE.
EVERYTHING'S CHANGED NOW!
NOT EVERYTHING.

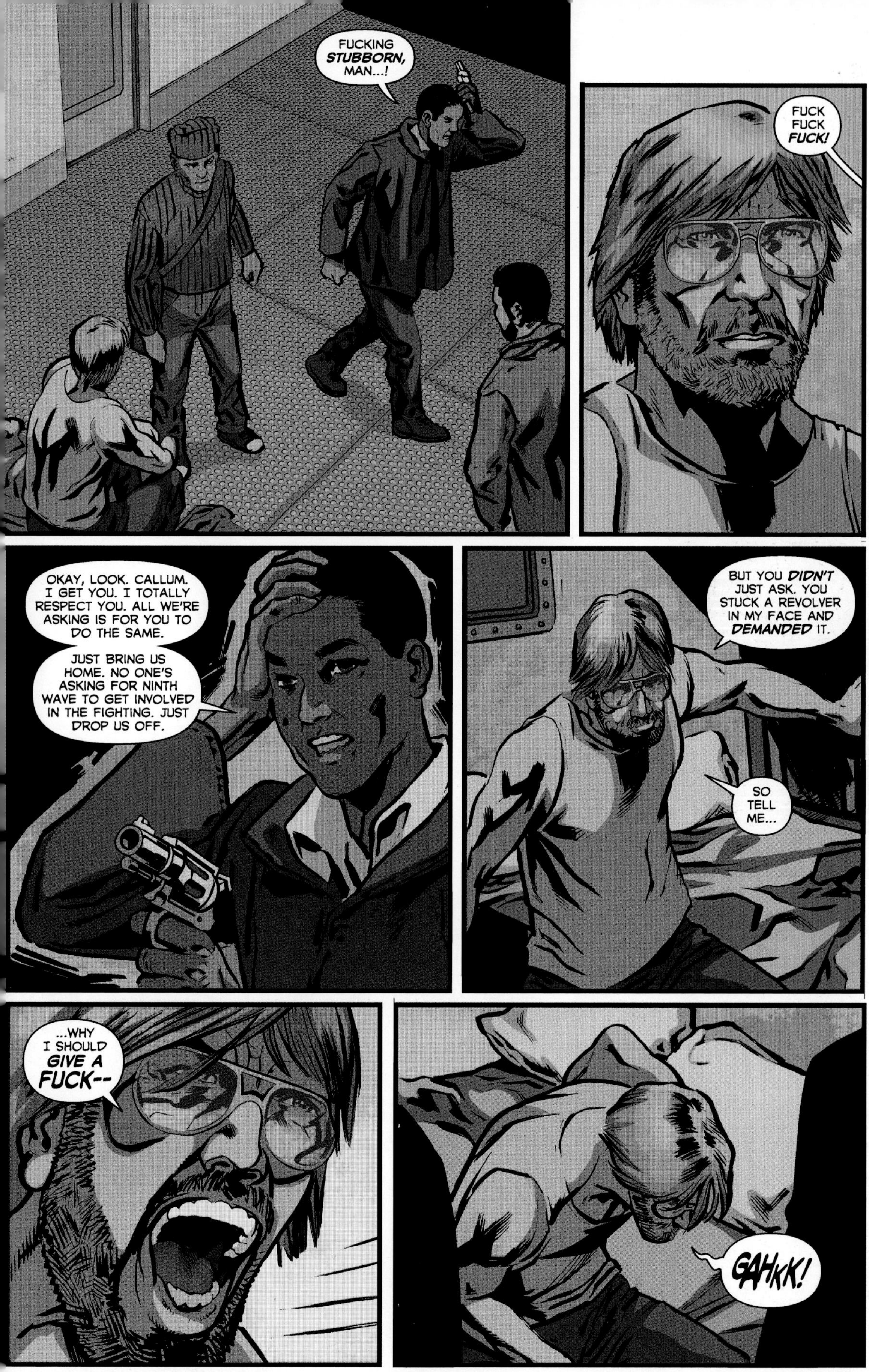
FUCKING STUBBORN, MAN...!
FUCK FUCK FUCK!
OKAY, LOOK. CALLUM. I GET YOU. I TOTALLY RESPECT YOU. ALL WE'RE ASKING IS FOR YOU TO DO THE SAME.
JUST BRING US HOME. NO ONE'S ASKING FOR NINTH WAVE TO GET INVOLVED IN THE FIGHTING. JUST DROP US OFF.
BUT YOU DIDN'T JUST ASK. YOU STUCK A REVOLVER IN MY FACE AND DEMANDED IT.
SO TELL ME...
...WHY I SHOULD GIVE A FUCK--
GAHKK!

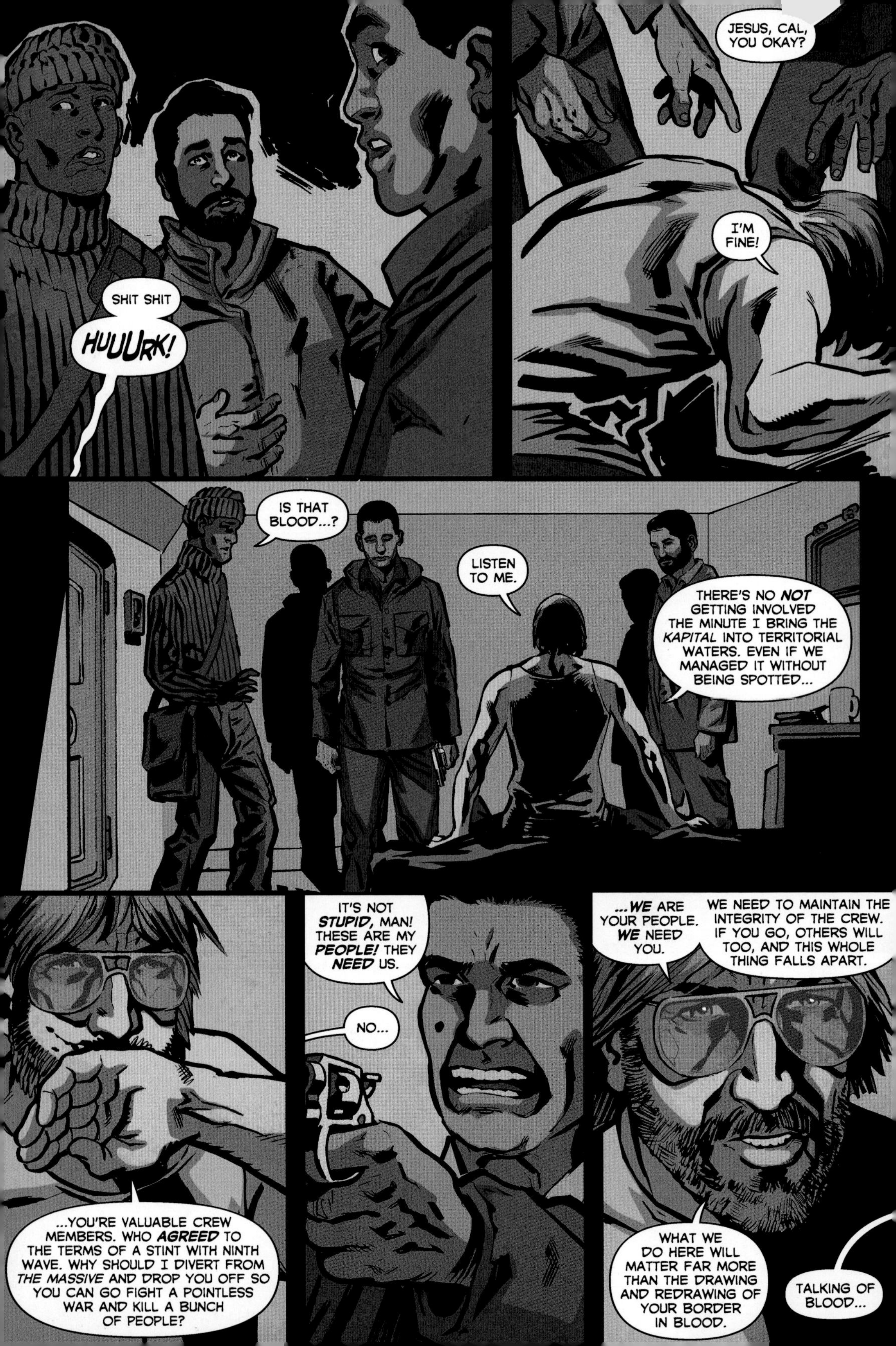
SHIT SHIT
HUUURK!
JESUS, CAL, YOU OKAY?
I'M FINE!
IS THAT BLOOD...?
LISTEN TO ME.
THERE'S NO NOT GETTING INVOLVED THE MINUTE I BRING THE KAPITAL INTO TERRITORIAL WATERS. EVEN IF WE MANAGED IT WITHOUT BEING SPOTTED...
...YOU'RE VALUABLE CREW MEMBERS. WHO AGREED TO THE TERMS OF A STINT WITH NINTH WAVE. WHY SHOULD I DIVERT FROM THE MASSIVE AND DROP YOU OFF SO YOU CAN GO FIGHT A POINTLESS WAR AND KILL A BUNCH OF PEOPLE?
IT'S NOT STUPID, MAN! THESE ARE MY PEOPLE! THEY NEED US.
NO...
...WE ARE YOUR PEOPLE. WE NEED YOU.
WE NEED TO MAINTAIN THE INTEGRITY OF THE CREW. IF YOU GO, OTHERS WILL TOO, AND THIS WHOLE THING FALLS APART.
WHAT WE DO HERE WILL MATTER FAR MORE THAN THE DRAWING AND REDRAWING OF YOUR BORDER IN BLOOD.
TALKING OF BLOOD...

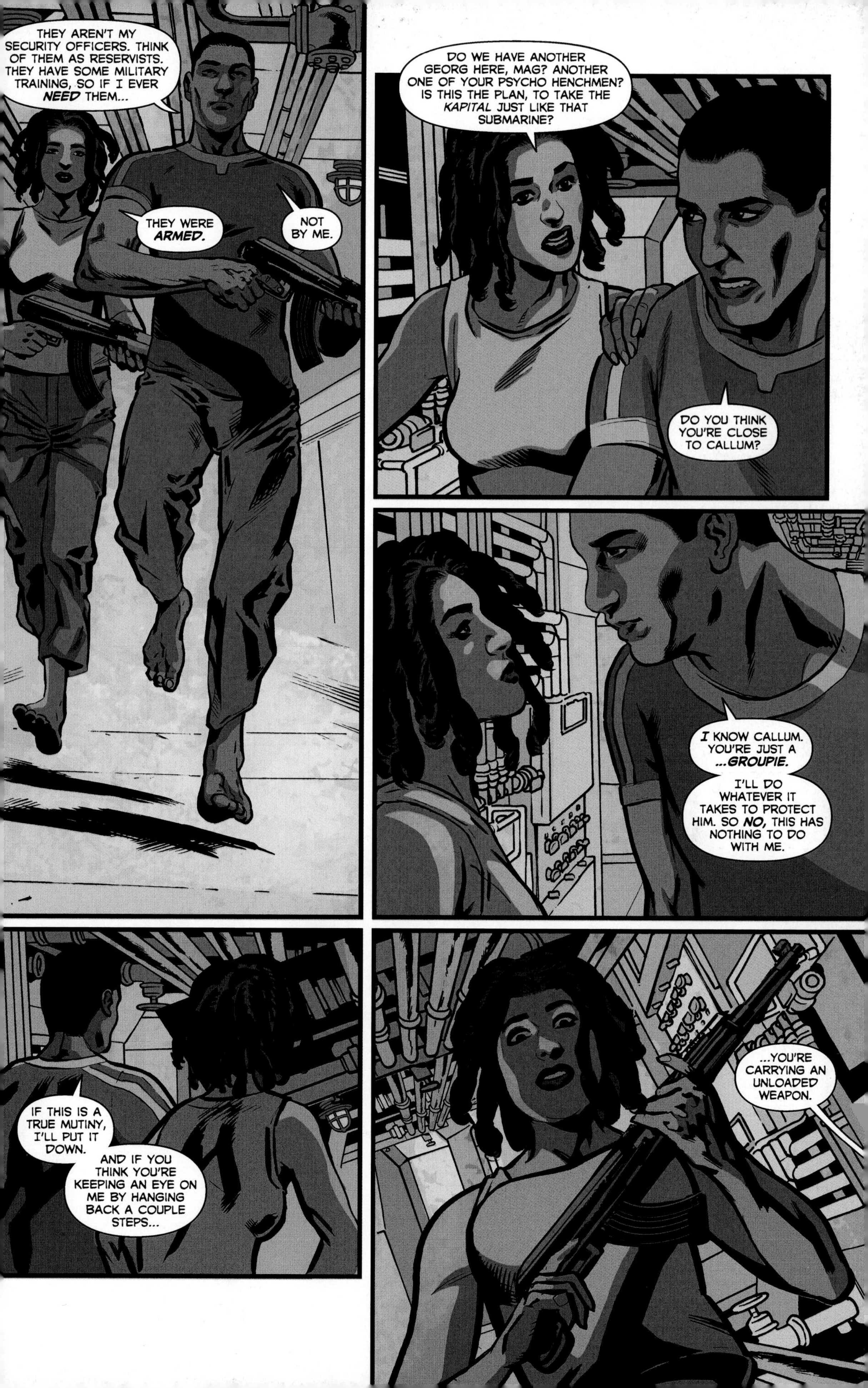
THEY AREN'T MY SECURITY OFFICERS. THINK OF THEM AS RESERVISTS. THEY HAVE SOME MILITARY TRAINING, SO IF I EVER NEED THEM...
THEY WERE ARMED.
NOT BY ME.
DO WE HAVE ANOTHER GEORG HERE, MAG? ANOTHER ONE OF YOUR PSYCHO HENCHMEN? IS THIS THE PLAN, TO TAKE THE KAPITAL JUST LIKE THAT SUBMARINE?
DO YOU THINK YOU'RE CLOSE TO CALLUM?
I KNOW CALLUM. YOU'RE JUST A ...GROUPIE.
I'LL DO WHATEVER IT TAKES TO PROTECT HIM. SO NO, THIS HAS NOTHING TO DO WITH ME.
IF THIS IS A TRUE MUTINY, I'LL PUT IT DOWN.
AND IF YOU THINK YOU'RE KEEPING AN EYE ON ME BY HANGING BACK A COUPLE STEPS...
...YOU'RE CARRYING AN UNLOADED WEAPON.

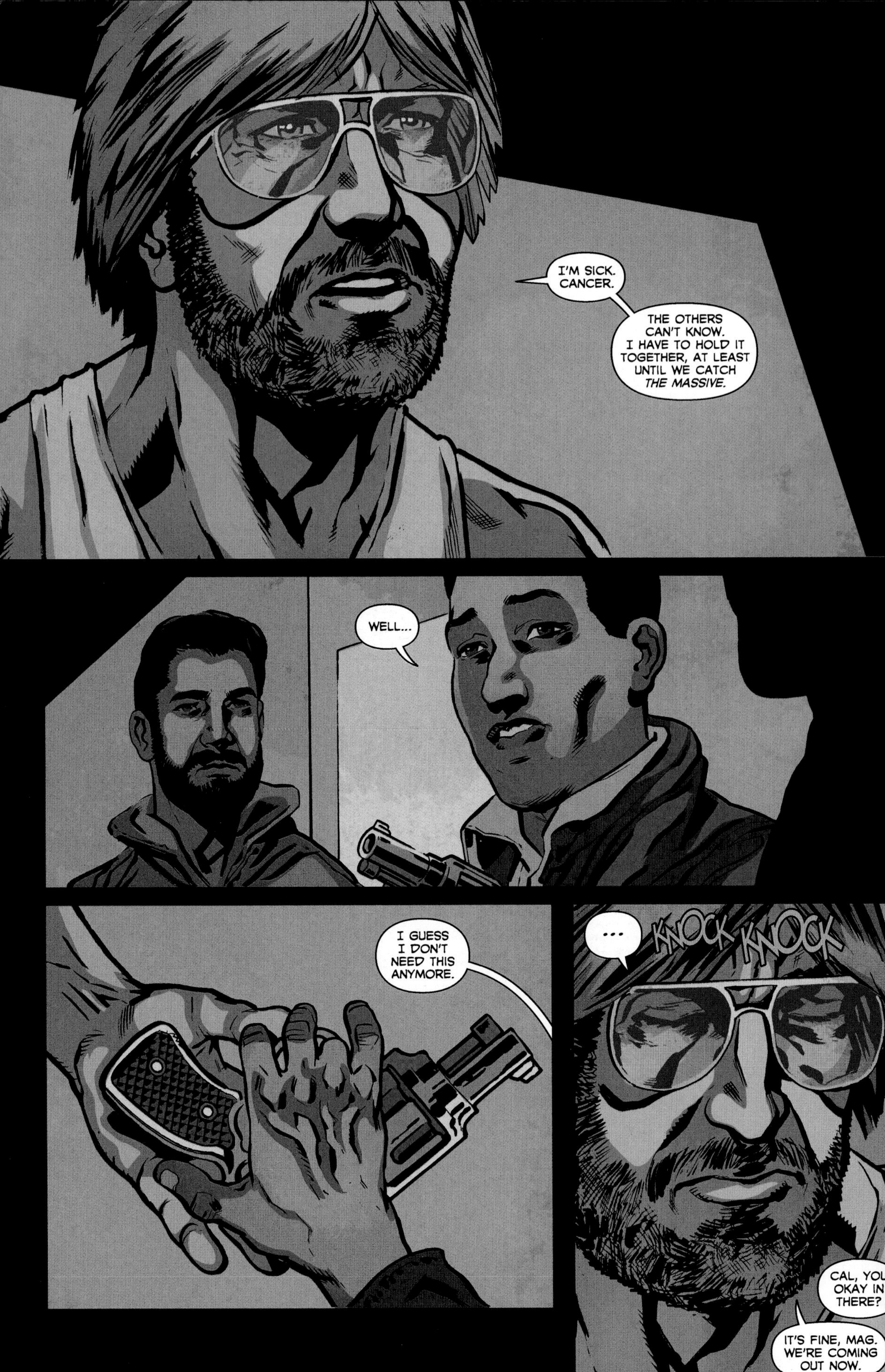
I'M SICK. CANCER.
THE OTHERS CAN'T KNOW. I HAVE TO HOLD IT TOGETHER, AT LEAST UNTIL WE CATCH *THE MASSIVE.*
WELL...
I GUESS I DON'T NEED THIS ANYMORE.
...
KNOCK KNOCK
CAL, YOU OKAY IN THERE?
IT'S FINE, MAG. WE'RE COMING OUT NOW.

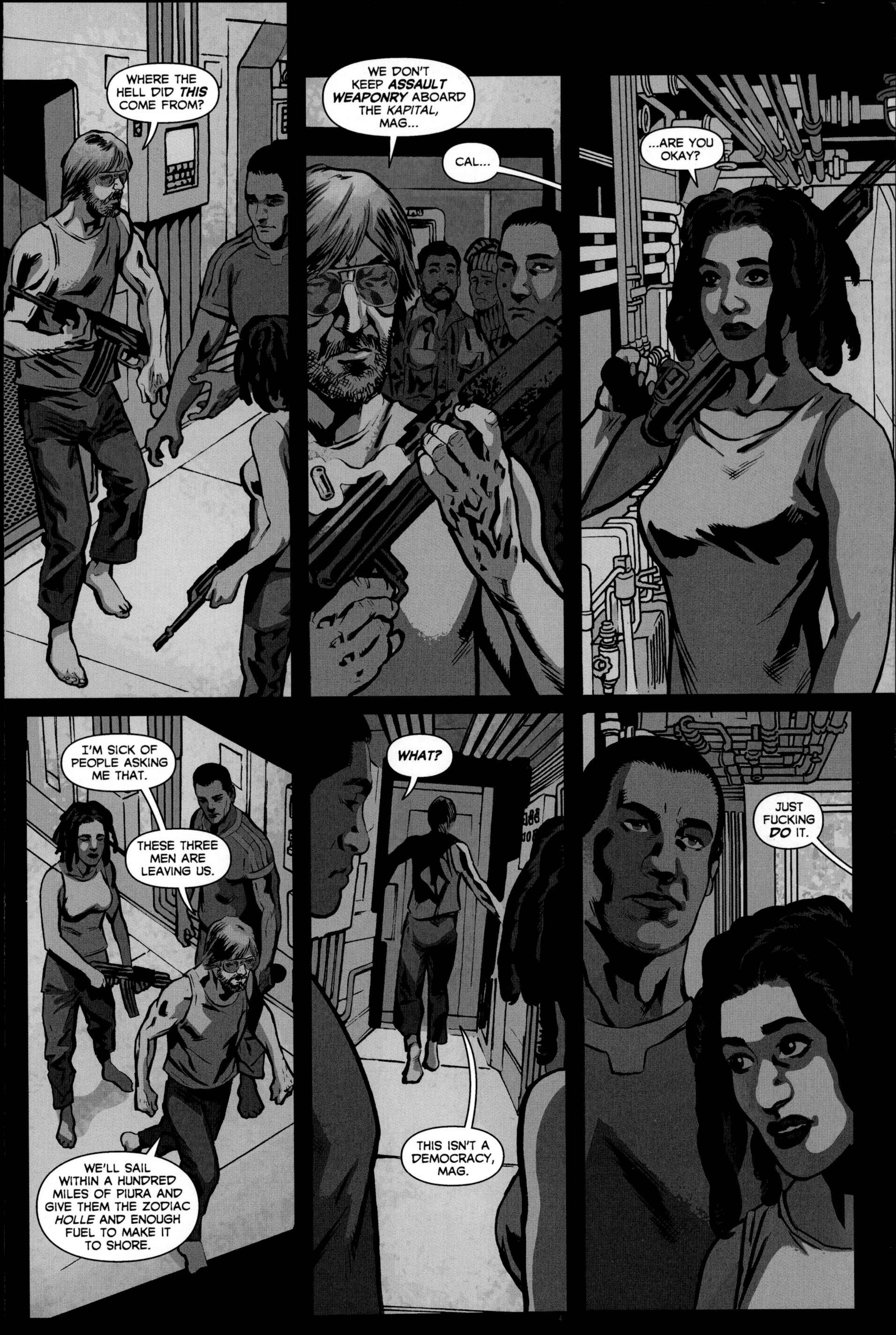
WHERE THE HELL DID *THIS* COME FROM?
WE DON'T KEEP **ASSAULT WEAPONRY** ABOARD THE *KAPITAL,* MAG...
CAL...
...ARE YOU OKAY?
I'M SICK OF PEOPLE ASKING ME THAT.
THESE THREE MEN ARE LEAVING US.
WE'LL SAIL WITHIN A HUNDRED MILES OF PIURA AND GIVE THEM THE ZODIAC *HOLLE* AND ENOUGH FUEL TO MAKE IT TO SHORE.
WHAT?
THIS ISN'T A DEMOCRACY, MAG.
JUST FUCKING ***DO*** IT.

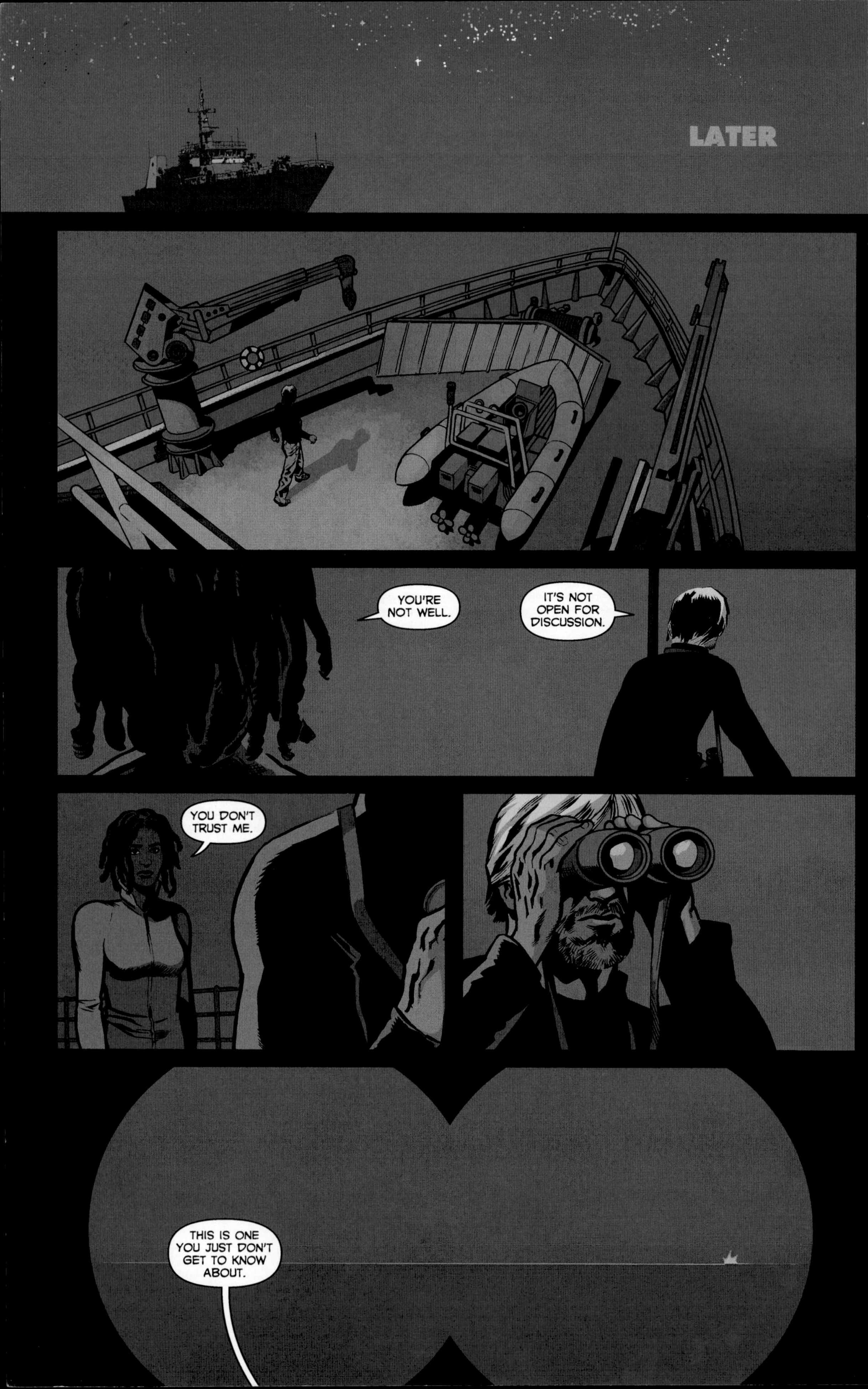
LATER
YOU'RE NOT WELL.
IT'S NOT OPEN FOR DISCUSSION.
YOU DON'T TRUST ME.
THIS IS ONE YOU JUST DON'T GET TO KNOW ABOUT.

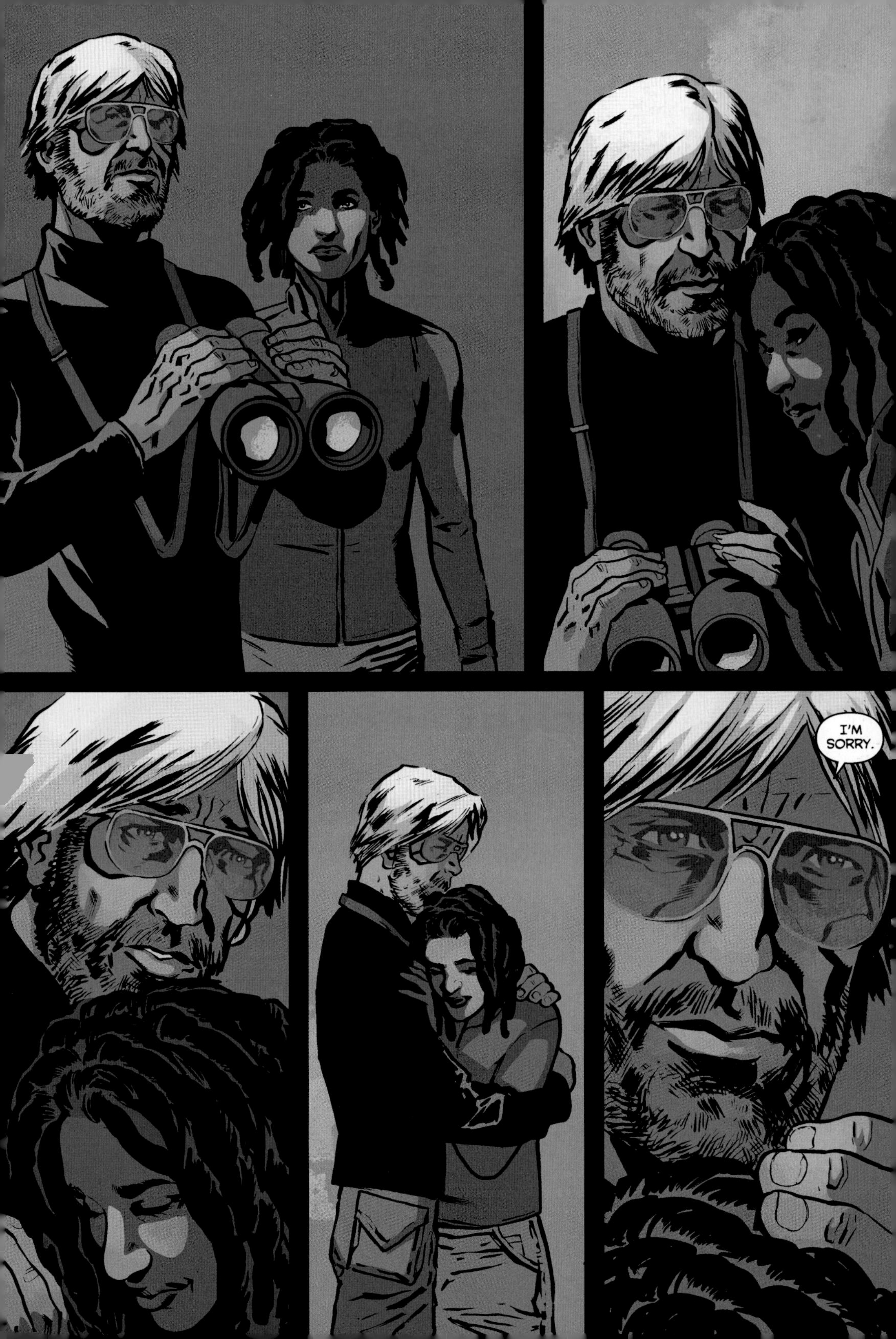
I'M SORRY.

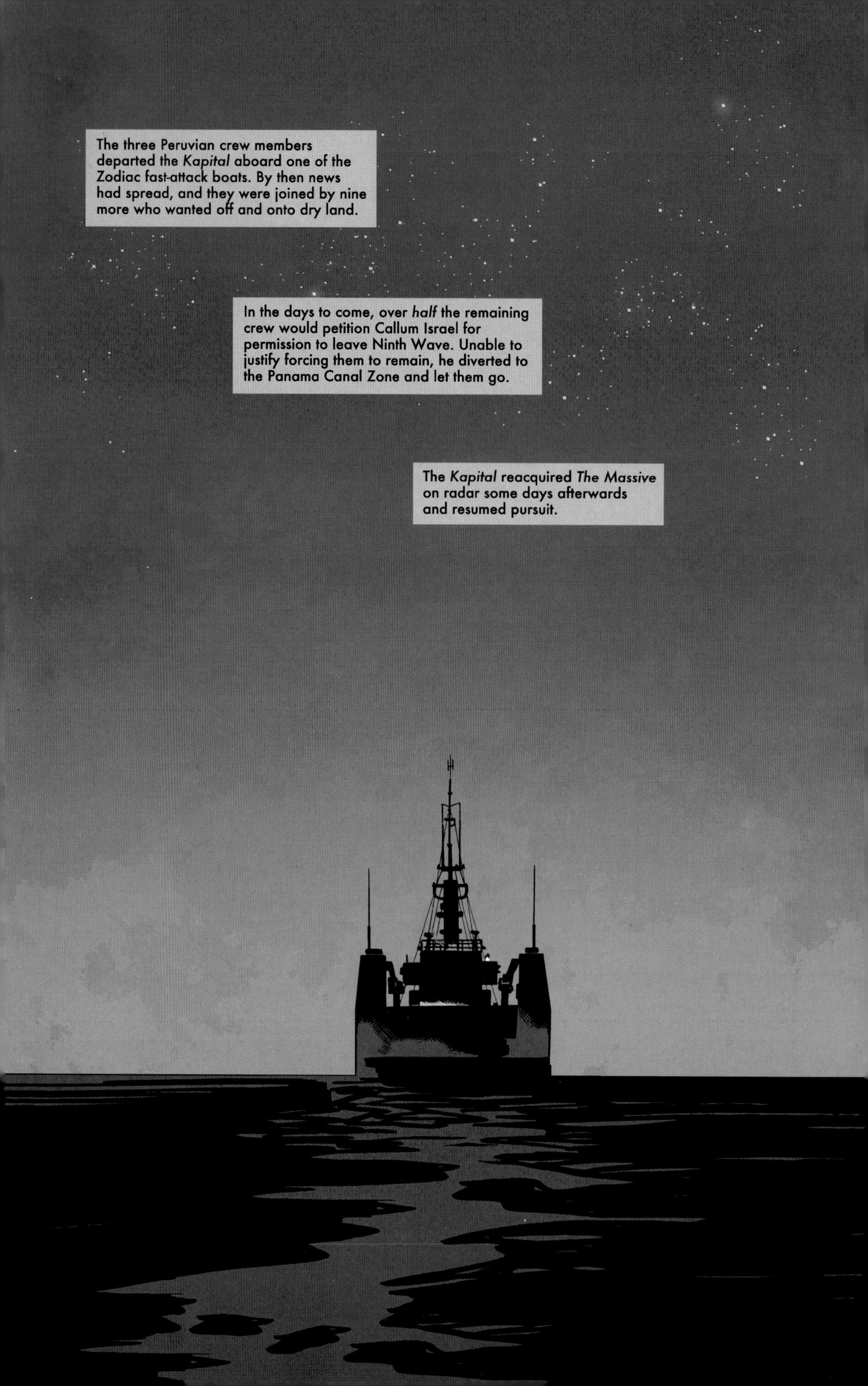
The three Peruvian crew members departed the *Kapital* aboard one of the Zodiac fast-attack boats. By then news had spread, and they were joined by nine more who wanted off and onto dry land.
In the days to come, over *half* the remaining crew would petition Callum Israel for permission to leave Ninth Wave. Unable to justify forcing them to remain, he diverted to the Panama Canal Zone and let them go.
The *Kapital* reacquired *The Massive* on radar some days afterwards and resumed pursuit.

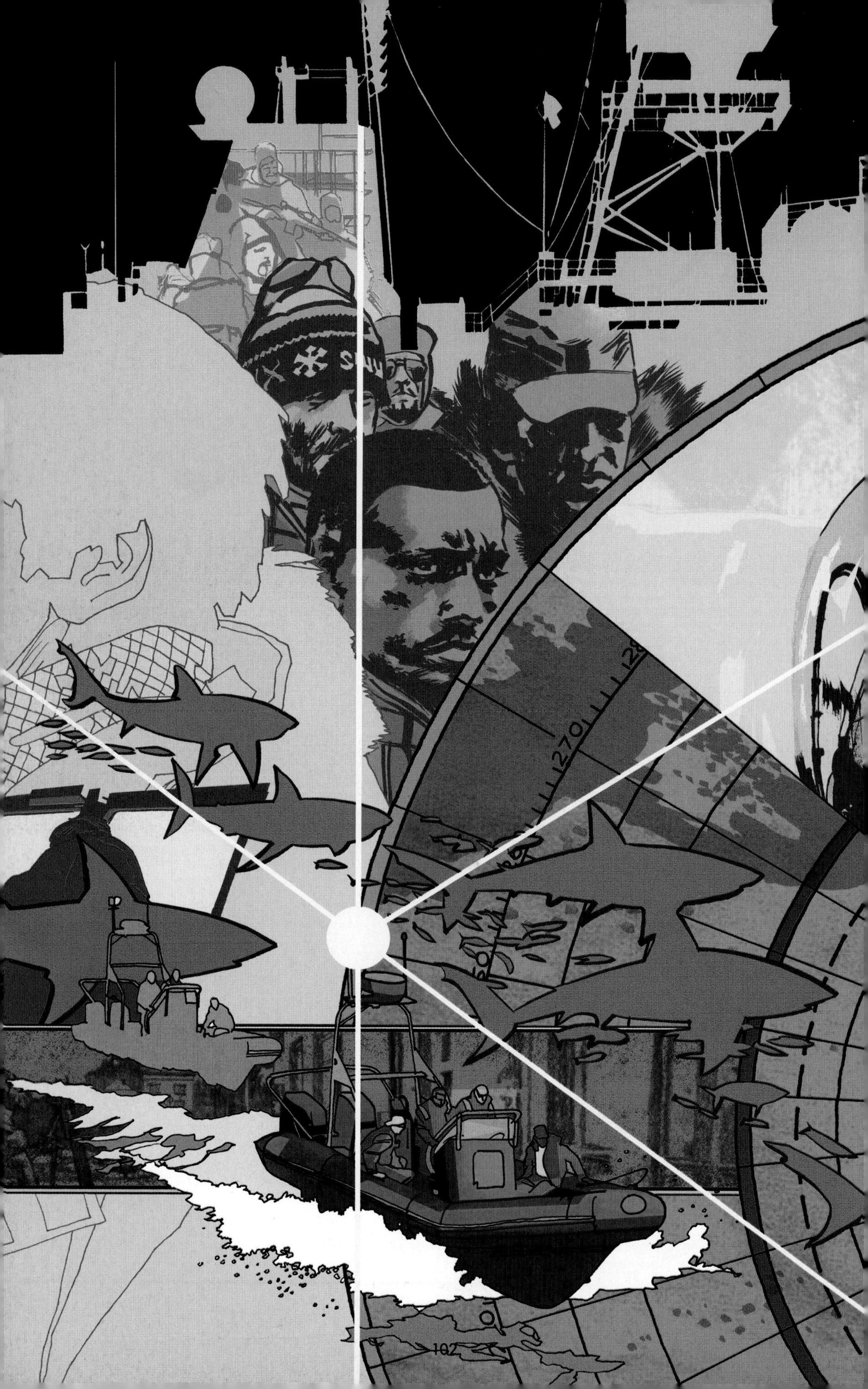
270

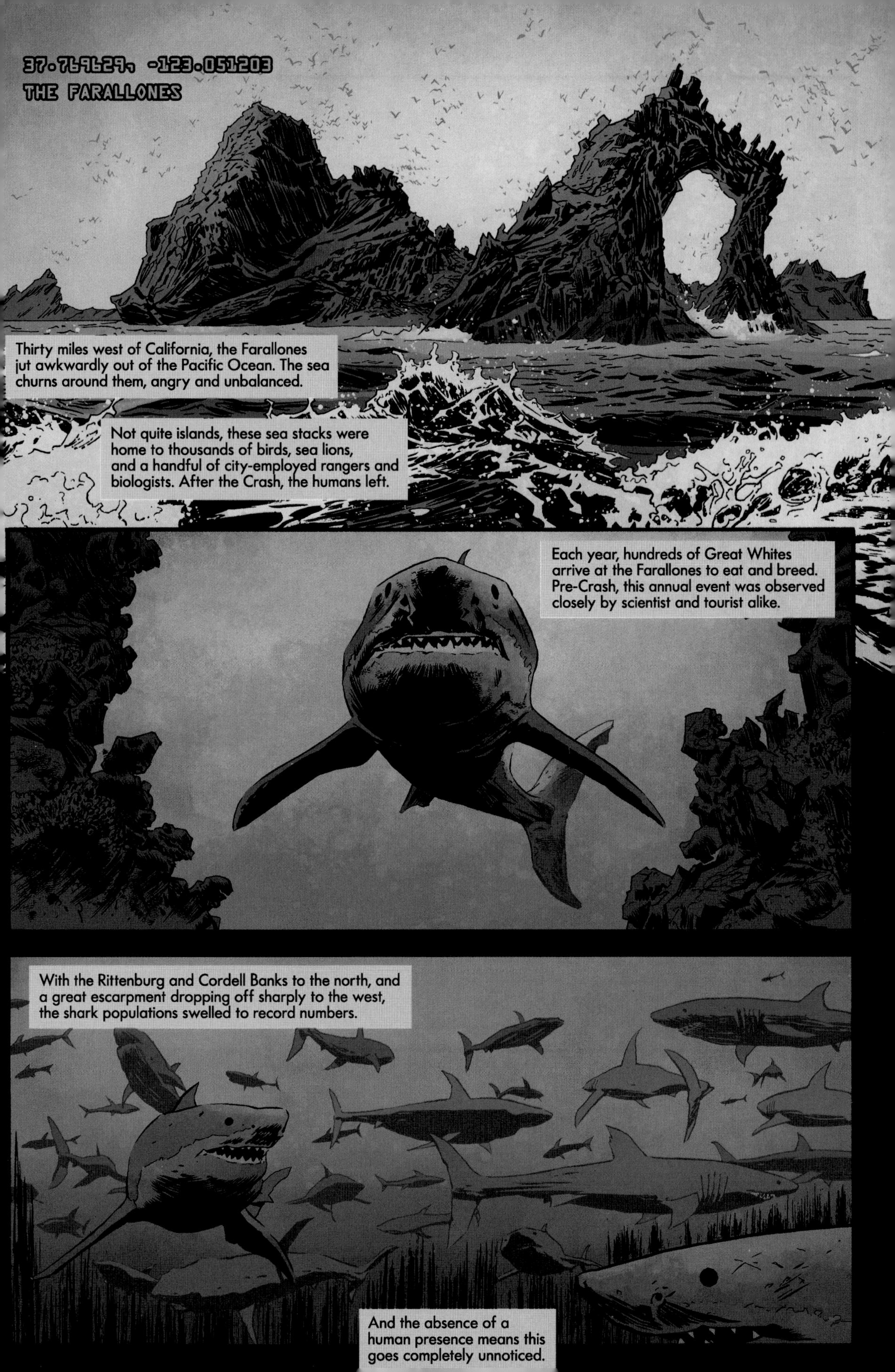
37.769629, -123.051203
THE FARALLONES
Thirty miles west of California, the Farallones jut awkwardly out of the Pacific Ocean. The sea churns around them, angry and unbalanced.
Not quite islands, these sea stacks were home to thousands of birds, sea lions, and a handful of city-employed rangers and biologists. After the Crash, the humans left.
Each year, hundreds of Great Whites arrive at the Farallones to eat and breed. Pre-Crash, this annual event was observed closely by scientist and tourist alike.
With the Rittenburg and Cordell Banks to the north, and a great escarpment dropping off sharply to the west, the shark populations swelled to record numbers.
And the absence of a human presence means this goes completely unnoticed.

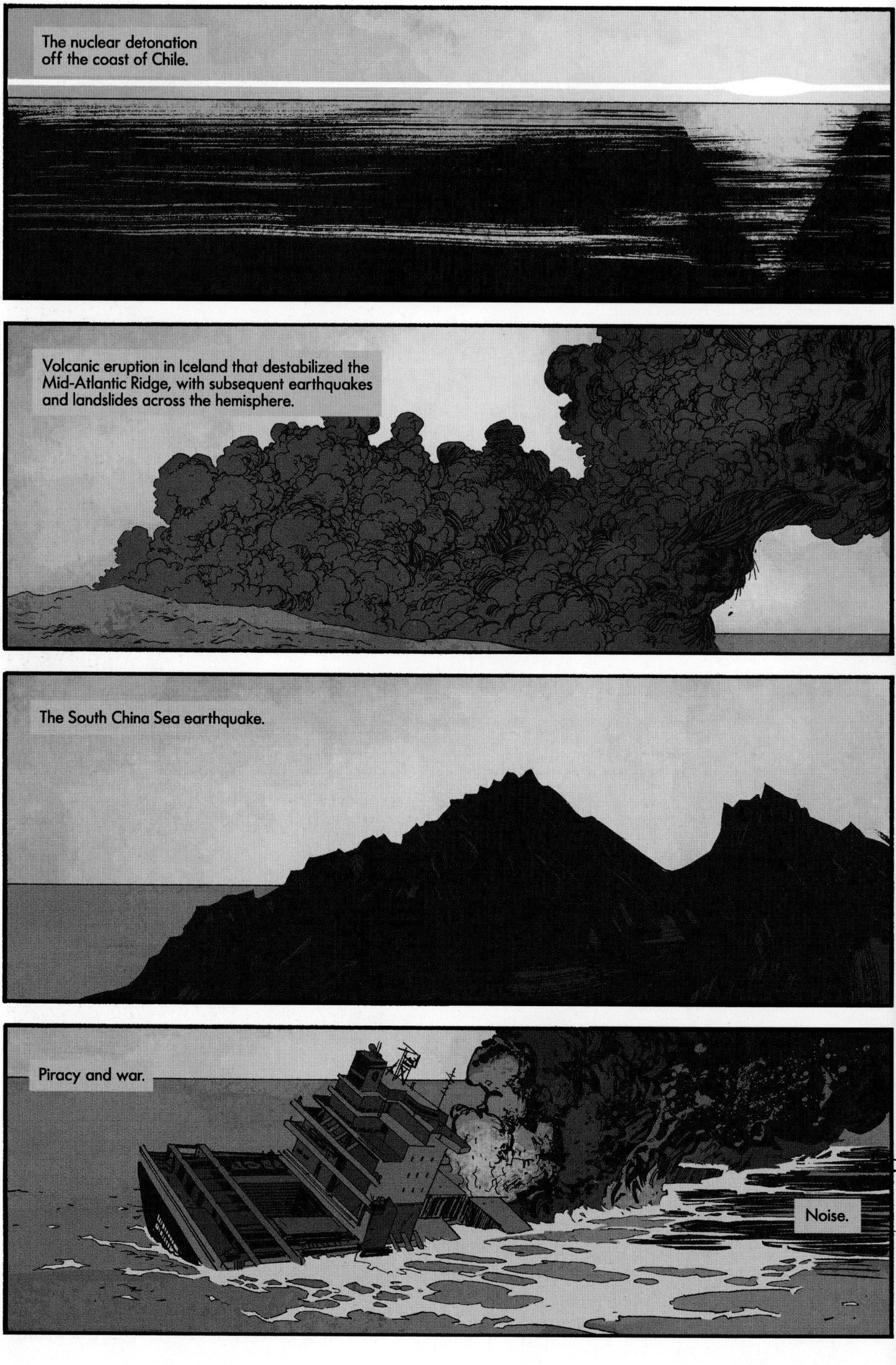
The nuclear detonation off the coast of Chile.
Volcanic eruption in Iceland that destabilized the Mid-Atlantic Ridge, with subsequent earthquakes and landslides across the hemisphere.
The South China Sea earthquake.
Piracy and war.
Noise.

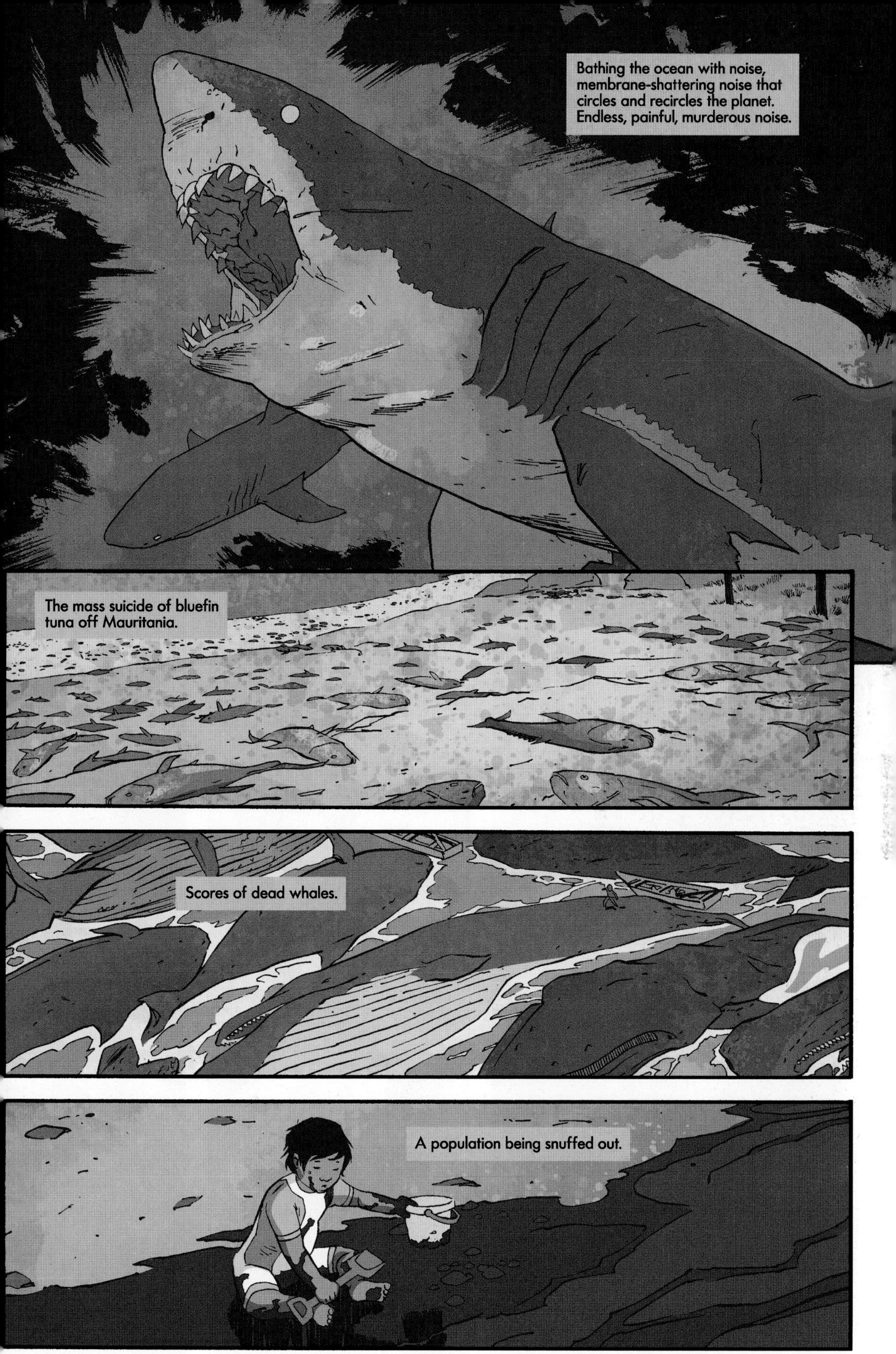
Bathing the ocean with noise, membrane-shattering noise that circles and recircles the planet. Endless, painful, murderous noise.
The mass suicide of bluefin tuna off Mauritania.
Scores of dead whales.
A population being snuffed out.

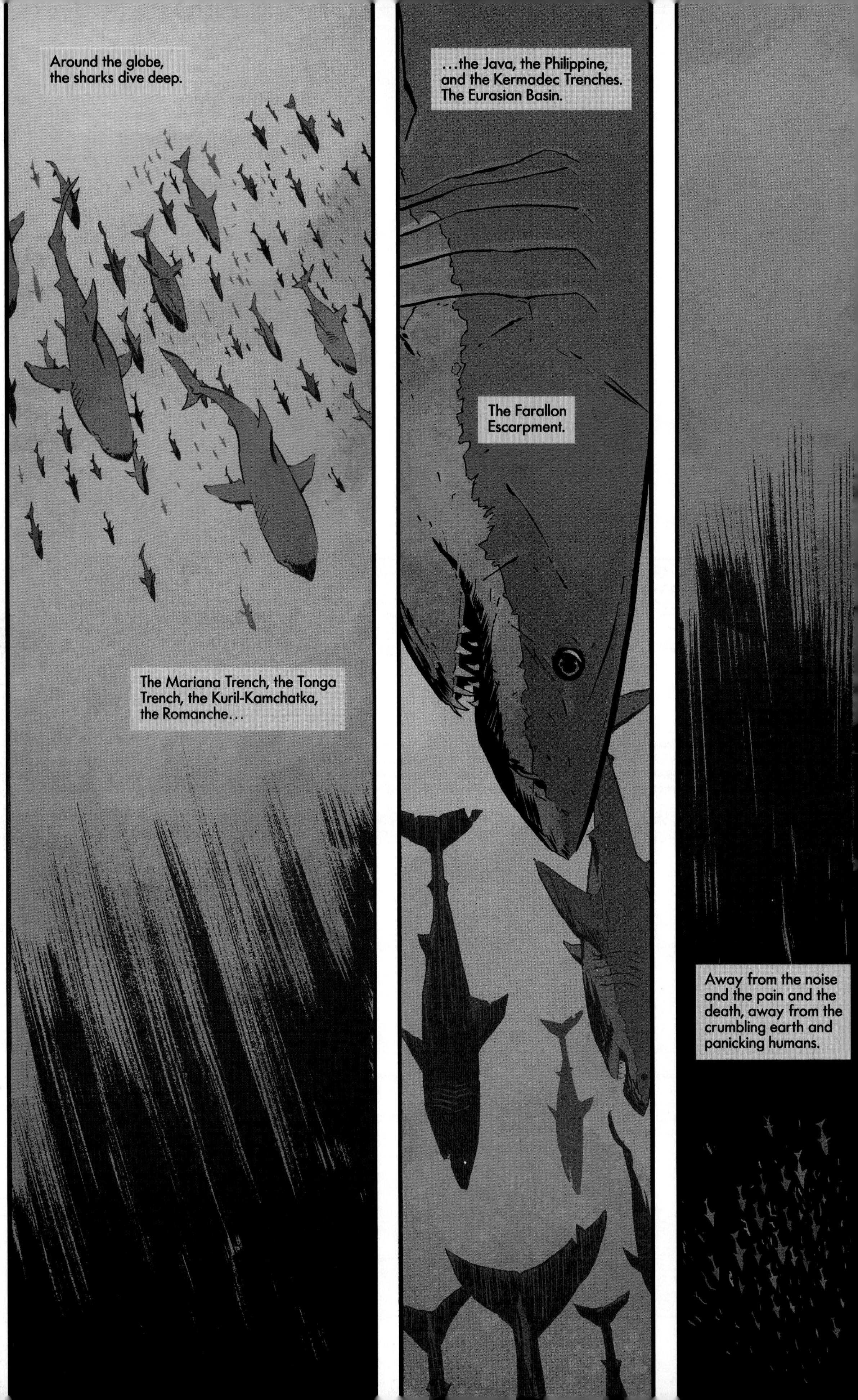
Around the globe, the sharks dive deep.
The Mariana Trench, the Tonga Trench, the Kuril-Kamchatka, the Romanche...
...the Java, the Philippine, and the Kermadec Trenches. The Eurasian Basin.
The Farallon Escarpment.
Away from the noise and the pain and the death, away from the crumbling earth and panicking humans.

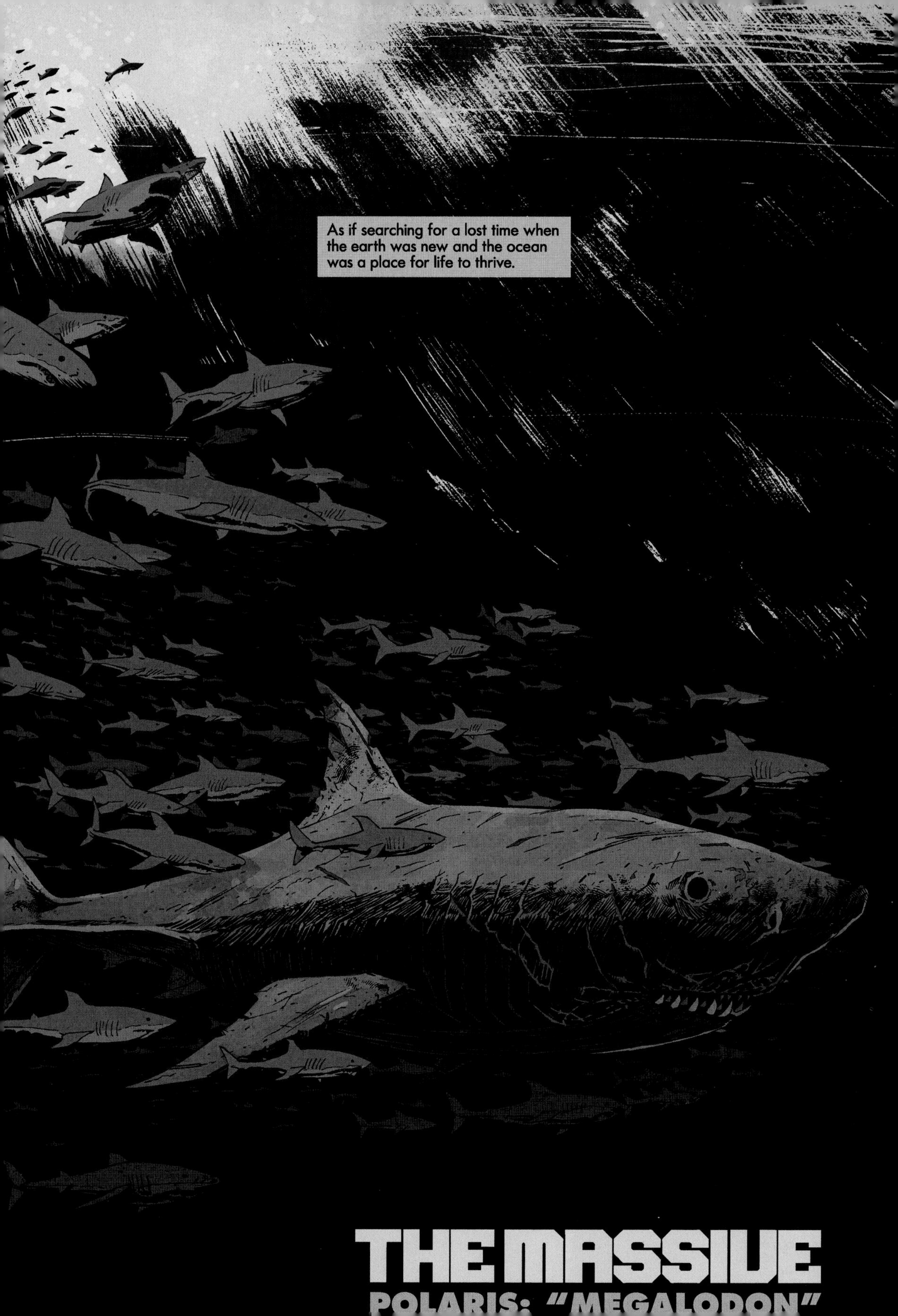
As if searching for a lost time when the earth was new and the ocean was a place for life to thrive.
THE MASSIVE
POLARIS: "MEGALODON"

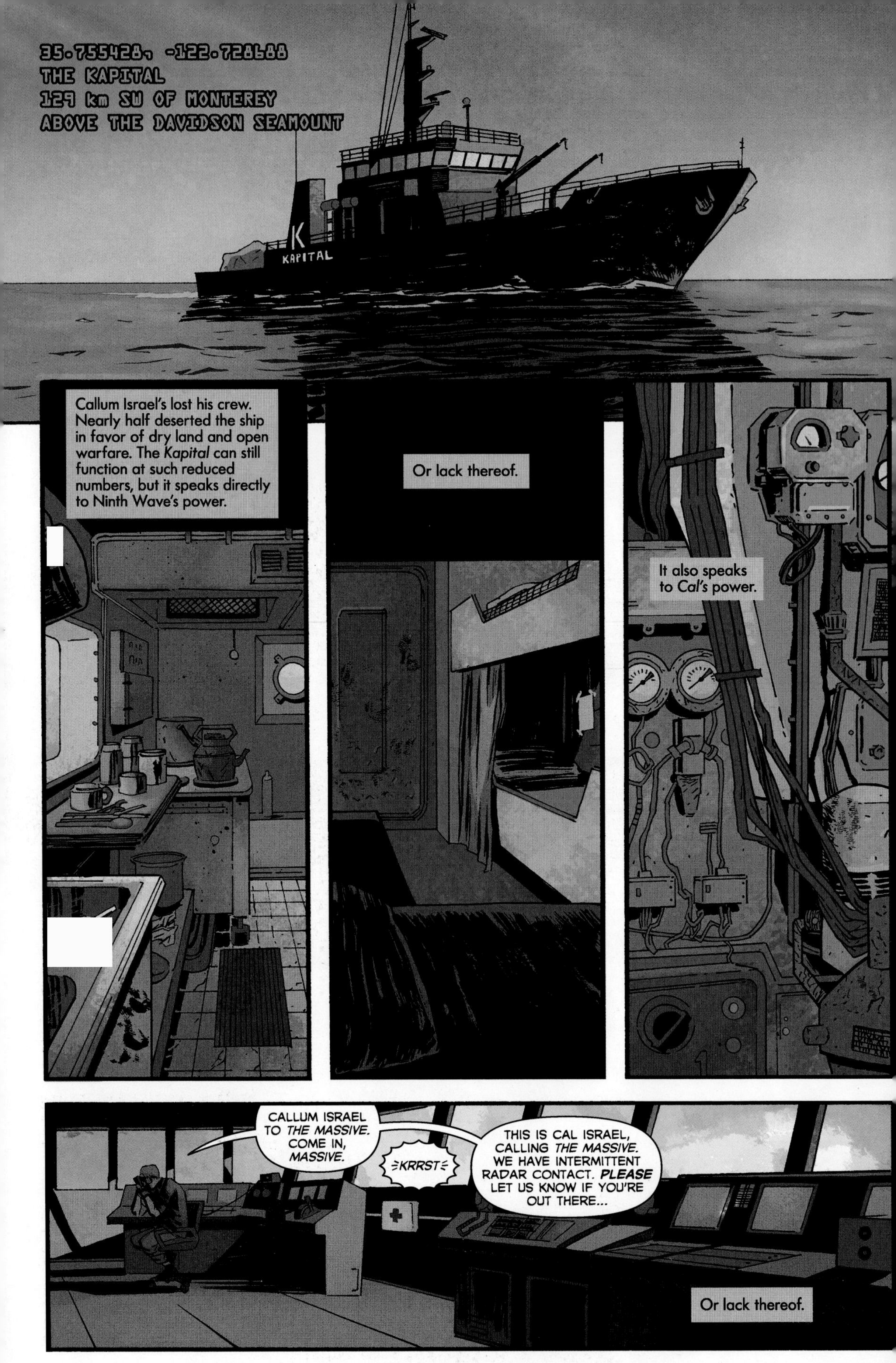
35.755428, -122.728688
THE KAPITAL
129 km SW OF MONTEREY
ABOVE THE DAVIDSON SEAMOUNT
KAPITAL
Callum Israel's lost his crew. Nearly half deserted the ship in favor of dry land and open warfare. The *Kapital* can still function at such reduced numbers, but it speaks directly to Ninth Wave's power.
Or lack thereof.
It also speaks to *Cal's* power.
CALLUM ISRAEL TO *THE MASSIVE.* COME IN, *MASSIVE.*
KRRST
THIS IS CAL ISRAEL, CALLING *THE MASSIVE.* WE HAVE INTERMITTENT RADAR CONTACT. ***PLEASE*** LET US KNOW IF YOU'RE OUT THERE...
Or lack thereof.

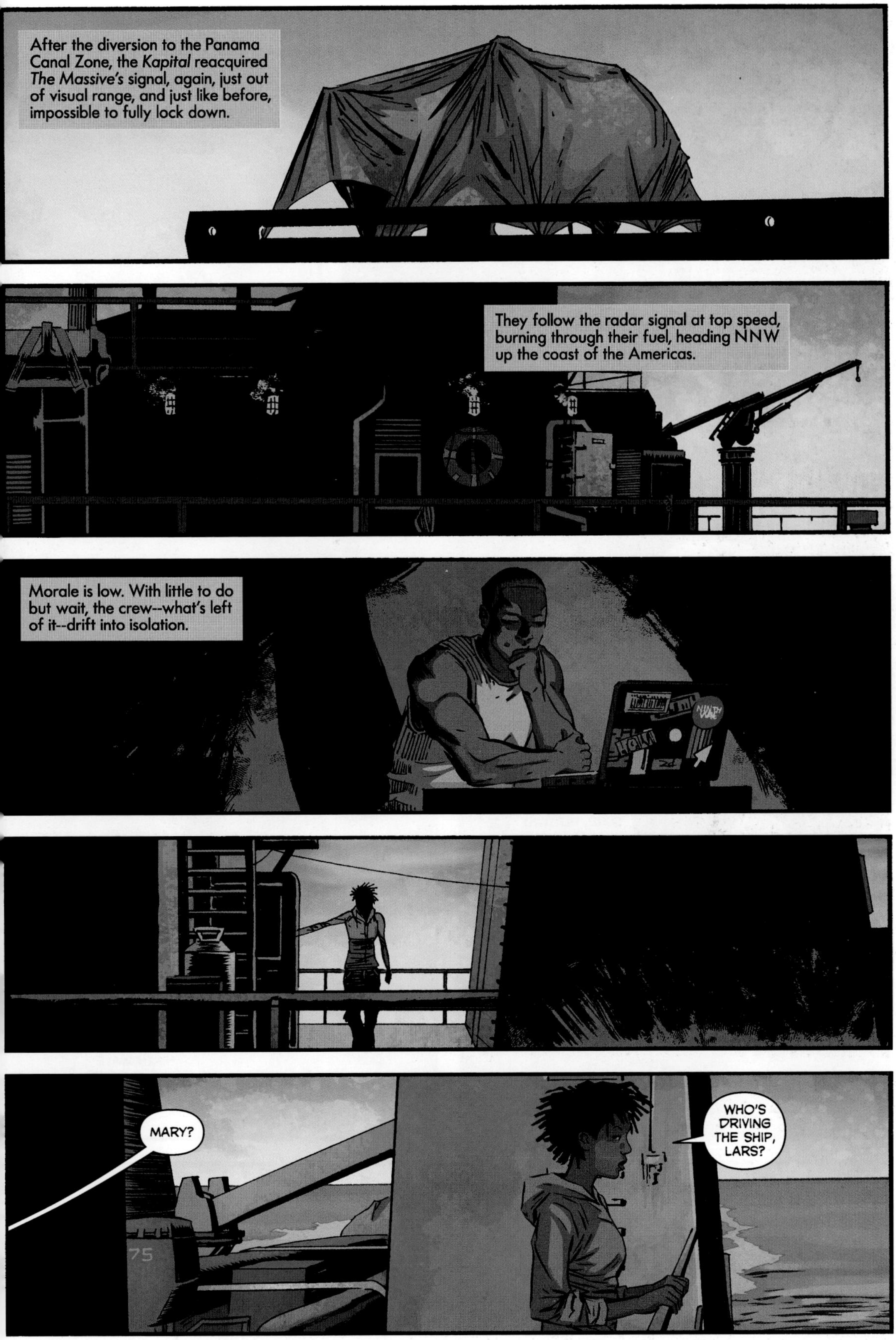
After the diversion to the Panama Canal Zone, the *Kapital* reacquired *The Massive's* signal, again, just out of visual range, and just like before, impossible to fully lock down.
They follow the radar signal at top speed, burning through their fuel, heading NNW up the coast of the Americas.
Morale is low. With little to do but wait, the crew--what's left of it--drift into isolation.
MARY?
WHO'S DRIVING THE SHIP, LARS?

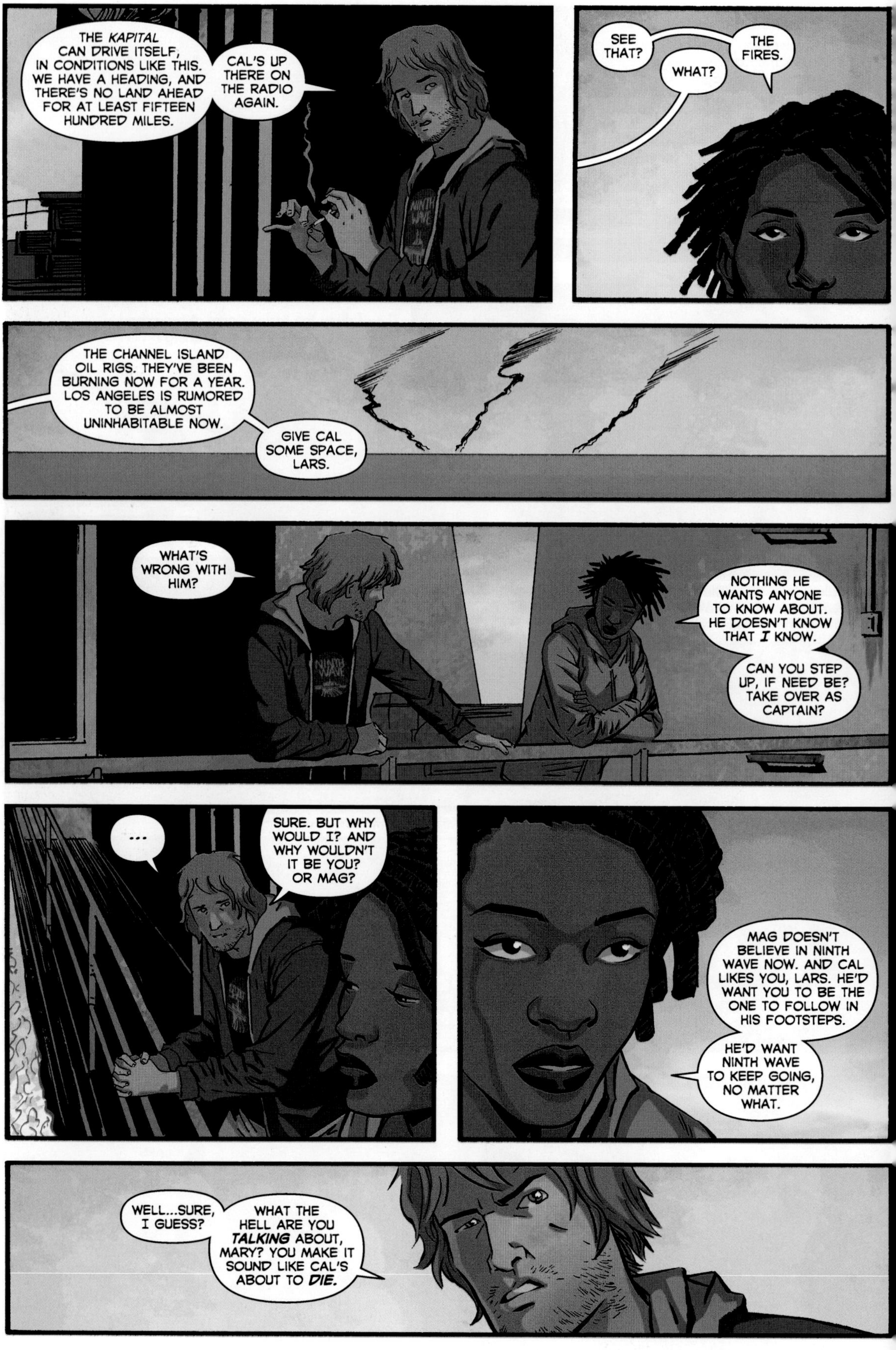
THE *KAPITAL* CAN DRIVE ITSELF, IN CONDITIONS LIKE THIS. WE HAVE A HEADING, AND THERE'S NO LAND AHEAD FOR AT LEAST FIFTEEN HUNDRED MILES.
CAL'S UP THERE ON THE RADIO AGAIN.
SEE THAT?
WHAT?
THE FIRES.
THE CHANNEL ISLAND OIL RIGS. THEY'VE BEEN BURNING NOW FOR A YEAR. LOS ANGELES IS RUMORED TO BE ALMOST UNINHABITABLE NOW.
GIVE CAL SOME SPACE, LARS.
WHAT'S WRONG WITH HIM?
NOTHING HE WANTS ANYONE TO KNOW ABOUT. HE DOESN'T KNOW THAT *I* KNOW.
CAN YOU STEP UP, IF NEED BE? TAKE OVER AS CAPTAIN?
...
SURE. BUT WHY WOULD I? AND WHY WOULDN'T IT BE YOU? OR MAG?
MAG DOESN'T BELIEVE IN NINTH WAVE NOW. AND CAL LIKES YOU, LARS. HE'D WANT YOU TO BE THE ONE TO FOLLOW IN HIS FOOTSTEPS.
HE'D WANT NINTH WAVE TO KEEP GOING, NO MATTER WHAT.
WELL...SURE, I GUESS?
WHAT THE HELL ARE YOU ***TALKING*** ABOUT, MARY? YOU MAKE IT SOUND LIKE CAL'S ABOUT TO ***DIE.***

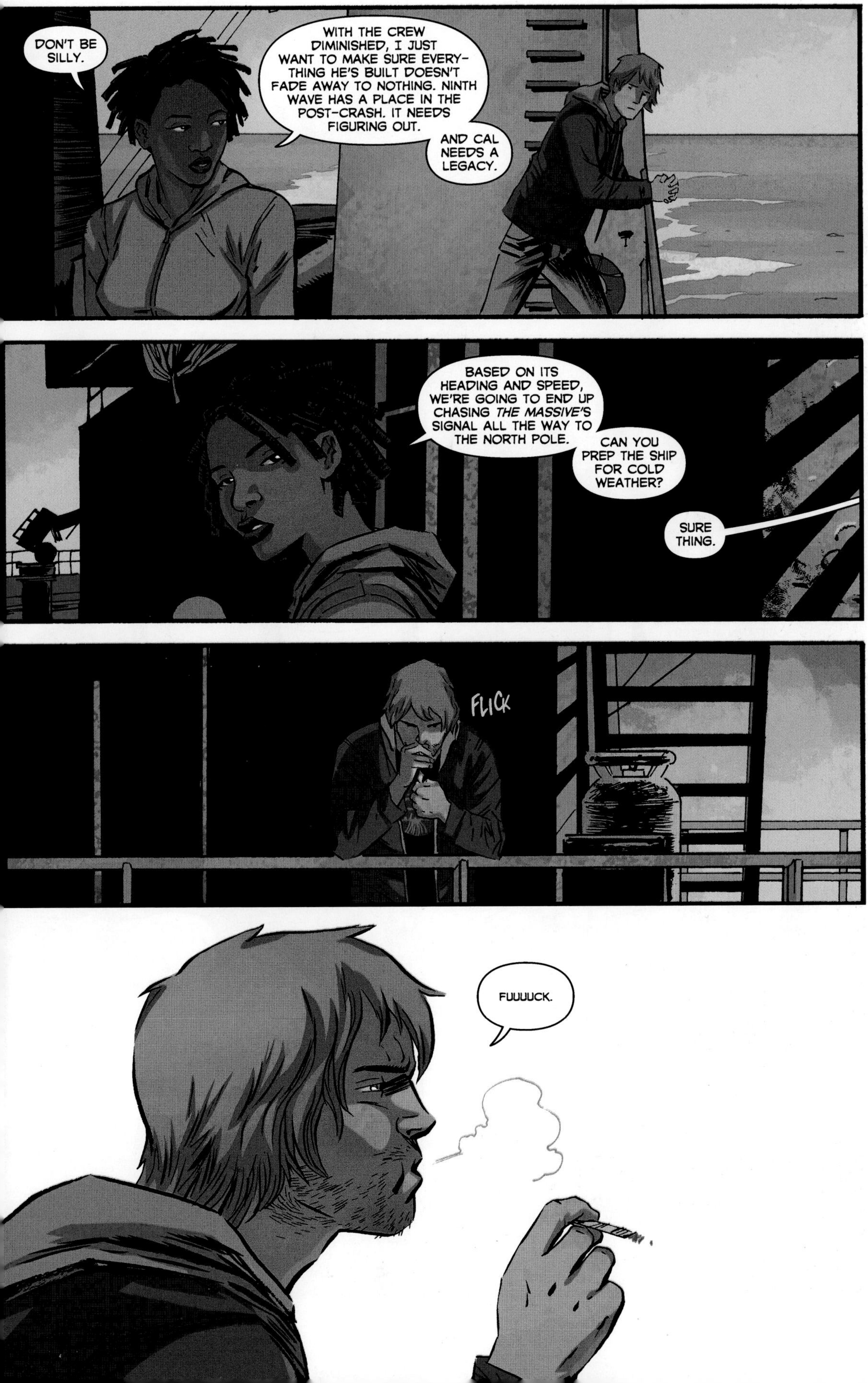
DON'T BE SILLY.
WITH THE CREW DIMINISHED, I JUST WANT TO MAKE SURE EVERY-THING HE'S BUILT DOESN'T FADE AWAY TO NOTHING. NINTH WAVE HAS A PLACE IN THE POST-CRASH. IT NEEDS FIGURING OUT.
AND CAL NEEDS A LEGACY.
BASED ON ITS HEADING AND SPEED, WE'RE GOING TO END UP CHASING *THE MASSIVE*'S SIGNAL ALL THE WAY TO THE NORTH POLE.
CAN YOU PREP THE SHIP FOR COLD WEATHER?
SURE THING.
FLICK
FUUUUCK.

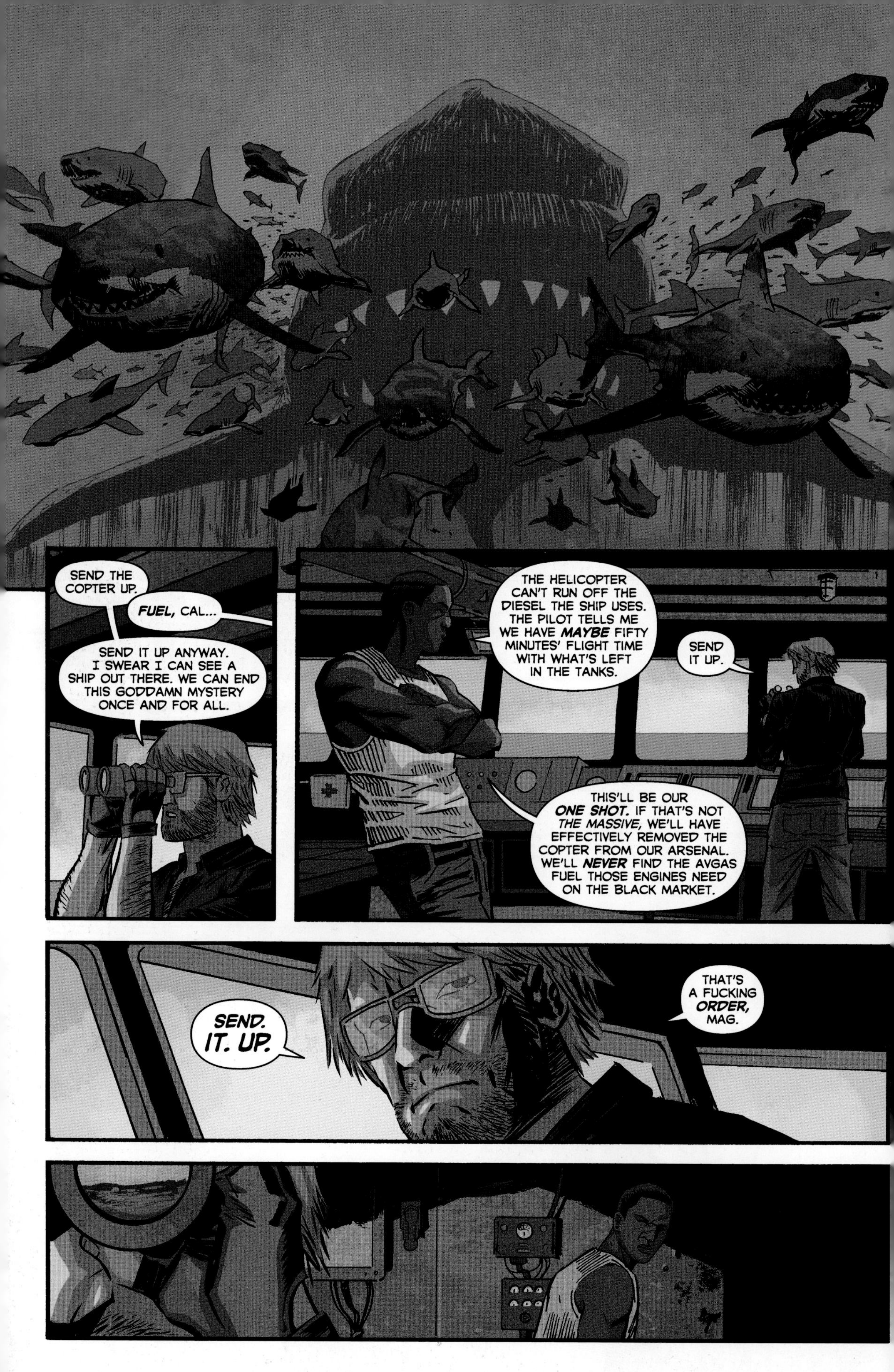
SEND THE COPTER UP.
FUEL, CAL...
SEND IT UP ANYWAY. I SWEAR I CAN SEE A SHIP OUT THERE. WE CAN END THIS GODDAMN MYSTERY ONCE AND FOR ALL.
THE HELICOPTER CAN'T RUN OFF THE DIESEL THE SHIP USES. THE PILOT TELLS ME WE HAVE MAYBE FIFTY MINUTES' FLIGHT TIME WITH WHAT'S LEFT IN THE TANKS.
SEND IT UP.
THIS'LL BE OUR ONE SHOT. IF THAT'S NOT THE MASSIVE, WE'LL HAVE EFFECTIVELY REMOVED THE COPTER FROM OUR ARSENAL. WE'LL NEVER FIND THE AVGAS FUEL THOSE ENGINES NEED ON THE BLACK MARKET.
SEND. IT. UP.
THAT'S A FUCKING ORDER, MAG.

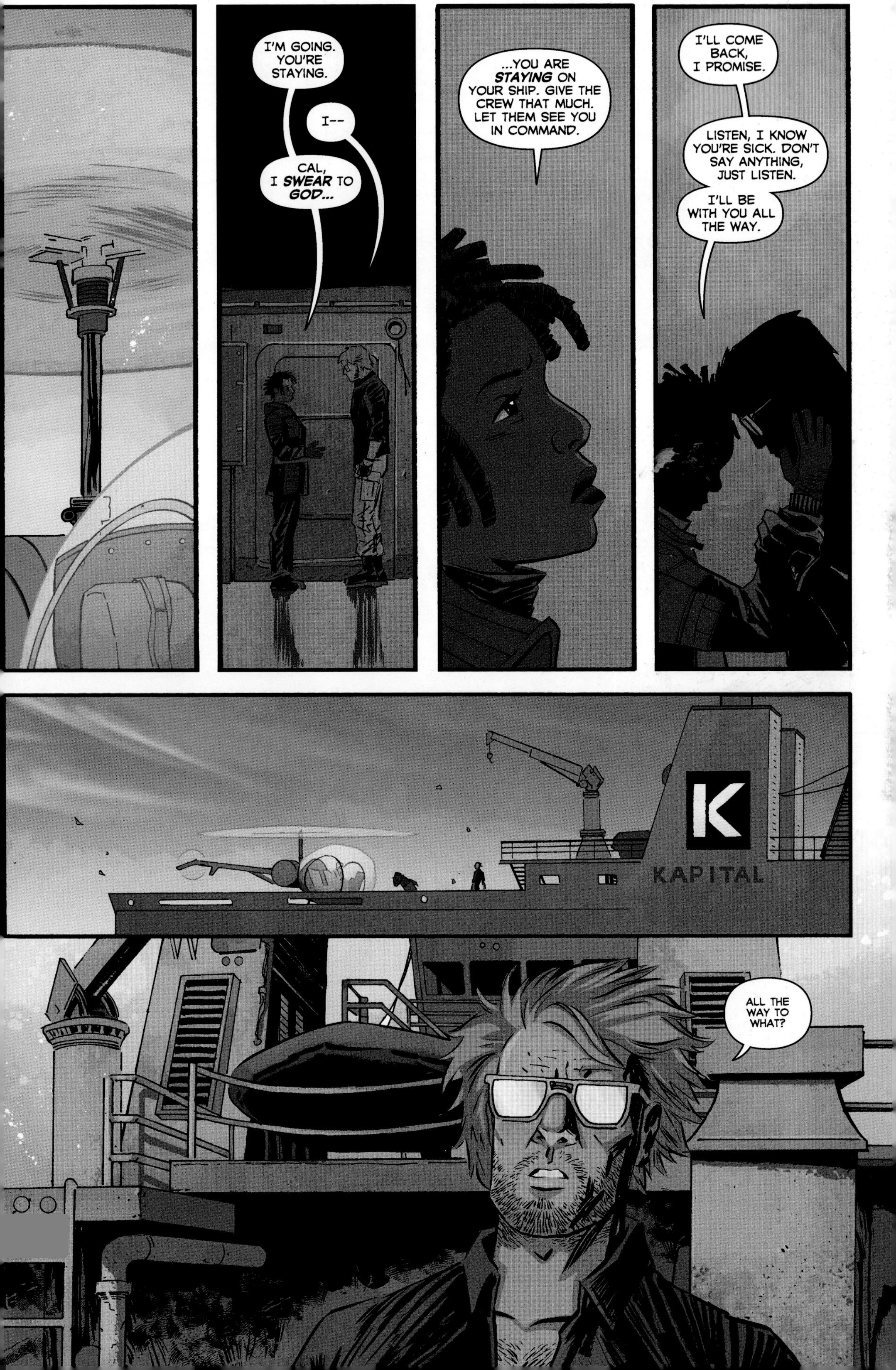
I'M GOING. YOU'RE STAYING.
I--
CAL, I SWEAR TO GOD...
...YOU ARE STAYING ON YOUR SHIP. GIVE THE CREW THAT MUCH. LET THEM SEE YOU IN COMMAND.
I'LL COME BACK, I PROMISE.
LISTEN, I KNOW YOU'RE SICK. DON'T SAY ANYTHING, JUST LISTEN.
I'LL BE WITH YOU ALL THE WAY.
K
KAPITAL
ALL THE WAY TO WHAT?

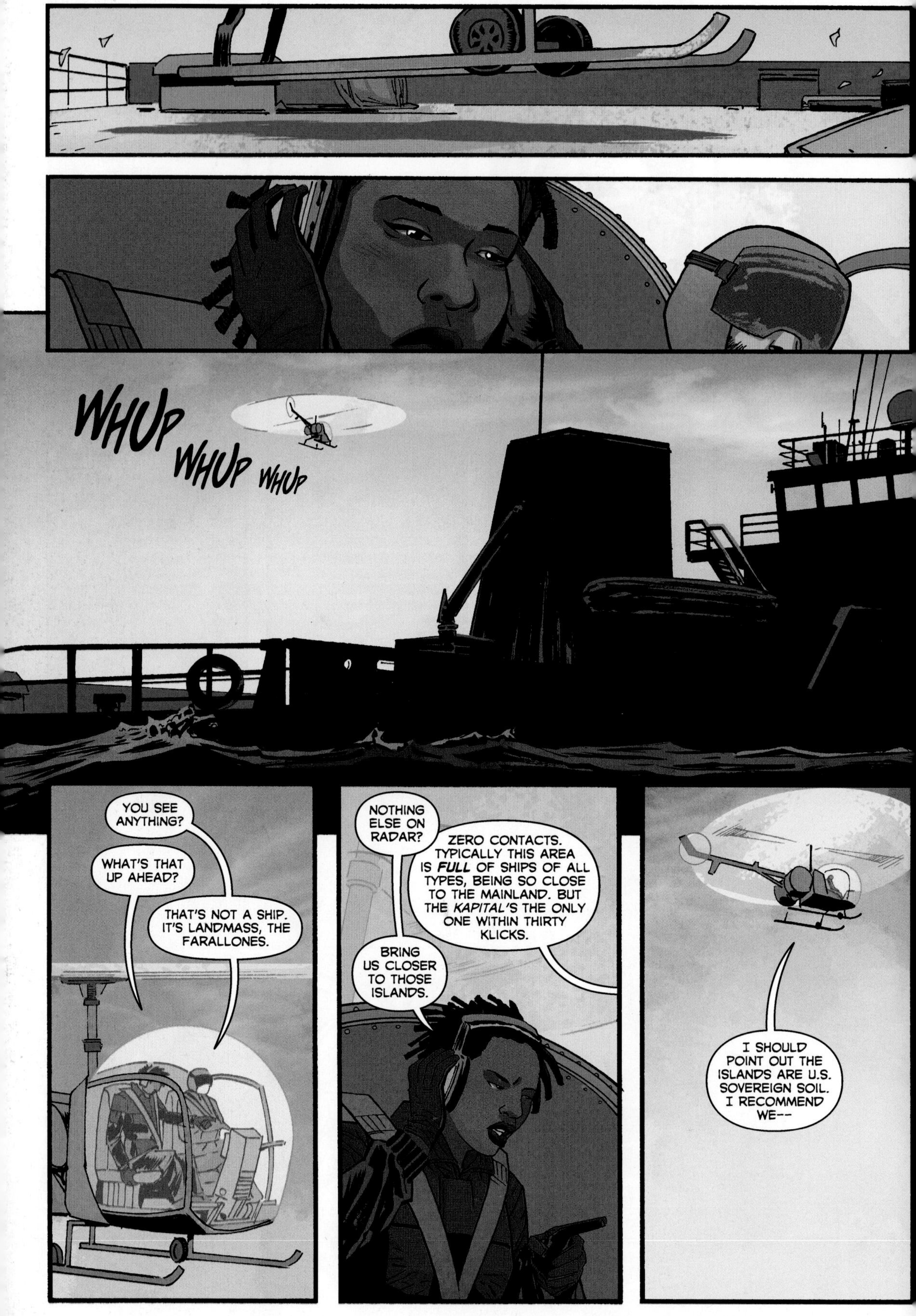

WHUP WHUP WHUP
YOU SEE ANYTHING?
WHAT'S THAT UP AHEAD?
THAT'S NOT A SHIP. IT'S LANDMASS, THE FARALLONES.
NOTHING ELSE ON RADAR?
ZERO CONTACTS. TYPICALLY THIS AREA IS *FULL* OF SHIPS OF ALL TYPES, BEING SO CLOSE TO THE MAINLAND. BUT THE *KAPITAL*'S THE ONLY ONE WITHIN THIRTY KLICKS.
BRING US CLOSER TO THOSE ISLANDS.
I SHOULD POINT OUT THE ISLANDS ARE U.S. SOVEREIGN SOIL. I RECOMMEND WE--

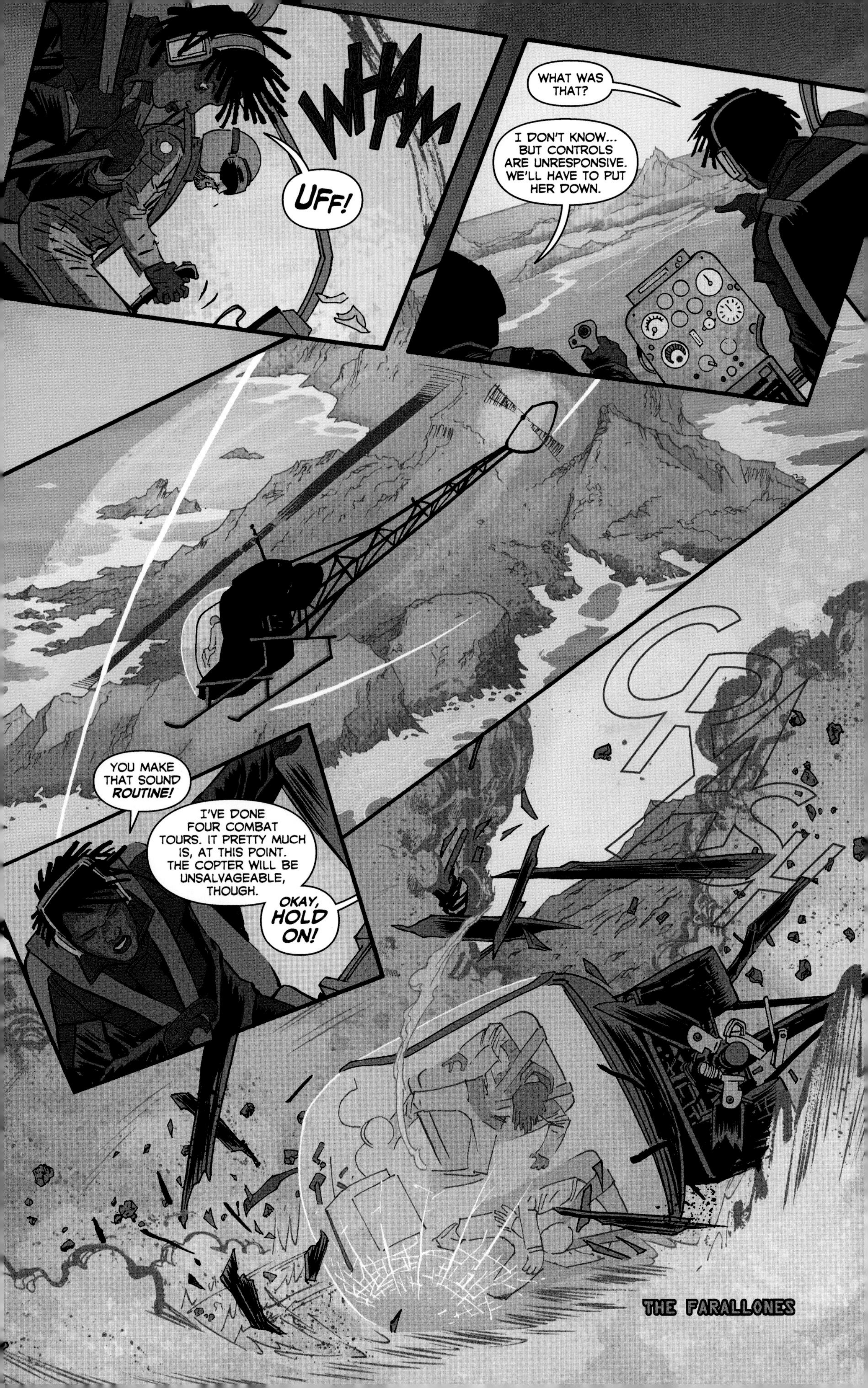
WHAM
UFF!
WHAT WAS THAT?
I DON'T KNOW... BUT CONTROLS ARE UNRESPONSIVE. WE'LL HAVE TO PUT HER DOWN.
YOU MAKE THAT SOUND ROUTINE!
I'VE DONE FOUR COMBAT TOURS. IT PRETTY MUCH IS, AT THIS POINT. THE COPTER WILL BE UNSALVAGEABLE, THOUGH.
OKAY, HOLD ON!
THE FARALLONES

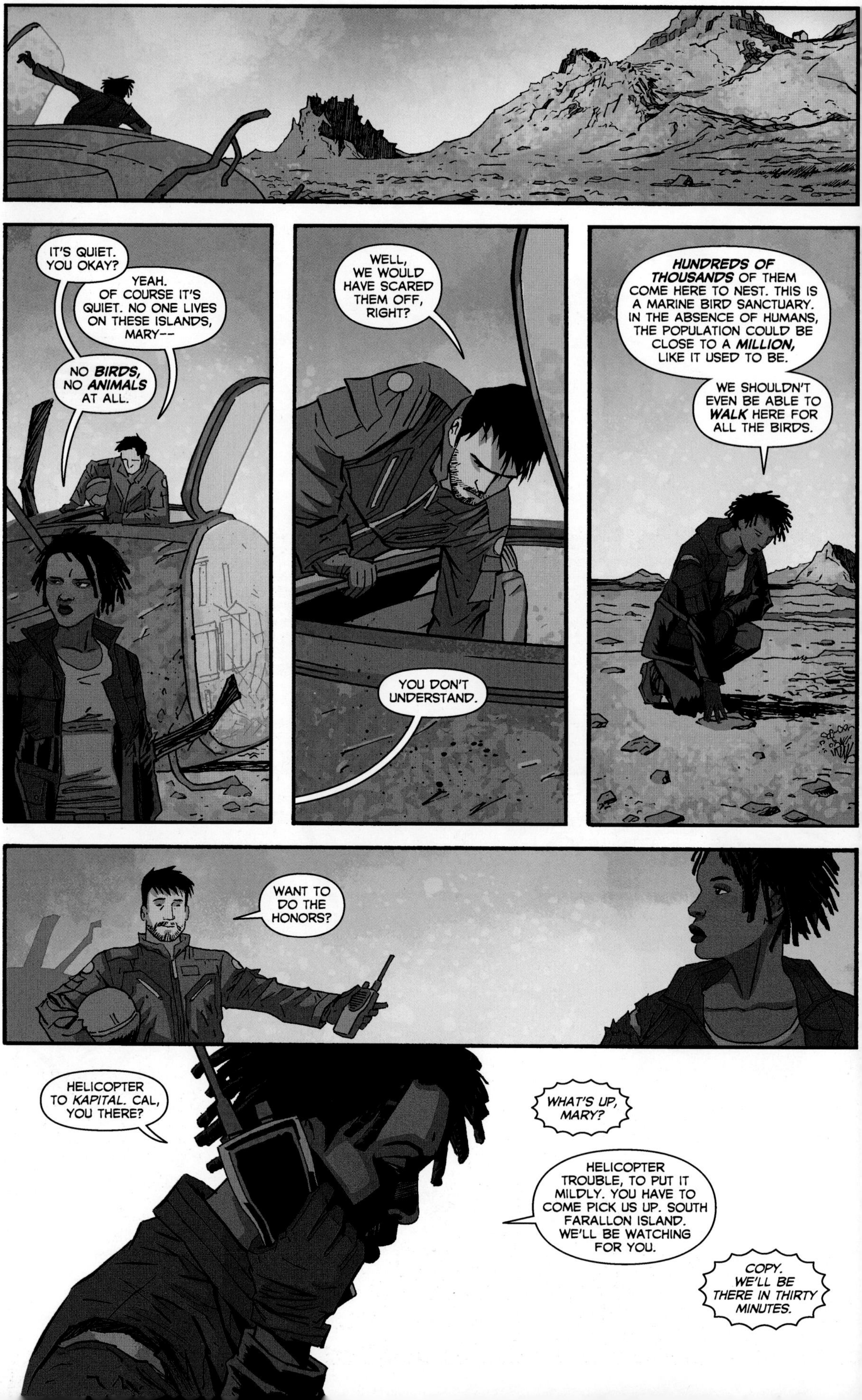
IT'S QUIET. YOU OKAY?
YEAH. OF COURSE IT'S QUIET. NO ONE LIVES ON THESE ISLANDS, MARY--
NO BIRDS, NO ANIMALS AT ALL.
WELL, WE WOULD HAVE SCARED THEM OFF, RIGHT?
YOU DON'T UNDERSTAND.
HUNDREDS OF THOUSANDS OF THEM COME HERE TO NEST. THIS IS A MARINE BIRD SANCTUARY. IN THE ABSENCE OF HUMANS, THE POPULATION COULD BE CLOSE TO A MILLION, LIKE IT USED TO BE.
WE SHOULDN'T EVEN BE ABLE TO WALK HERE FOR ALL THE BIRDS.
WANT TO DO THE HONORS?
HELICOPTER TO KAPITAL. CAL, YOU THERE?
WHAT'S UP, MARY?
HELICOPTER TROUBLE, TO PUT IT MILDLY. YOU HAVE TO COME PICK US UP. SOUTH FARALLON ISLAND. WE'LL BE WATCHING FOR YOU.
COPY. WE'LL BE THERE IN THIRTY MINUTES.

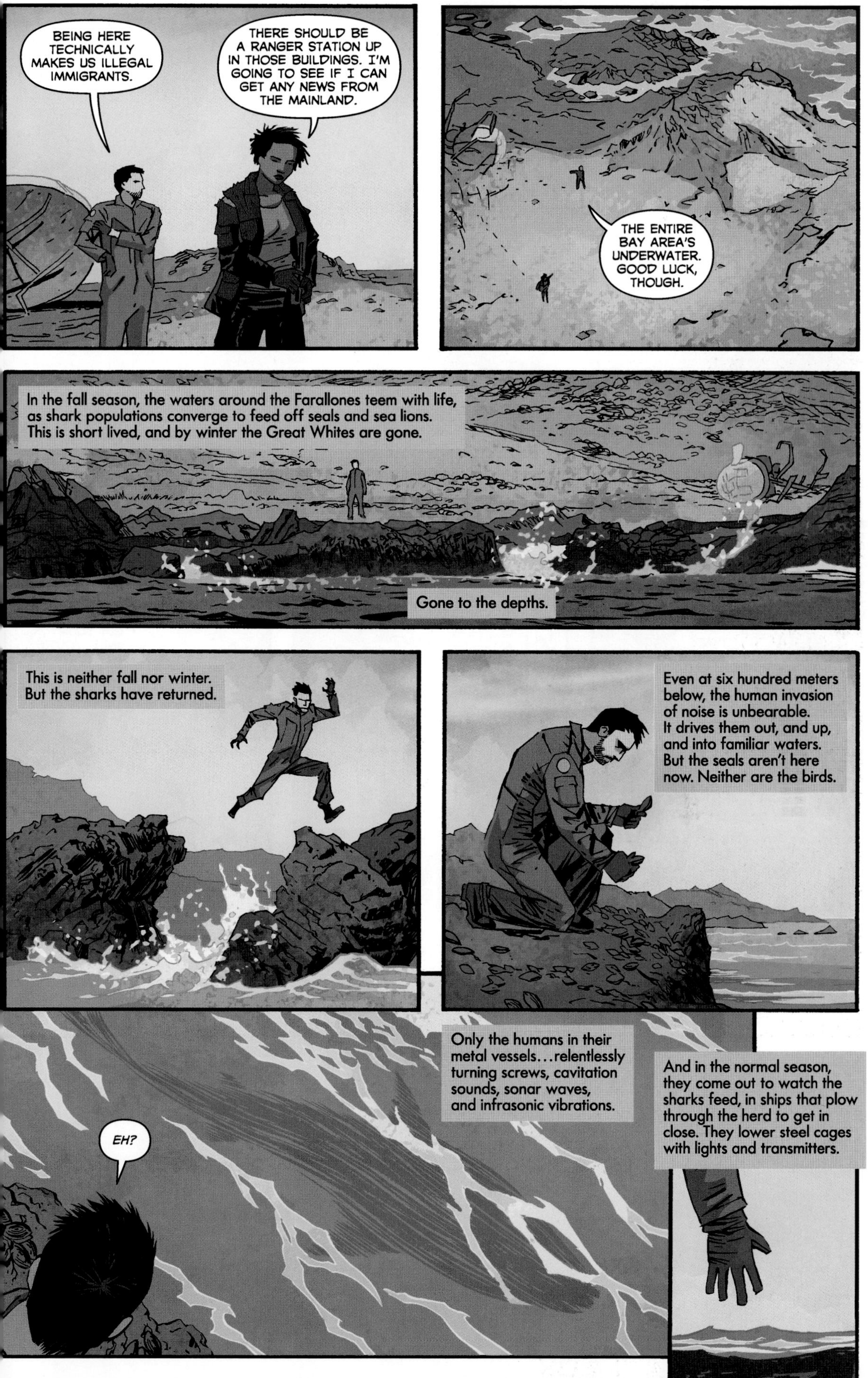
BEING HERE TECHNICALLY MAKES US ILLEGAL IMMIGRANTS.
THERE SHOULD BE A RANGER STATION UP IN THOSE BUILDINGS. I'M GOING TO SEE IF I CAN GET ANY NEWS FROM THE MAINLAND.
THE ENTIRE BAY AREA'S UNDERWATER. GOOD LUCK, THOUGH.
In the fall season, the waters around the Farallones teem with life, as shark populations converge to feed off seals and sea lions. This is short lived, and by winter the Great Whites are gone.
Gone to the depths.
This is neither fall nor winter. But the sharks have returned.
Even at six hundred meters below, the human invasion of noise is unbearable. It drives them out, and up, and into familiar waters. But the seals aren't here now. Neither are the birds.
Only the humans in their metal vessels...relentlessly turning screws, cavitation sounds, sonar waves, and infrasonic vibrations.
EH?
And in the normal season, they come out to watch the sharks feed, in ships that plow through the herd to get in close. They lower steel cages with lights and transmitters.

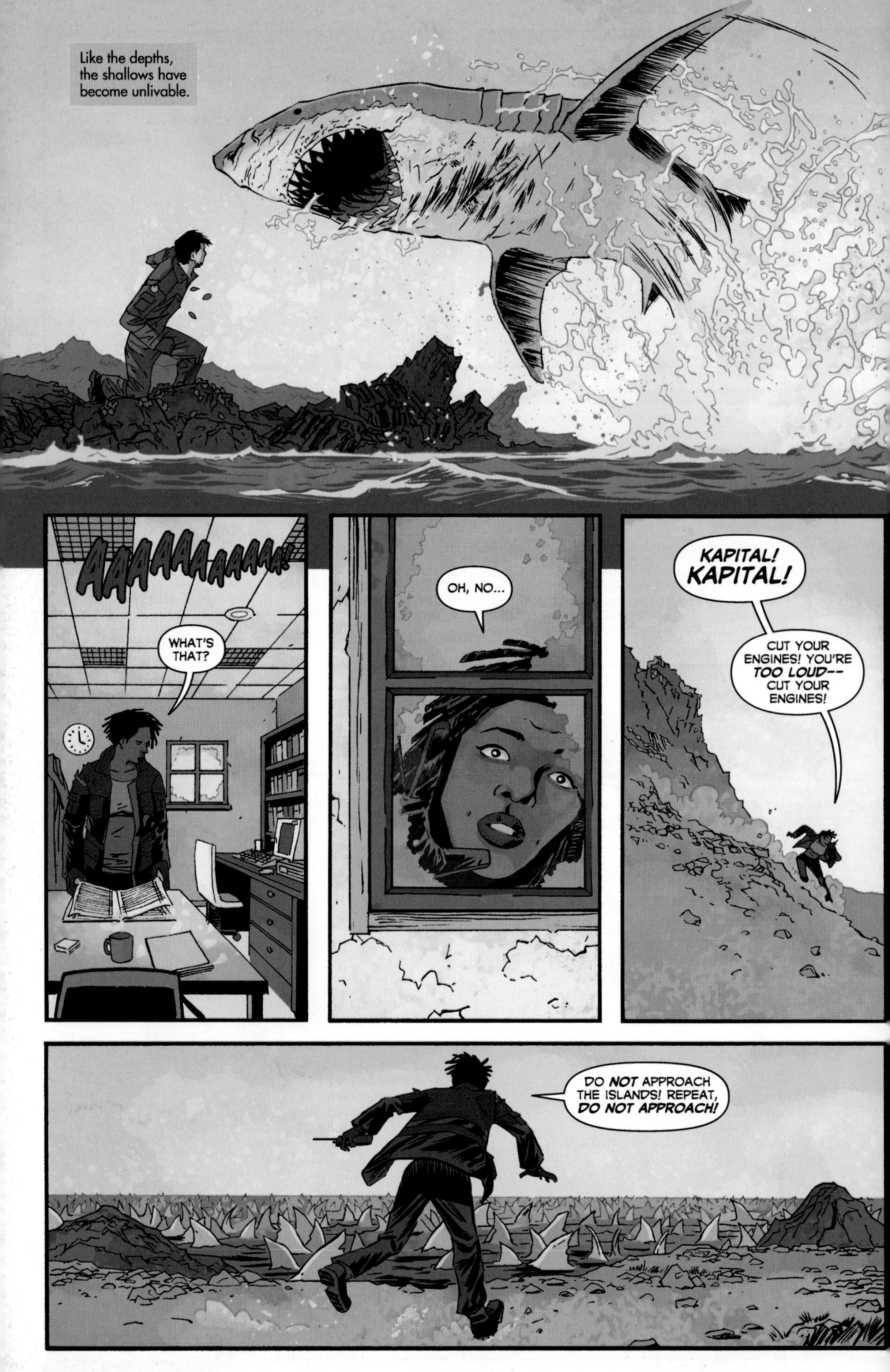
Like the depths, the shallows have become unlivable.
AAAAAAAAAAAA!
WHAT'S THAT?
OH, NO...
KAPITAL! KAPITAL!
CUT YOUR ENGINES! YOU'RE *TOO LOUD*-- CUT YOUR ENGINES!
DO **NOT** APPROACH THE ISLANDS! REPEAT, ***DO NOT APPROACH!***

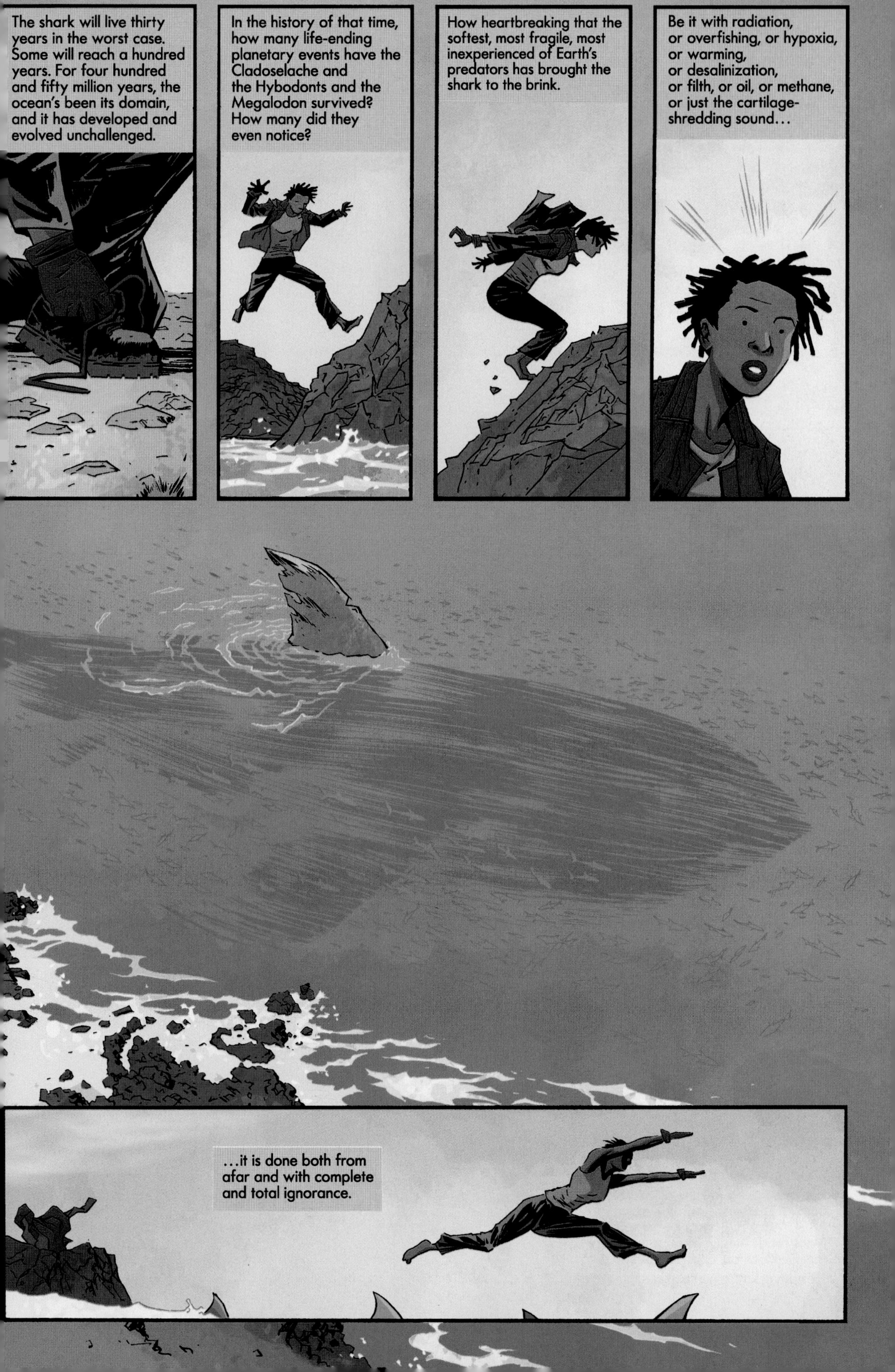
The shark will live thirty years in the worst case. Some will reach a hundred years. For four hundred and fifty million years, the ocean's been its domain, and it has developed and evolved unchallenged.
In the history of that time, how many life-ending planetary events have the Cladoselache and the Hybodonts and the Megalodon survived? How many did they even notice?
How heartbreaking that the softest, most fragile, most inexperienced of Earth's predators has brought the shark to the brink.
Be it with radiation, or overfishing, or hypoxia, or warming, or desalinization, or filth, or oil, or methane, or just the cartilage-shredding sound...
...it is done both from afar and with complete and total ignorance.

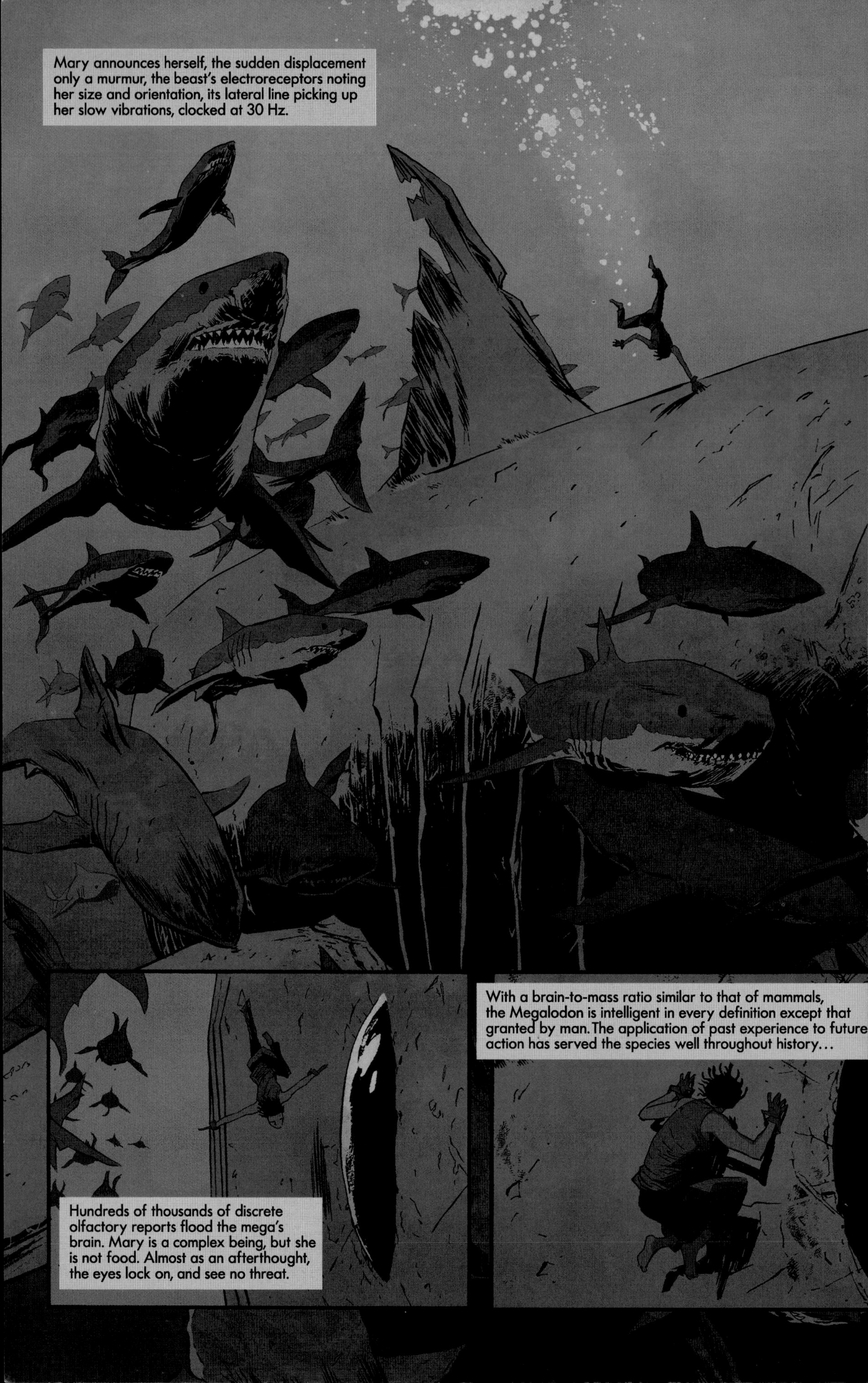

Mary announces herself, the sudden displacement only a murmur, the beast's electroreceptors noting her size and orientation, its lateral line picking up her slow vibrations, clocked at 30 Hz.
Hundreds of thousands of discrete olfactory reports flood the mega's brain. Mary is a complex being, but she is not food. Almost as an afterthought, the eyes lock on, and see no threat.
With a brain-to-mass ratio similar to that of mammals, the Megalodon is intelligent in every definition except that granted by man. The application of past experience to future action has served the species well throughout history…

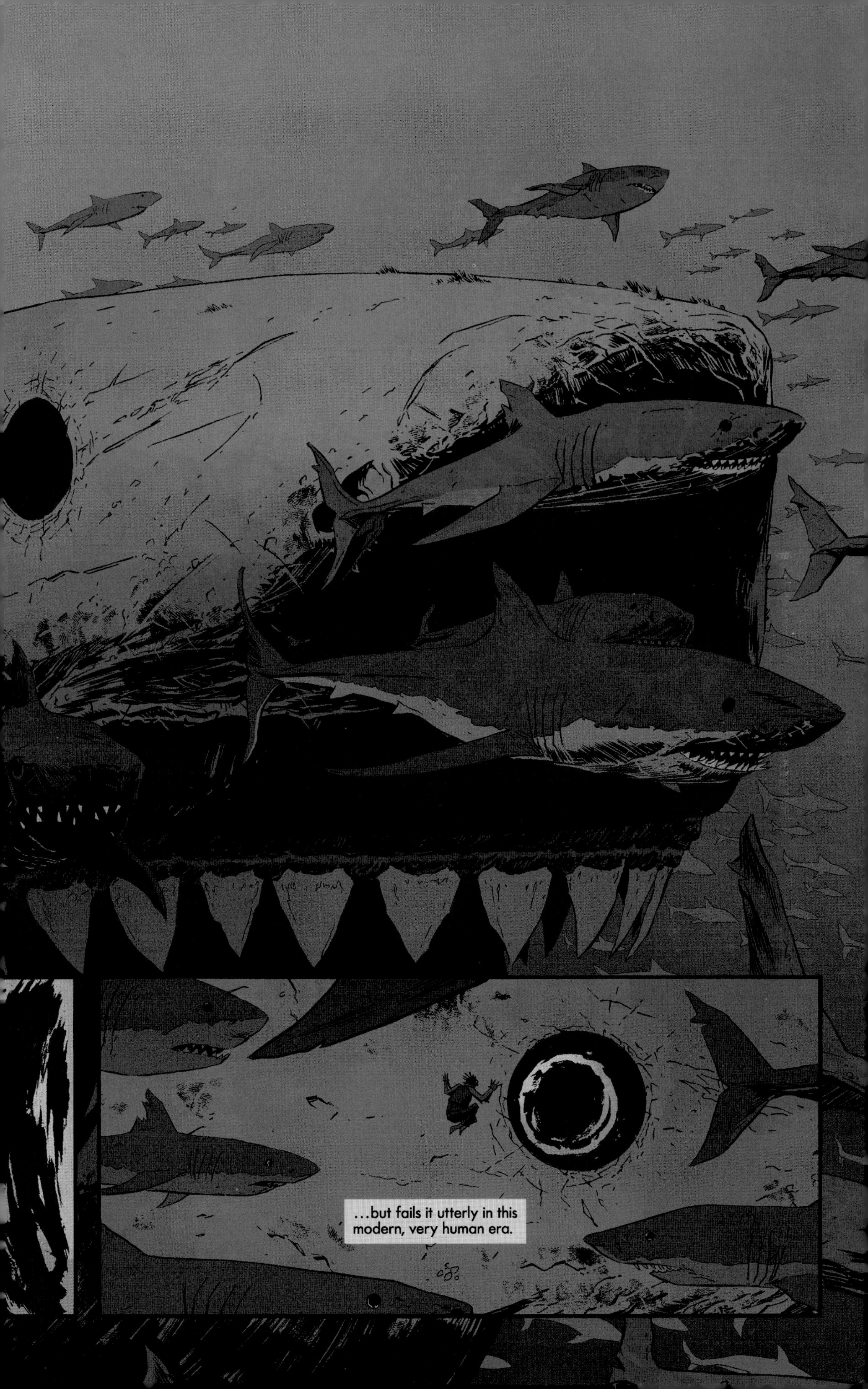
...but fails it utterly in this modern, very human era.

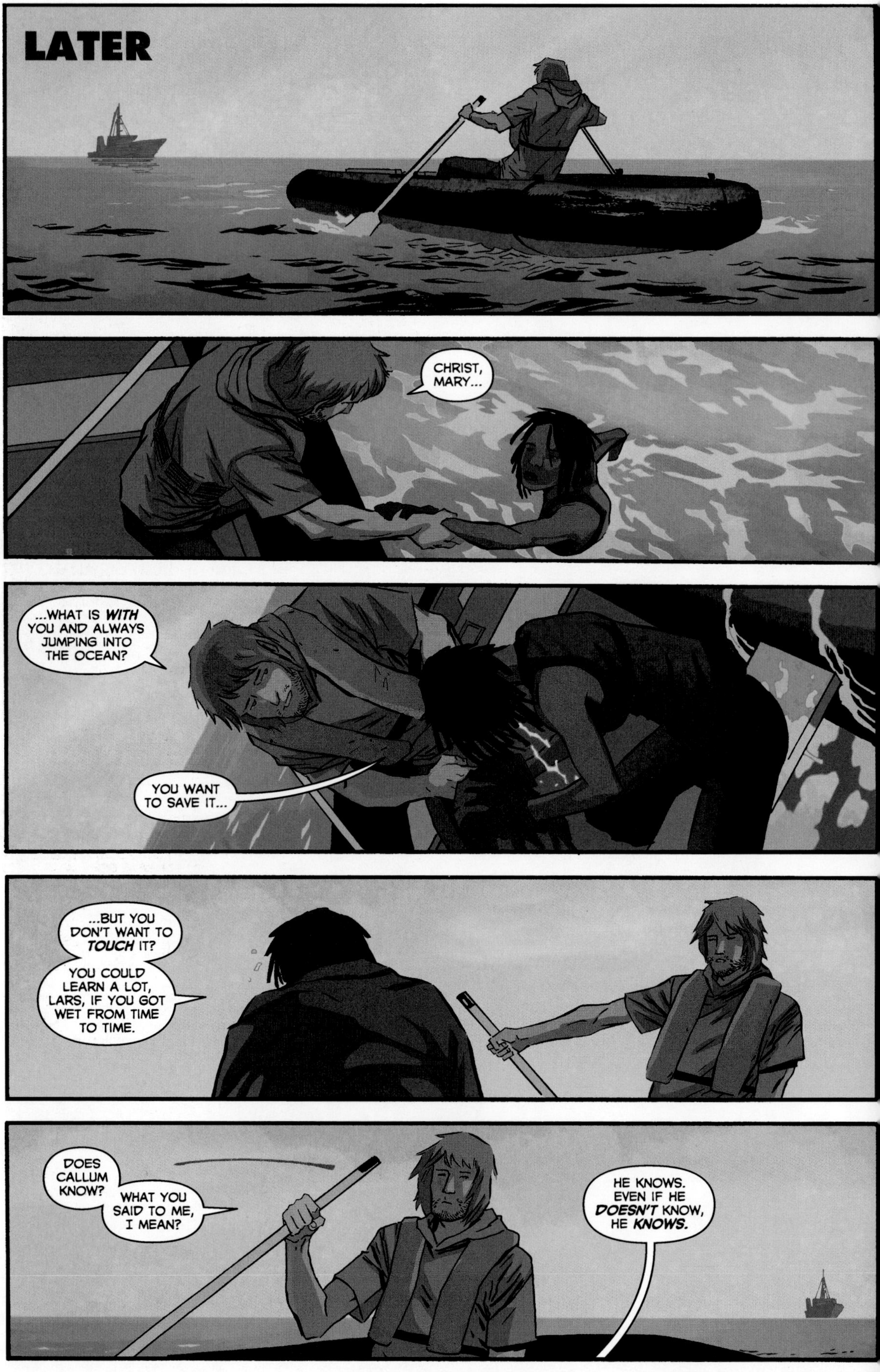
LATER
CHRIST, MARY...
...WHAT IS WITH YOU AND ALWAYS JUMPING INTO THE OCEAN?
YOU WANT TO SAVE IT...
...BUT YOU DON'T WANT TO TOUCH IT?
YOU COULD LEARN A LOT, LARS, IF YOU GOT WET FROM TIME TO TIME.
DOES CALLUM KNOW?
WHAT YOU SAID TO ME, I MEAN?
HE KNOWS. EVEN IF HE DOESN'T KNOW, HE KNOWS.

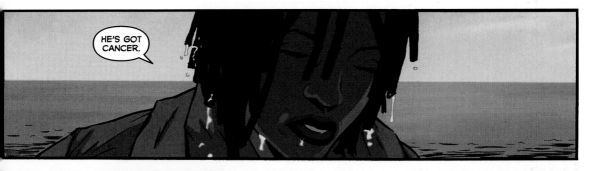

HE'S GOT CANCER.

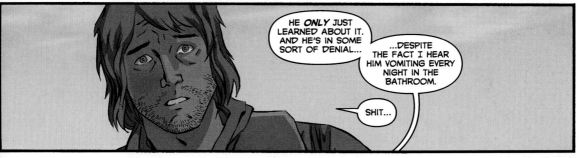

HE *ONLY* JUST LEARNED ABOUT IT. AND HE'S IN SOME SORT OF DENIAL...

...DESPITE THE FACT I HEAR HIM VOMITING EVERY NIGHT IN THE BATHROOM.

SHIT...

...WHAT HAPPENED?

WE ALL OWE A TOXIC DEBT TO OUR BODIES, ACTIVISTS ESPECIALLY. AT SOME POINT IN THE PAST HE WAS EXPOSED TO SOMETHING HE SHOULDN'T HAVE BEEN, AND THERE'S A PRICE YOU HAVE TO PAY FOR THAT.

HOW SICK IS HE?

PRETTY SICK. WE CAN HIDE IT FOR NOW, BUT NOT FOR LONG. RIGHT NOW ONLY YOU AND I KNOW ABOUT IT.

HE'S GOING TO NEED OUR HELP, BUT UNTIL THEN YOU HAVE TO BE QUIET ABOUT IT.

GIVE HIM THE DIGNITY OF THESE LAST FEW MONTHS OF WORK.

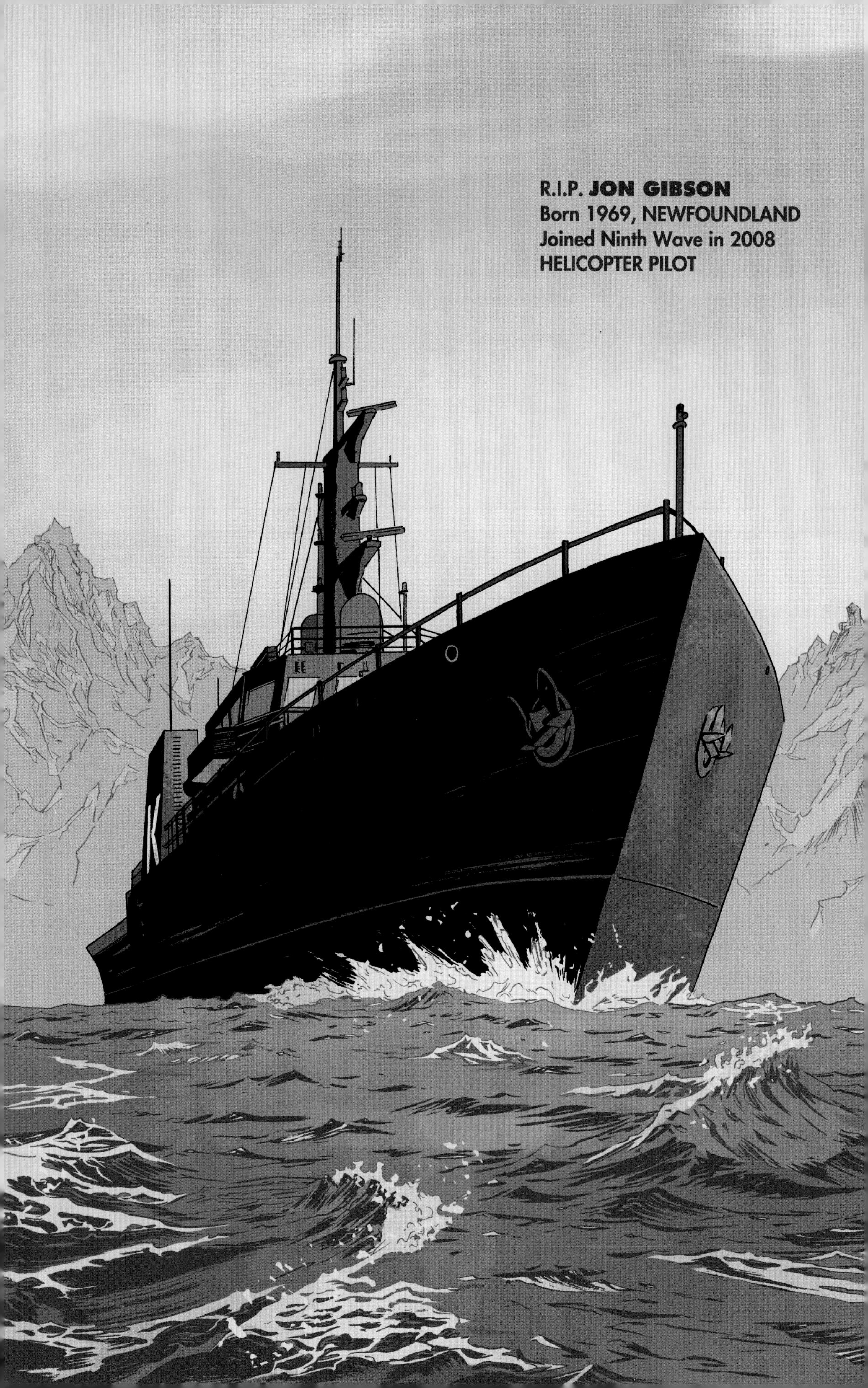
R.I.P. JON GIBSON
Born 1969, NEWFOUNDLAND
Joined Ninth Wave in 2008
HELICOPTER PILOT

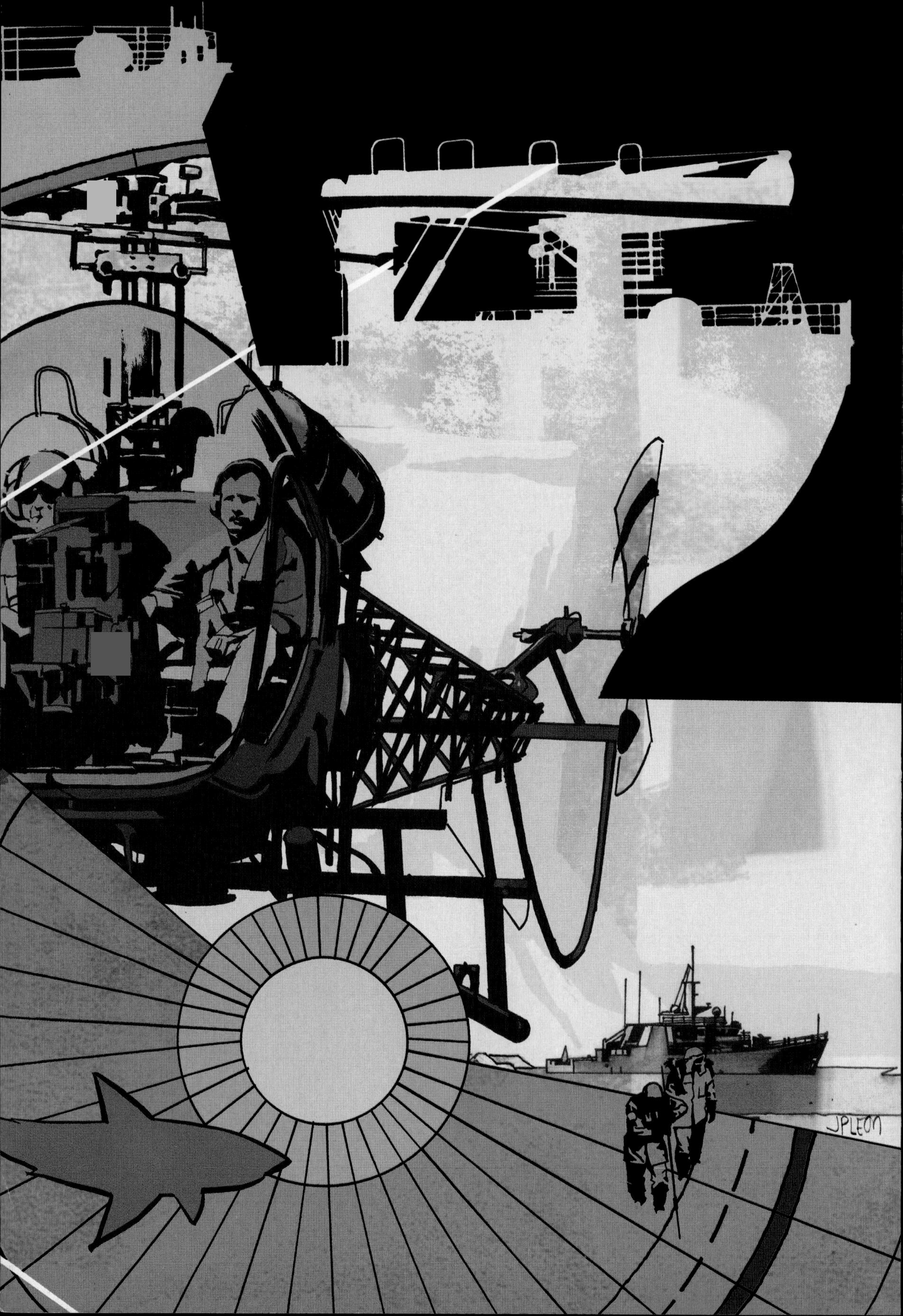
JPLEON

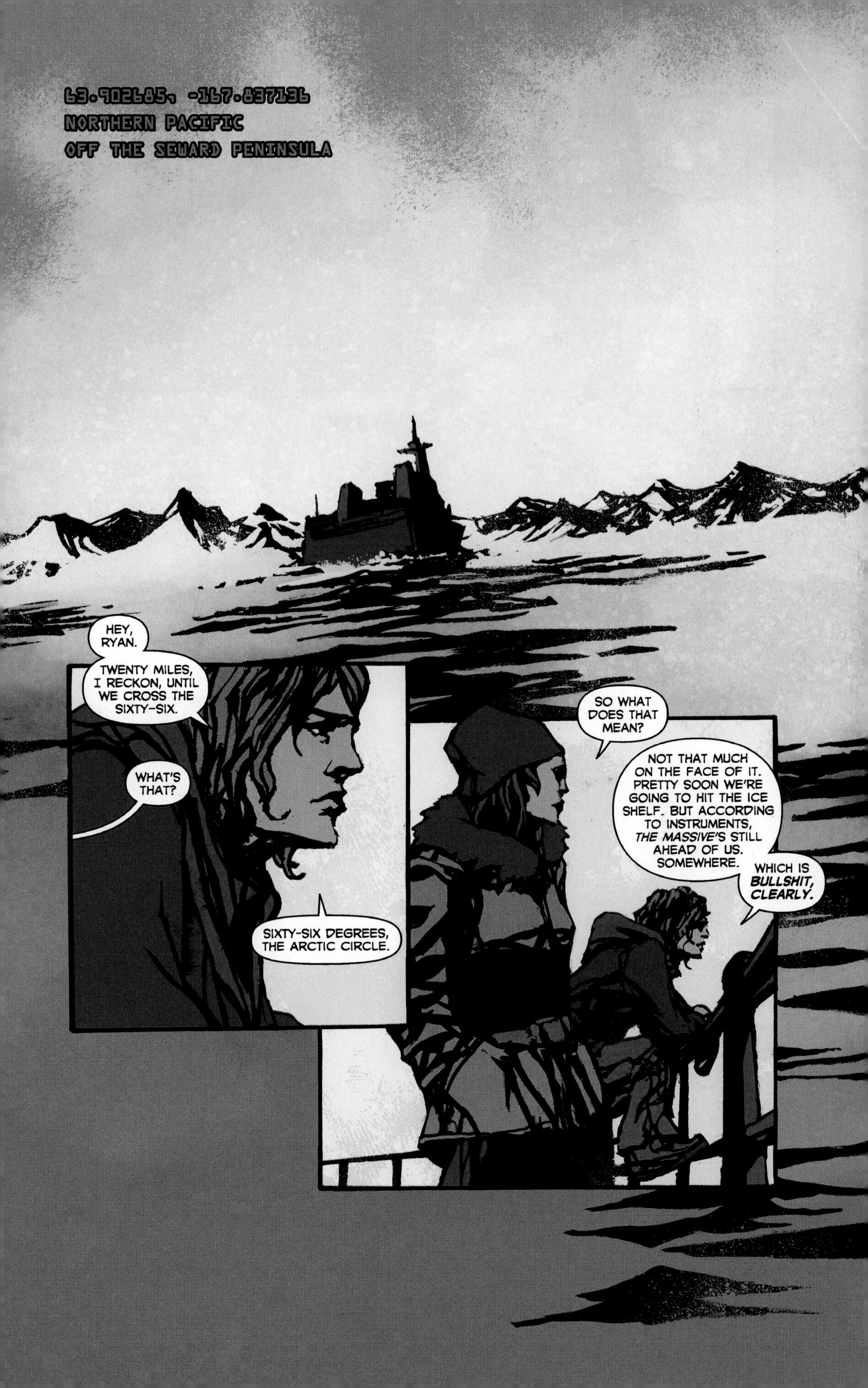
63.902685, -167.837136
NORTHERN PACIFIC
OFF THE SEWARD PENINSULA
HEY, RYAN.
TWENTY MILES, I RECKON, UNTIL WE CROSS THE SIXTY-SIX.
WHAT'S THAT?
SIXTY-SIX DEGREES, THE ARCTIC CIRCLE.
SO WHAT DOES THAT MEAN?
NOT THAT MUCH ON THE FACE OF IT. PRETTY SOON WE'RE GOING TO HIT THE ICE SHELF. BUT ACCORDING TO INSTRUMENTS, *THE MASSIVE'S* STILL AHEAD OF US. SOMEWHERE.
WHICH IS *BULLSHIT, CLEARLY.*

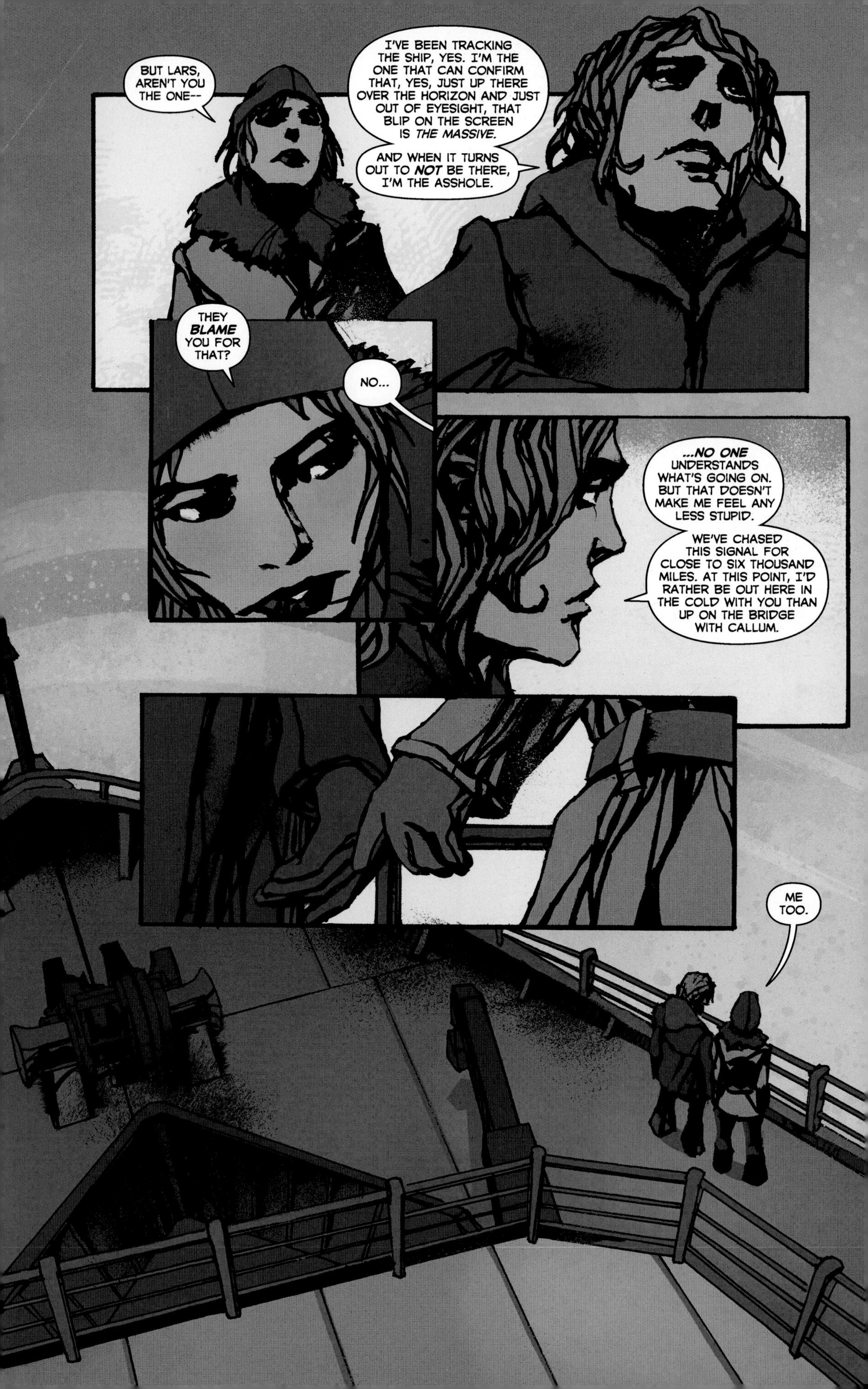

BUT LARS, AREN'T YOU THE ONE--
I'VE BEEN TRACKING THE SHIP, YES. I'M THE ONE THAT CAN CONFIRM THAT, YES, JUST UP THERE OVER THE HORIZON AND JUST OUT OF EYESIGHT, THAT BLIP ON THE SCREEN IS *THE MASSIVE.*
AND WHEN IT TURNS OUT TO ***NOT*** BE THERE, I'M THE ASSHOLE.
THEY ***BLAME*** YOU FOR THAT?
NO...
...NO ONE UNDERSTANDS WHAT'S GOING ON. BUT THAT DOESN'T MAKE ME FEEL ANY LESS STUPID.
WE'VE CHASED THIS SIGNAL FOR CLOSE TO SIX THOUSAND MILES. AT THIS POINT, I'D RATHER BE OUT HERE IN THE COLD WITH YOU THAN UP ON THE BRIDGE WITH CALLUM.
ME TOO.

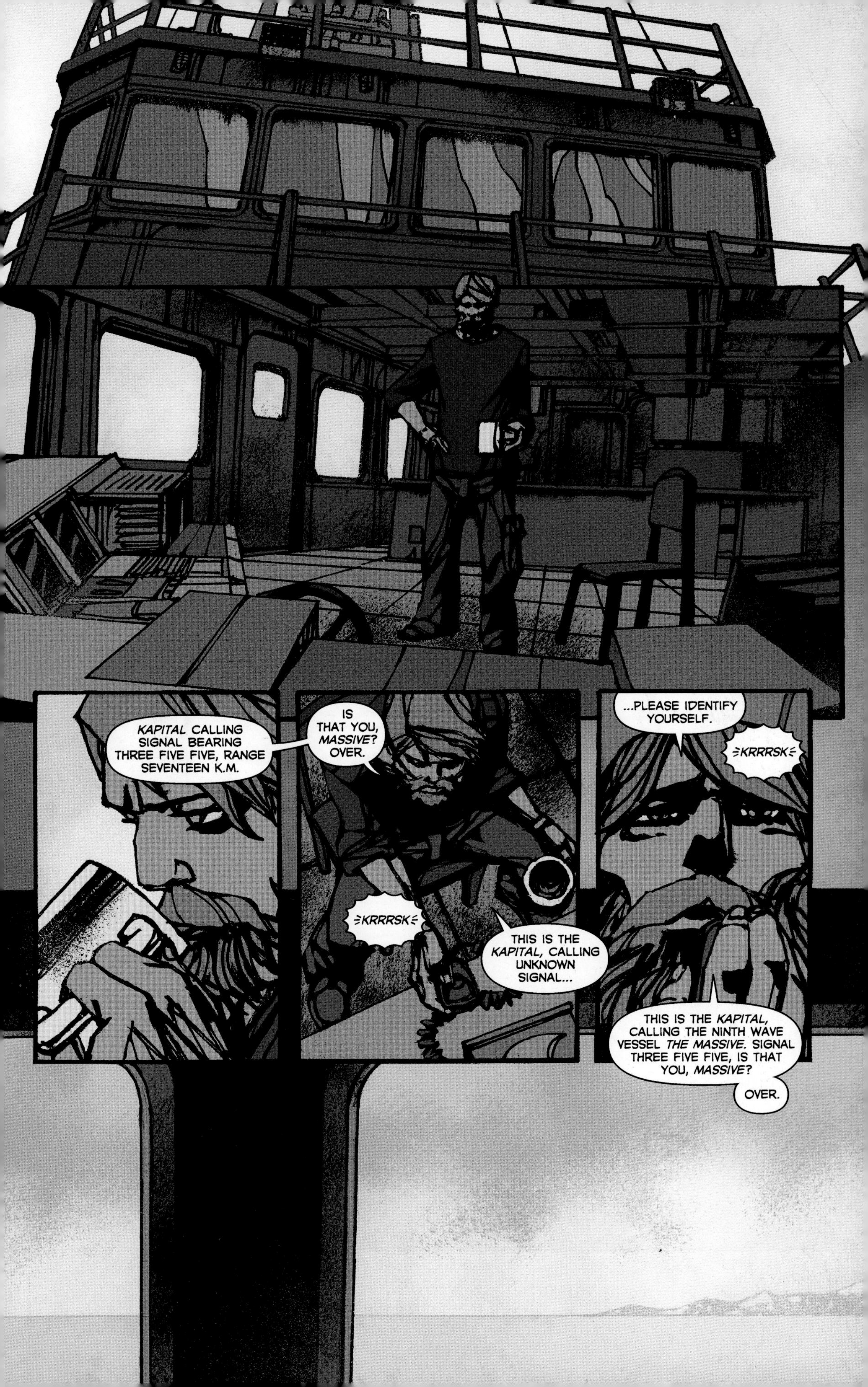
KAPITAL CALLING SIGNAL BEARING THREE FIVE FIVE, RANGE SEVENTEEN K.M.
IS THAT YOU, MASSIVE? OVER.
KRRRSK
THIS IS THE KAPITAL, CALLING UNKNOWN SIGNAL...
...PLEASE IDENTIFY YOURSELF.
KRRRSK
THIS IS THE KAPITAL, CALLING THE NINTH WAVE VESSEL THE MASSIVE. SIGNAL THREE FIVE FIVE, IS THAT YOU, MASSIVE?
OVER.

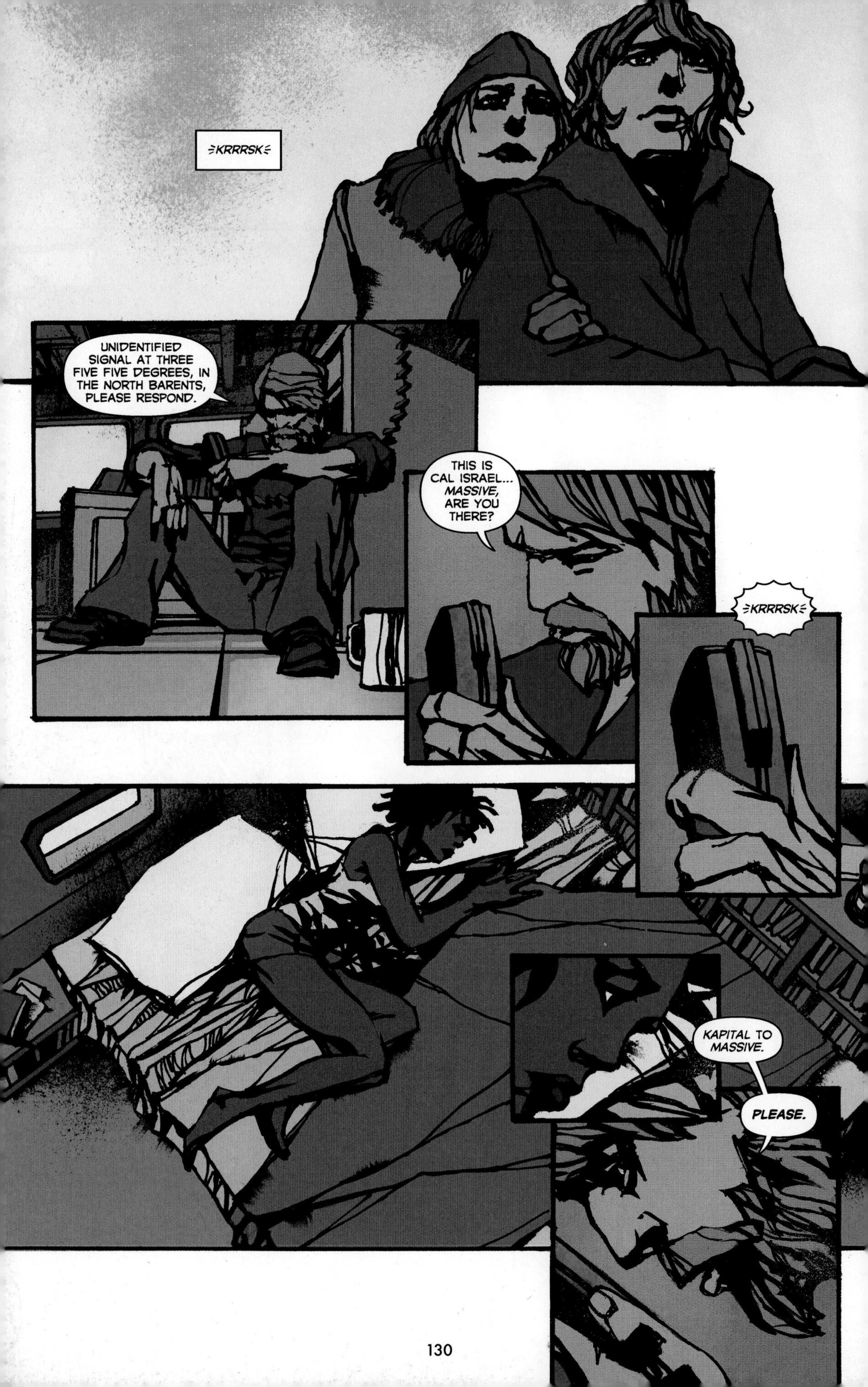

KRRRSK
UNIDENTIFIED SIGNAL AT THREE FIVE FIVE DEGREES, IN THE NORTH BARENTS, PLEASE RESPOND.
THIS IS CAL ISRAEL... MASSIVE, ARE YOU THERE?
KRRRSK
KAPITAL TO MASSIVE.
PLEASE.

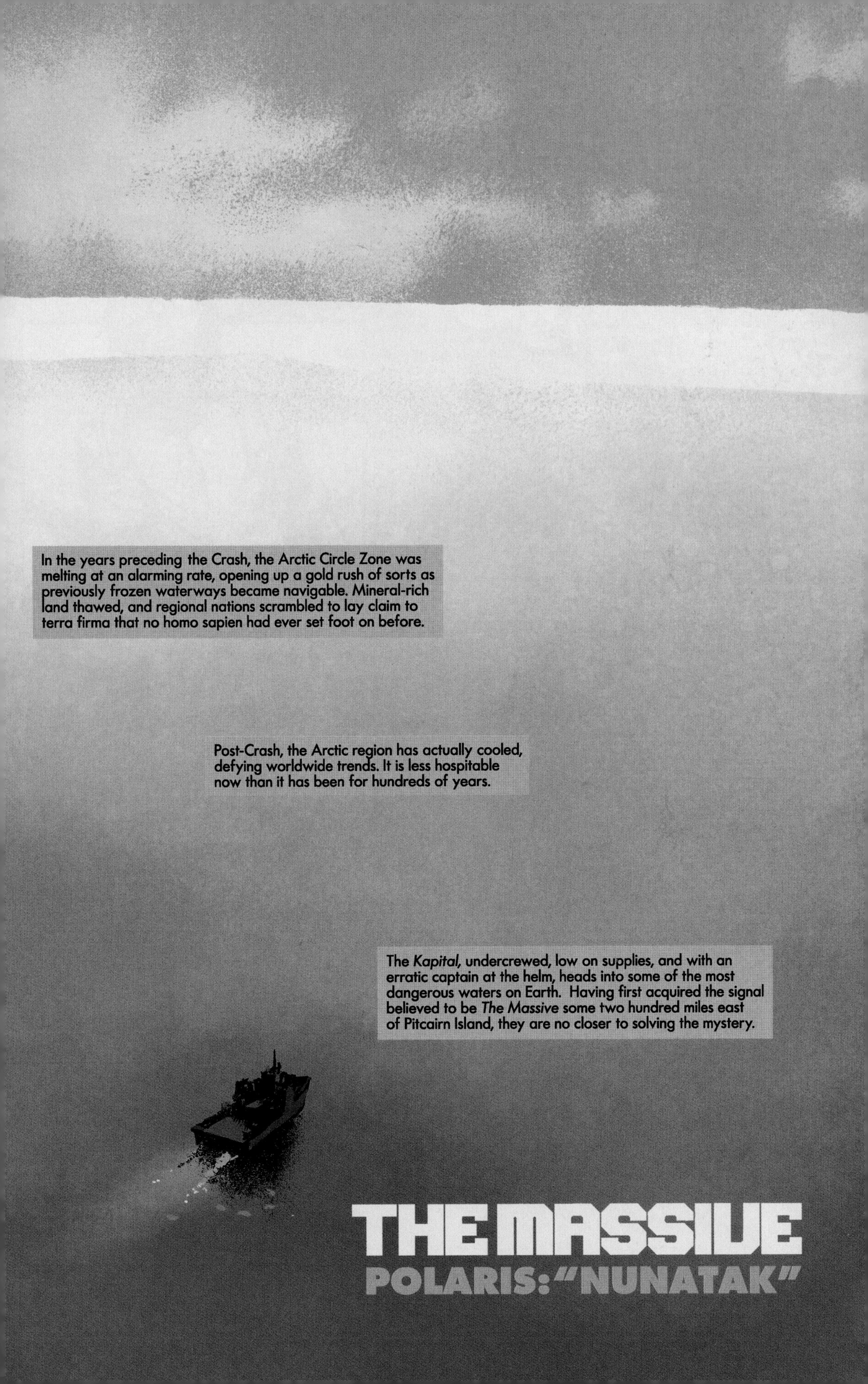
In the years preceding the Crash, the Arctic Circle Zone was melting at an alarming rate, opening up a gold rush of sorts as previously frozen waterways became navigable. Mineral-rich land thawed, and regional nations scrambled to lay claim to terra firma that no homo sapien had ever set foot on before.
Post-Crash, the Arctic region has actually cooled, defying worldwide trends. It is less hospitable now than it has been for hundreds of years.
The *Kapital,* undercrewed, low on supplies, and with an erratic captain at the helm, heads into some of the most dangerous waters on Earth. Having first acquired the signal believed to be *The Massive* some two hundred miles east of Pitcairn Island, they are no closer to solving the mystery.
THE MASSIVE
POLARIS: "NUNATAK"

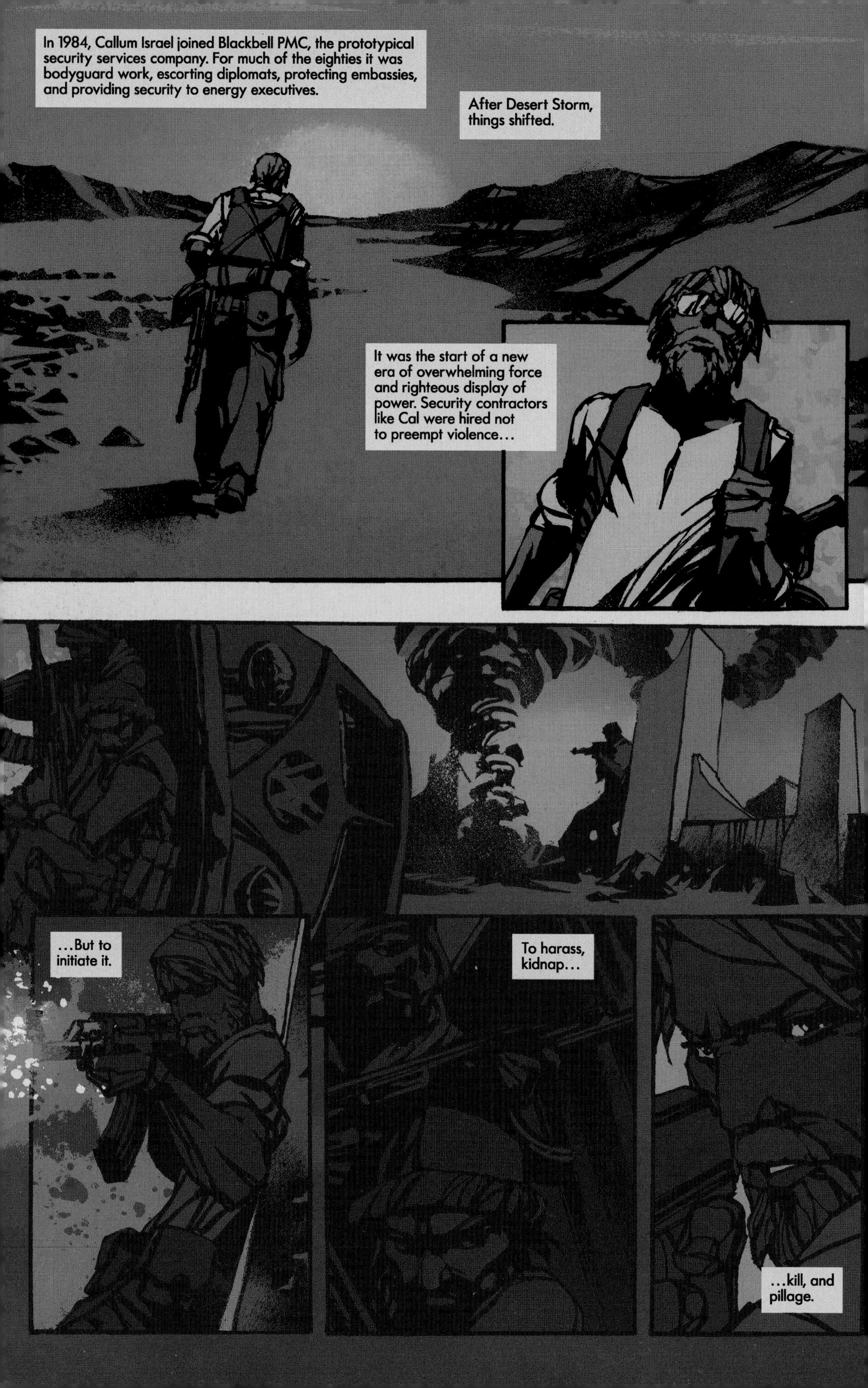
In 1984, Callum Israel joined Blackbell PMC, the prototypical security services company. For much of the eighties it was bodyguard work, escorting diplomats, protecting embassies, and providing security to energy executives.
After Desert Storm, things shifted.
It was the start of a new era of overwhelming force and righteous display of power. Security contractors like Cal were hired not to preempt violence…
…But to initiate it.
To harass, kidnap…
…kill, and pillage.

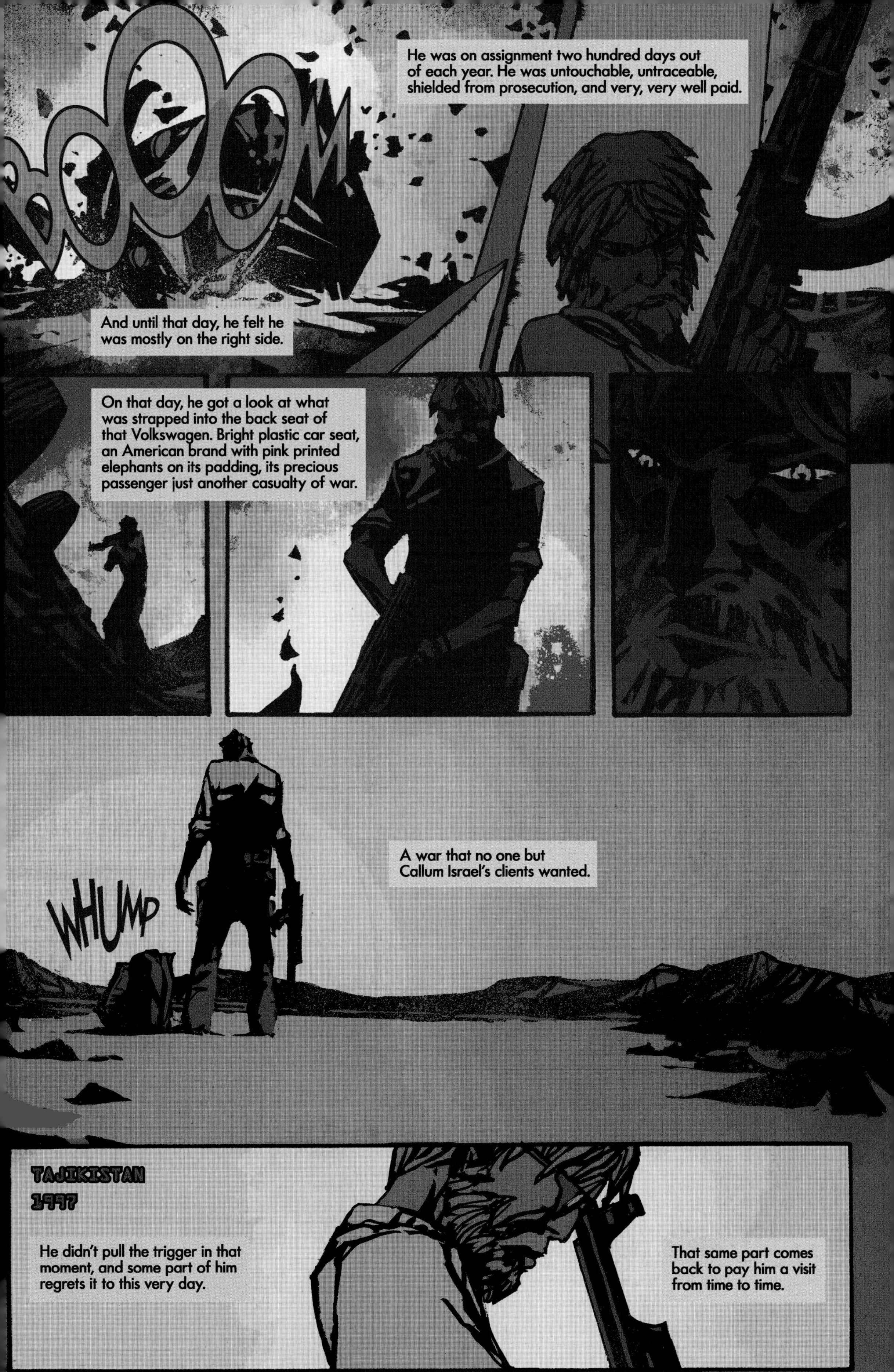

BOOOOM
He was on assignment two hundred days out of each year. He was untouchable, untraceable, shielded from prosecution, and very, very well paid.
And until that day, he felt he was mostly on the right side.
On that day, he got a look at what was strapped into the back seat of that Volkswagen. Bright plastic car seat, an American brand with pink printed elephants on its padding, its precious passenger just another casualty of war.
WHUMP
A war that no one but Callum Israel's clients wanted.
TAJIKISTAN
1997
He didn't pull the trigger in that moment, and some part of him regrets it to this very day.
That same part comes back to pay him a visit from time to time.

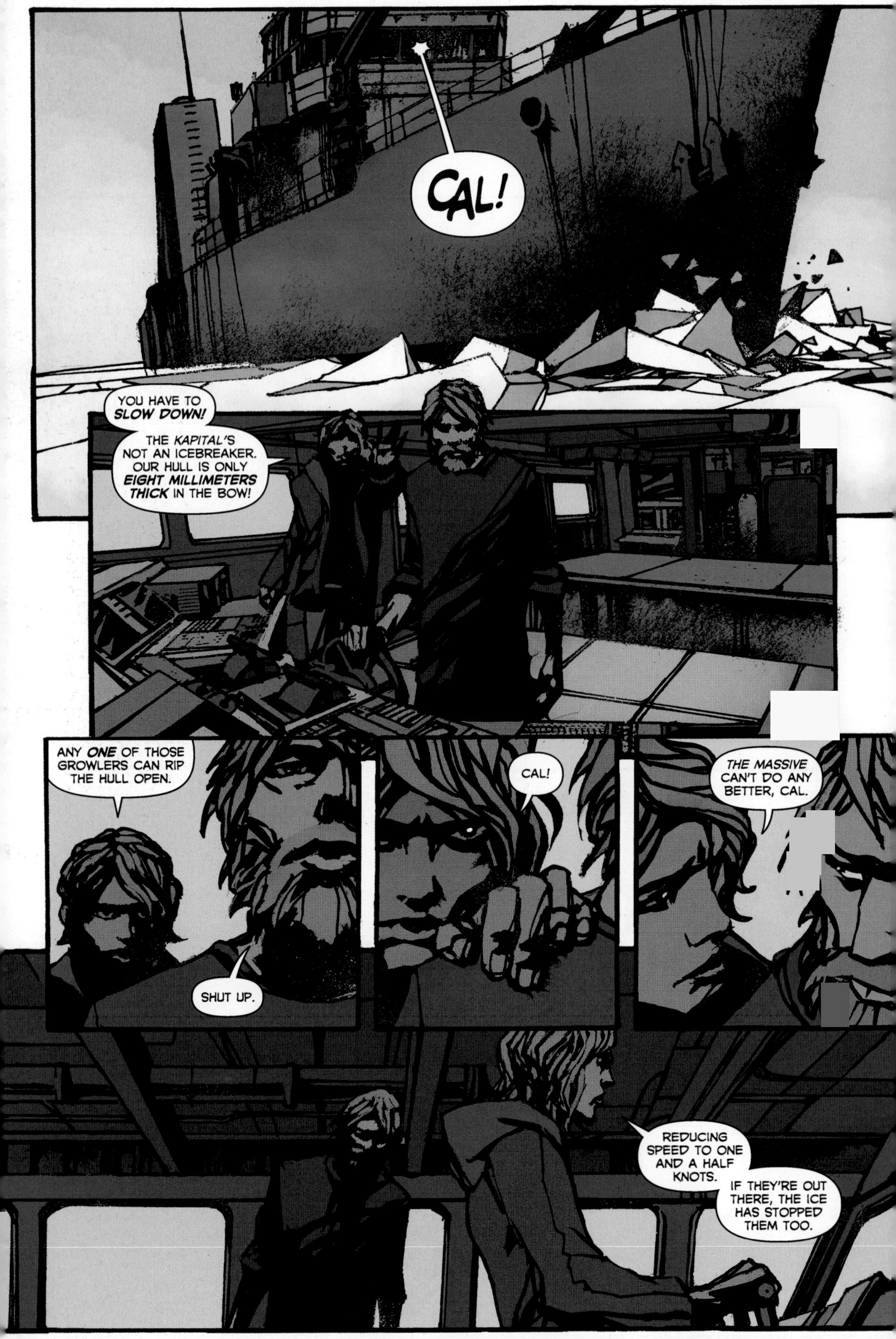
CAL!
YOU HAVE TO SLOW DOWN!
THE KAPITAL'S NOT AN ICEBREAKER. OUR HULL IS ONLY EIGHT MILLIMETERS THICK IN THE BOW!
ANY ONE OF THOSE GROWLERS CAN RIP THE HULL OPEN.
SHUT UP.
CAL!
THE MASSIVE CAN'T DO ANY BETTER, CAL.
REDUCING SPEED TO ONE AND A HALF KNOTS.
IF THEY'RE OUT THERE, THE ICE HAS STOPPED THEM TOO.

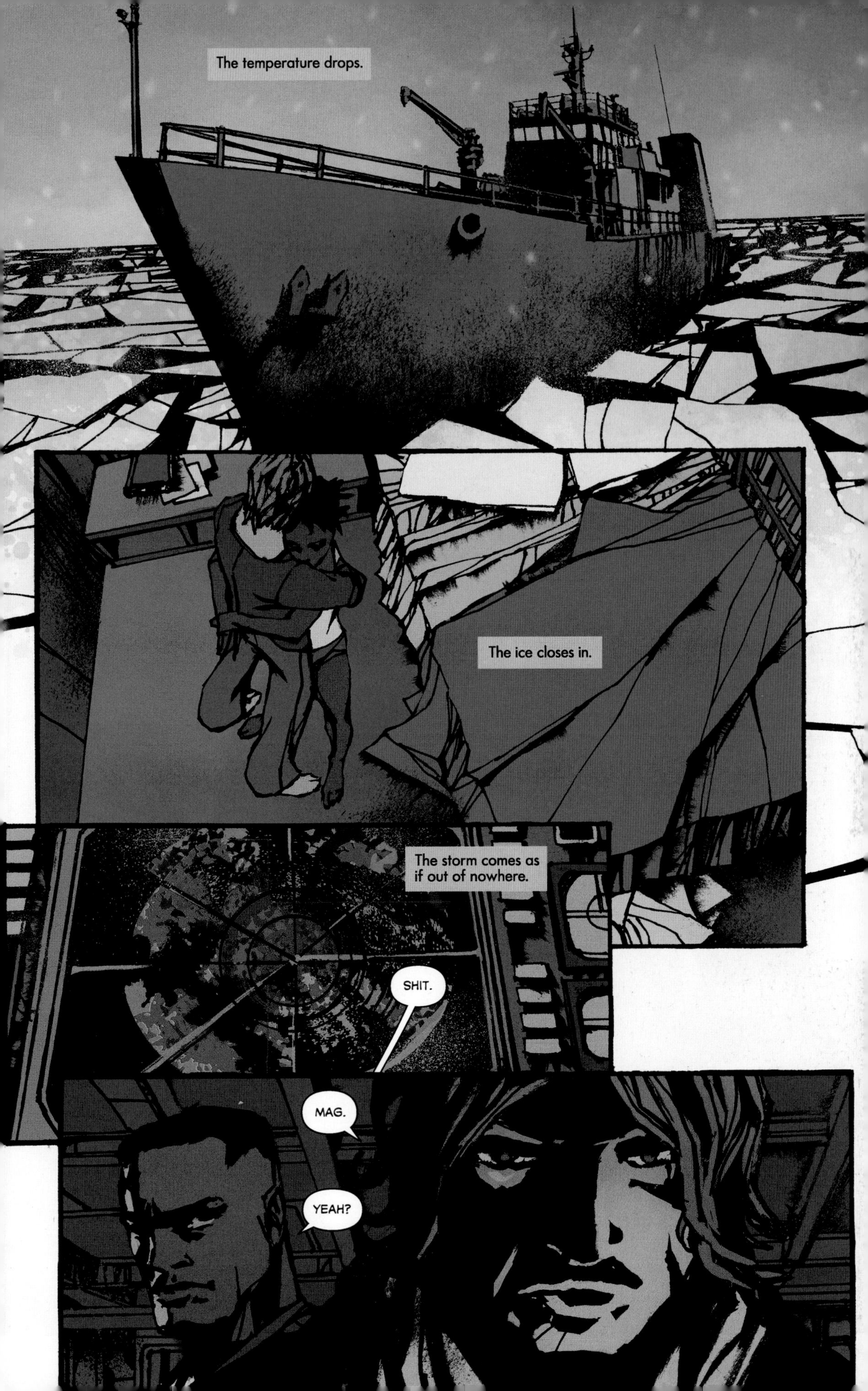
The temperature drops.
The ice closes in.
The storm comes as if out of nowhere.
SHIT.
MAG.
YEAH?

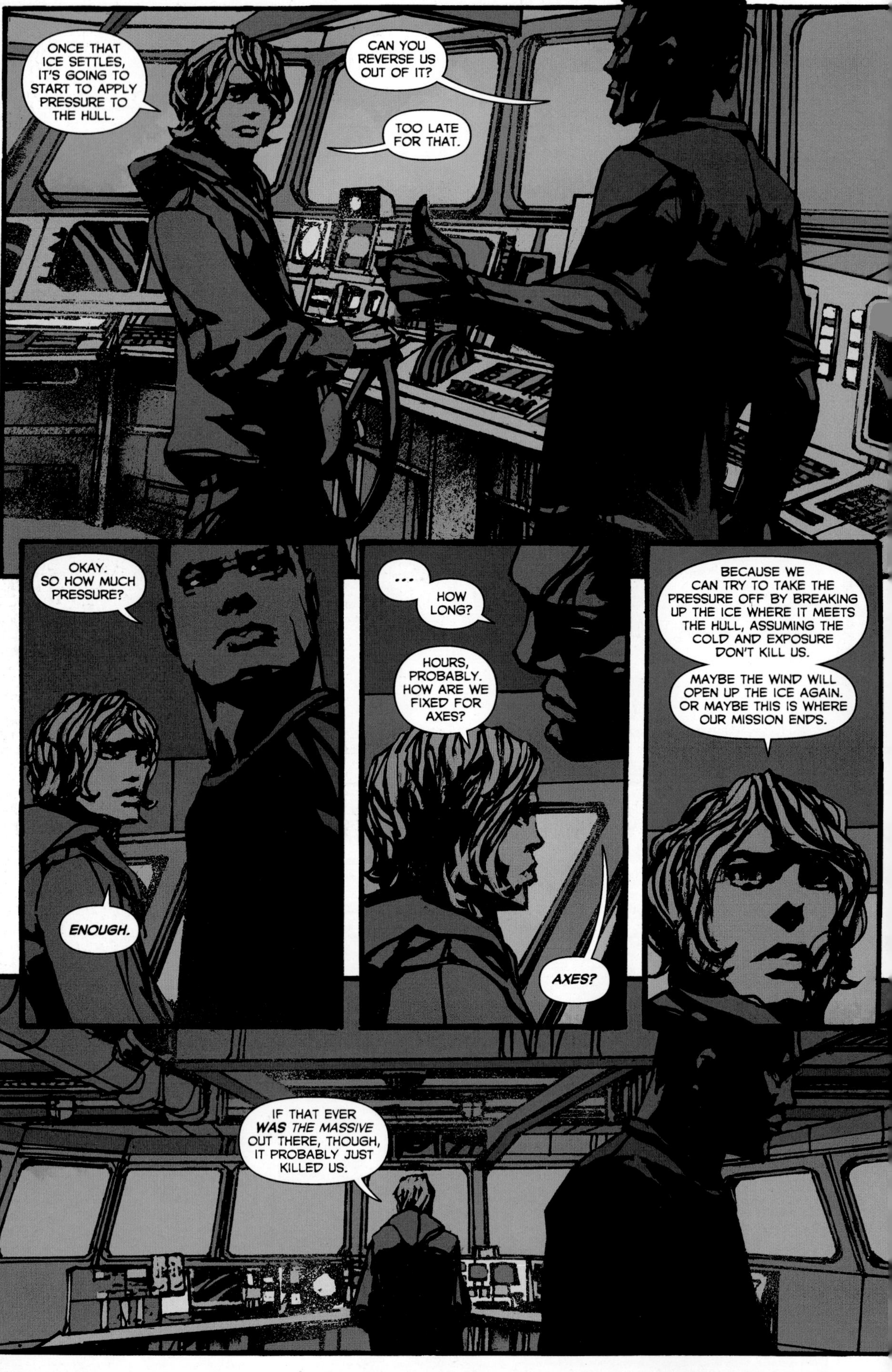

ONCE THAT ICE SETTLES, IT'S GOING TO START TO APPLY PRESSURE TO THE HULL.
CAN YOU REVERSE US OUT OF IT?
TOO LATE FOR THAT.
OKAY. SO HOW MUCH PRESSURE?
ENOUGH.
...
HOW LONG?
HOURS, PROBABLY. HOW ARE WE FIXED FOR AXES?
AXES?
BECAUSE WE CAN TRY TO TAKE THE PRESSURE OFF BY BREAKING UP THE ICE WHERE IT MEETS THE HULL, ASSUMING THE COLD AND EXPOSURE DON'T KILL US.
MAYBE THE WIND WILL OPEN UP THE ICE AGAIN. OR MAYBE THIS IS WHERE OUR MISSION ENDS.
IF THAT EVER **WAS** *THE MASSIVE* OUT THERE, THOUGH, IT PROBABLY JUST KILLED US.

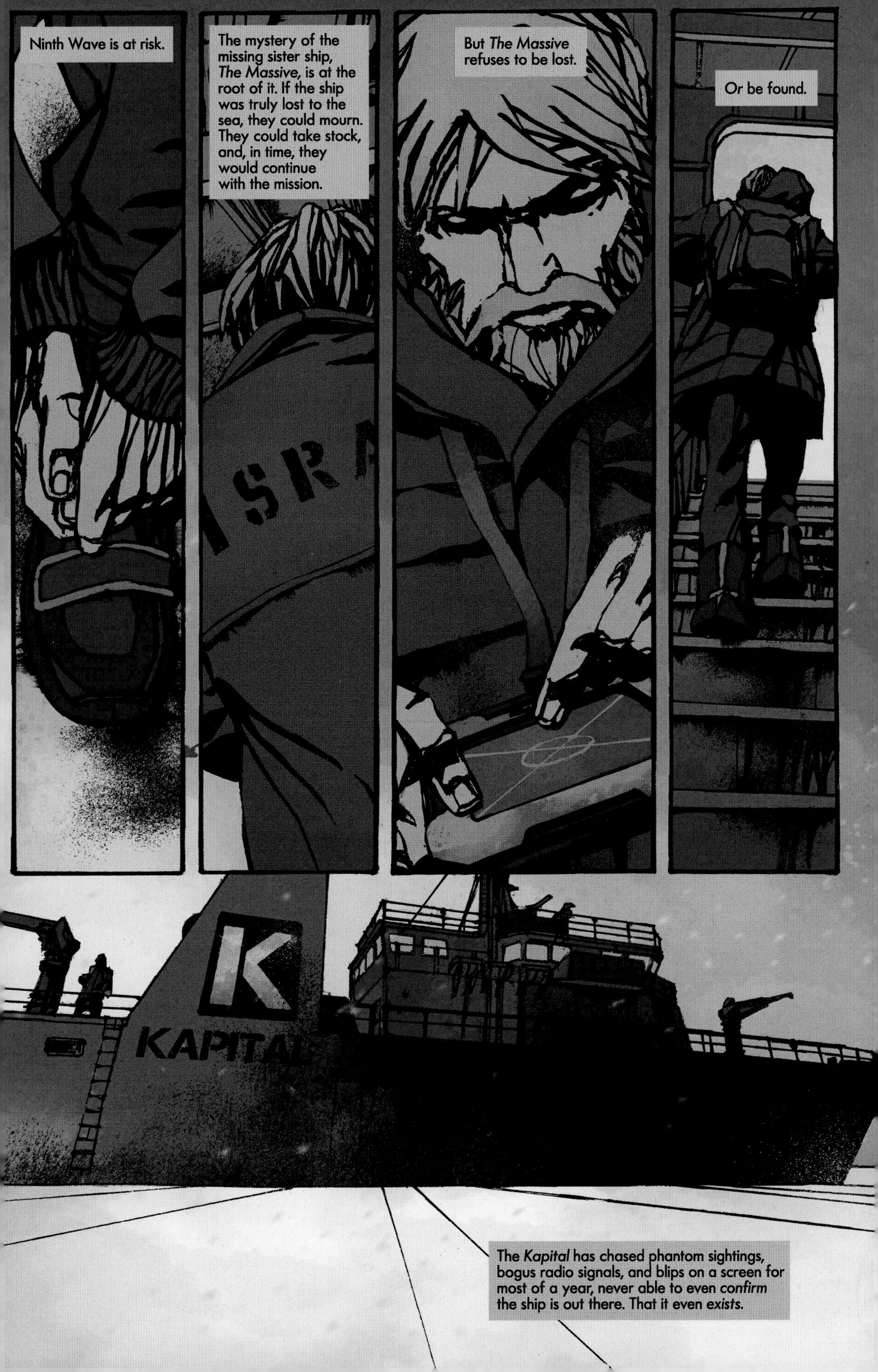
Ninth Wave is at risk.
The mystery of the missing sister ship, *The Massive*, is at the root of it. If the ship was truly lost to the sea, they could mourn. They could take stock, and, in time, they would continue with the mission.
ISRA
But *The Massive* refuses to be lost.
Or be found.
K
KAPITAL
The *Kapital* has chased phantom sightings, bogus radio signals, and blips on a screen for most of a year, never able to even *confirm* the ship is out there. That it even *exists*.

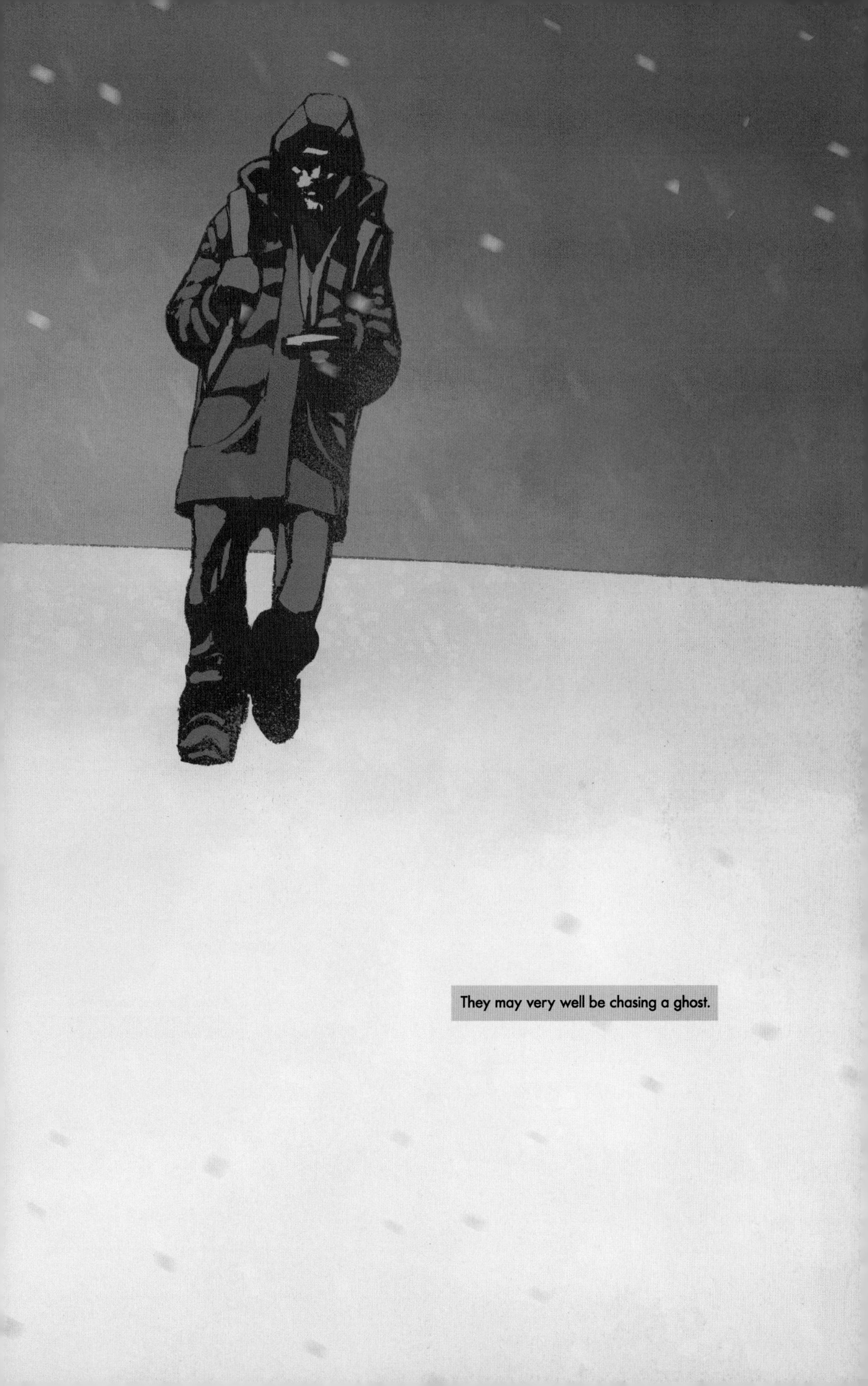
They may very well be chasing a ghost.

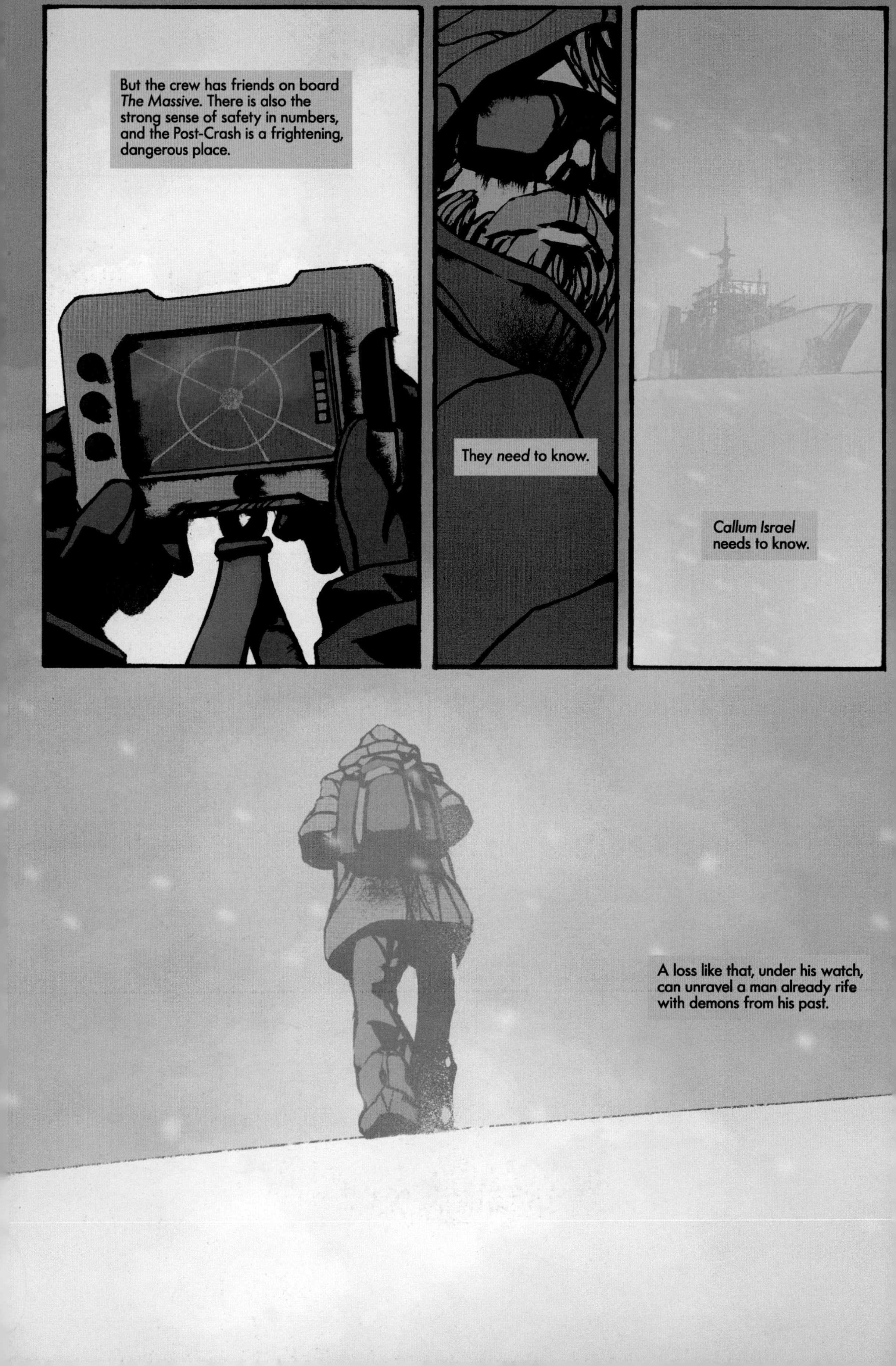
But the crew has friends on board *The Massive*. There is also the strong sense of safety in numbers, and the Post-Crash is a frightening, dangerous place.
They *need* to know.
Callum Israel needs to know.
A loss like that, under his watch, can unravel a man already rife with demons from his past.

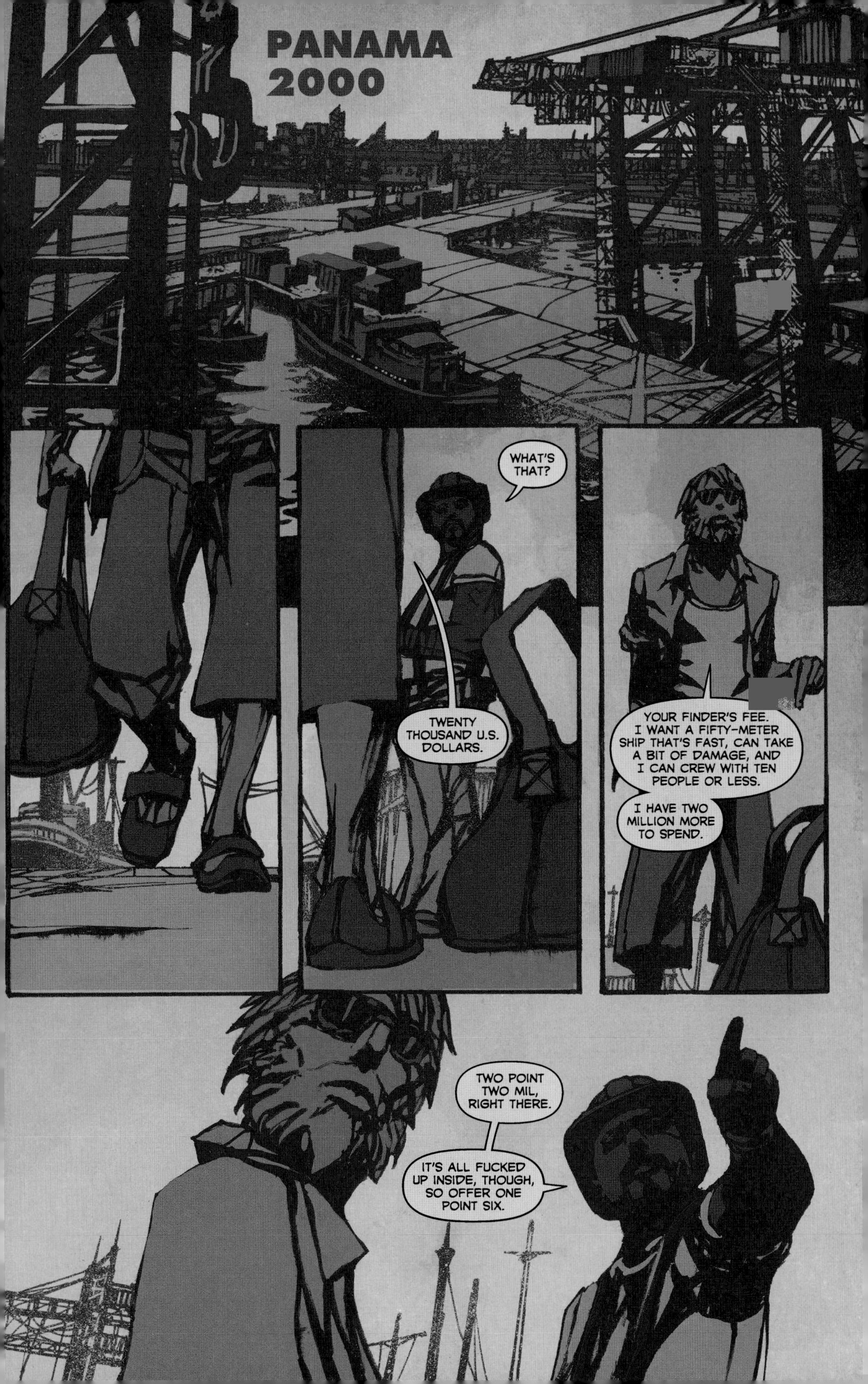
PANAMA 2000
WHAT'S THAT?
TWENTY THOUSAND U.S. DOLLARS.
YOUR FINDER'S FEE. I WANT A FIFTY-METER SHIP THAT'S FAST, CAN TAKE A BIT OF DAMAGE, AND I CAN CREW WITH TEN PEOPLE OR LESS.
I HAVE TWO MILLION MORE TO SPEND.
TWO POINT TWO MIL, RIGHT THERE.
IT'S ALL FUCKED UP INSIDE, THOUGH, SO OFFER ONE POINT SIX.

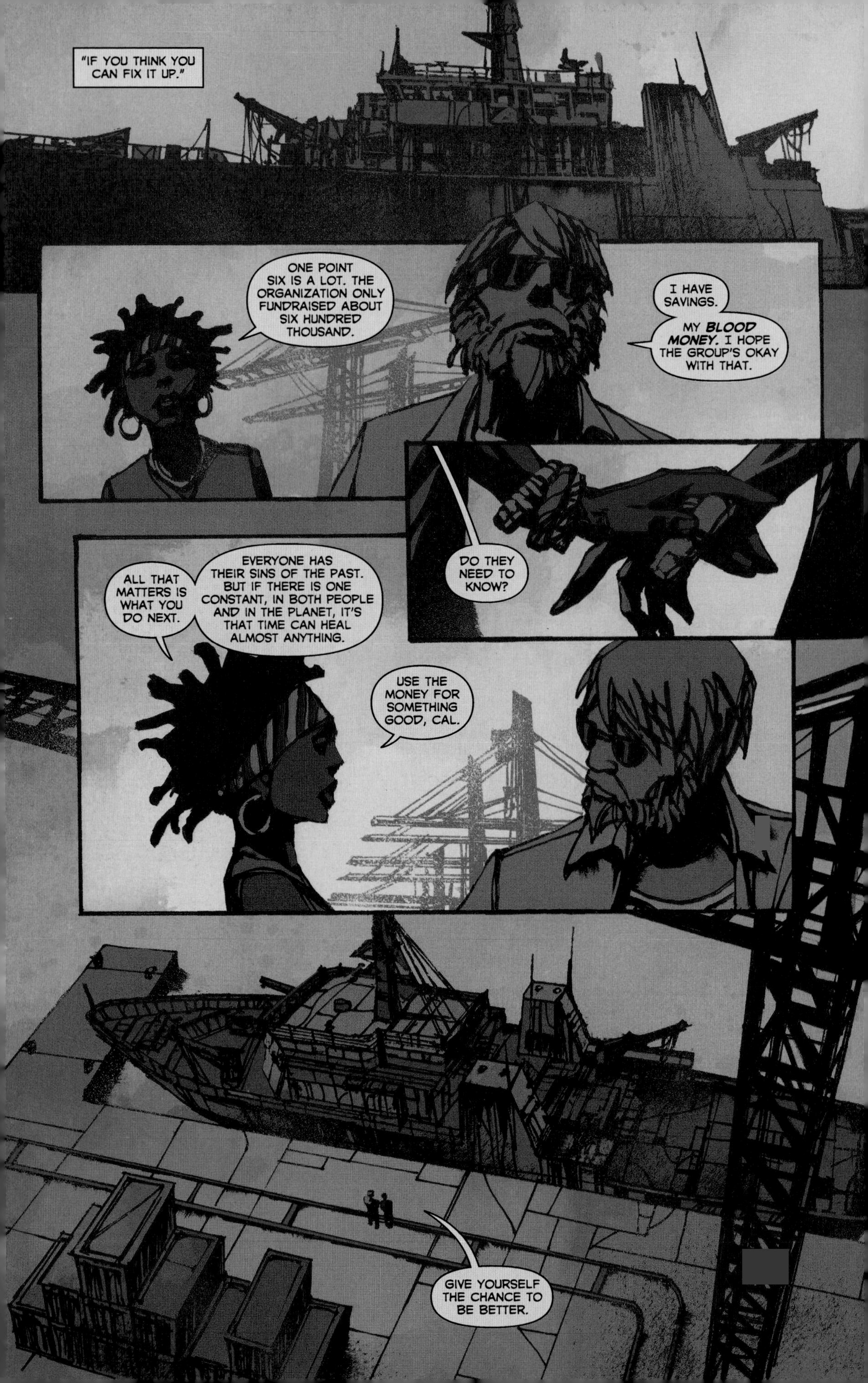

"IF YOU THINK YOU CAN FIX IT UP."
ONE POINT SIX IS A LOT. THE ORGANIZATION ONLY FUNDRAISED ABOUT SIX HUNDRED THOUSAND.
I HAVE SAVINGS.
MY **BLOOD MONEY.** I HOPE THE GROUP'S OKAY WITH THAT.
DO THEY NEED TO KNOW?
ALL THAT MATTERS IS WHAT YOU DO NEXT.
EVERYONE HAS THEIR SINS OF THE PAST. BUT IF THERE IS ONE CONSTANT, IN BOTH PEOPLE AND IN THE PLANET, IT'S THAT TIME CAN HEAL ALMOST ANYTHING.
USE THE MONEY FOR SOMETHING GOOD, CAL.
GIVE YOURSELF THE CHANCE TO BE BETTER.

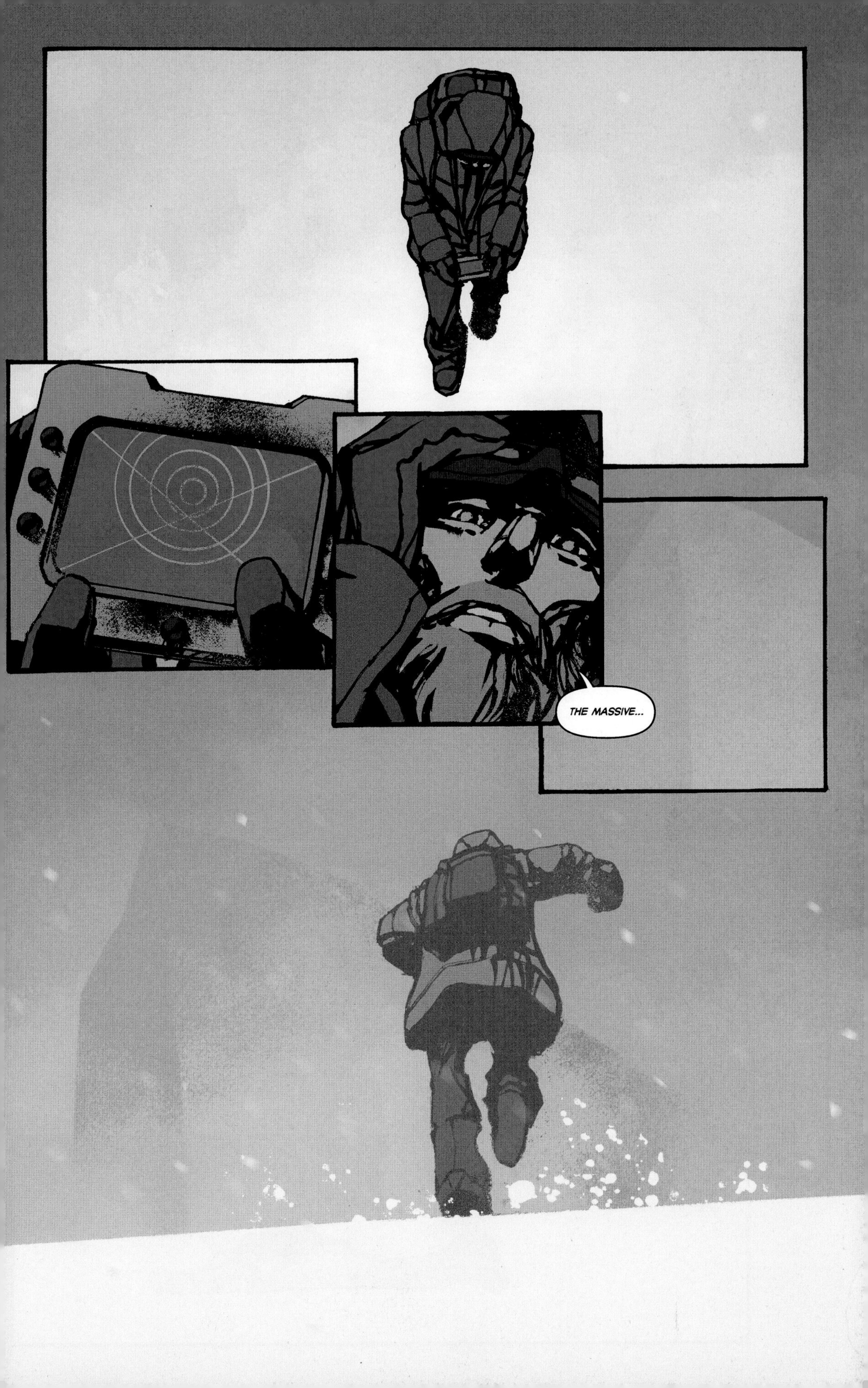
THE MASSIVE...

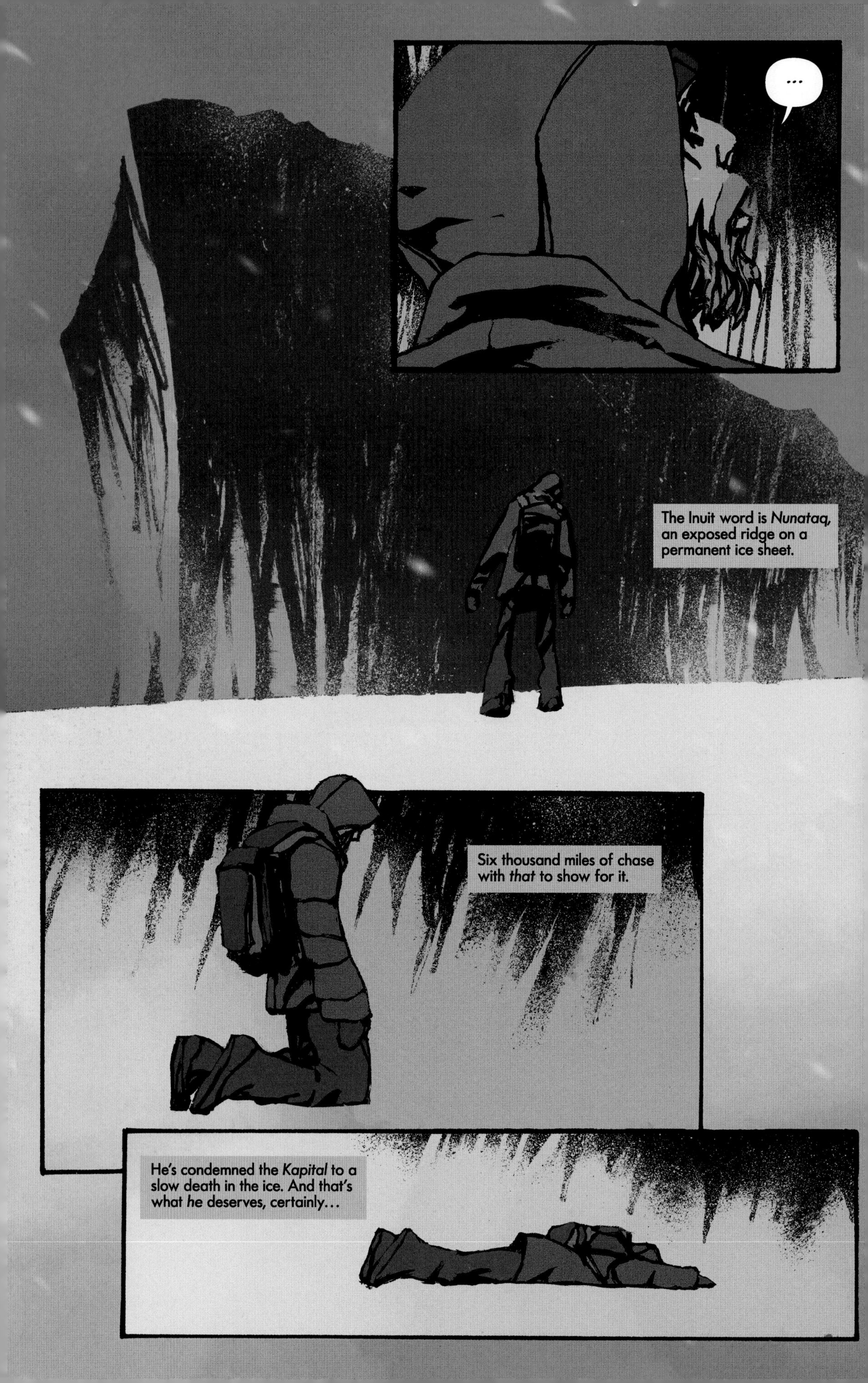
...
The Inuit word is *Nunataq*, an exposed ridge on a permanent ice sheet.
Six thousand miles of chase with *that* to show for it.
He's condemned the *Kapital* to a slow death in the ice. And that's what *he* deserves, certainly...

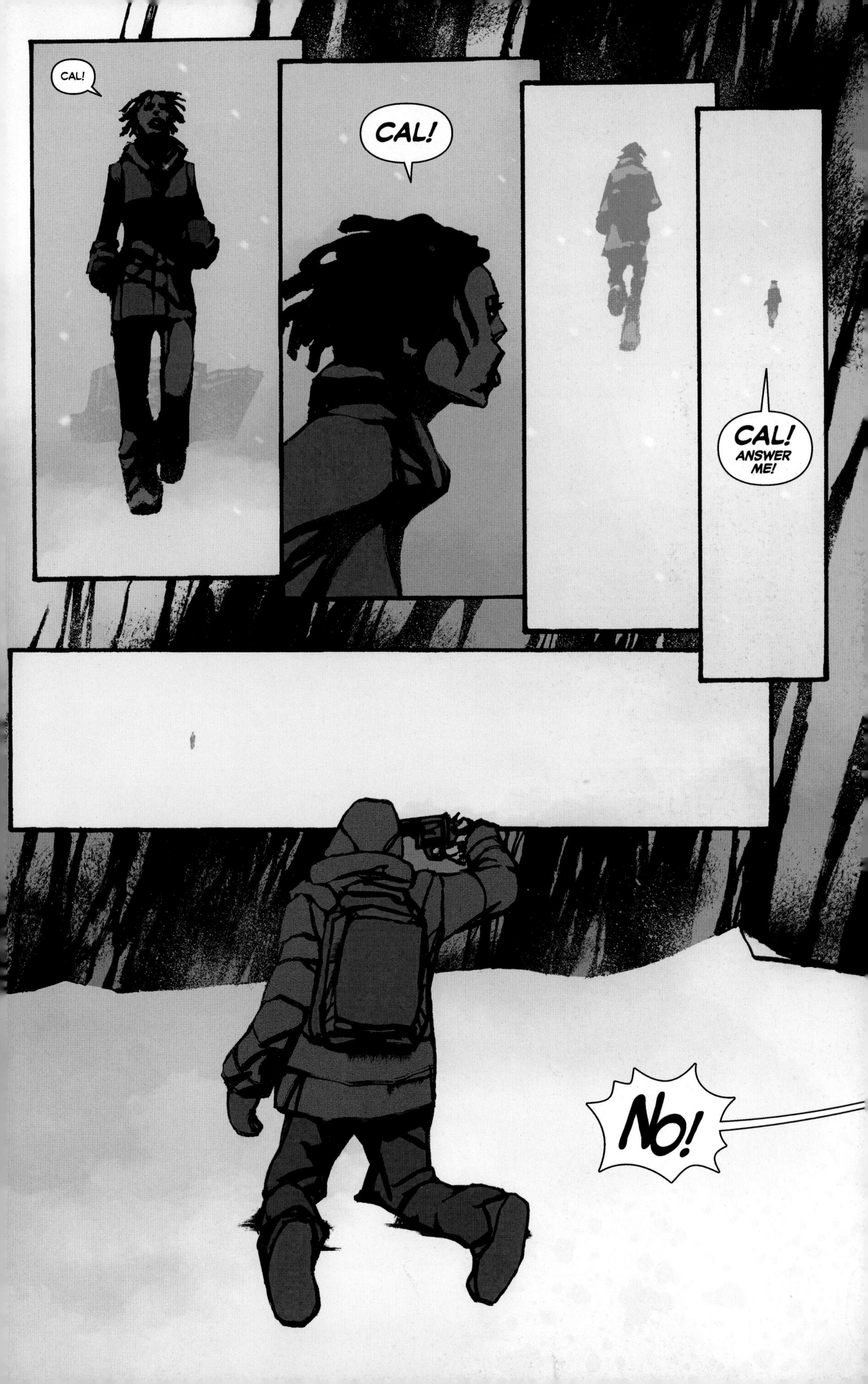
CAL!
CAL!
CAL! ANSWER ME!
No!

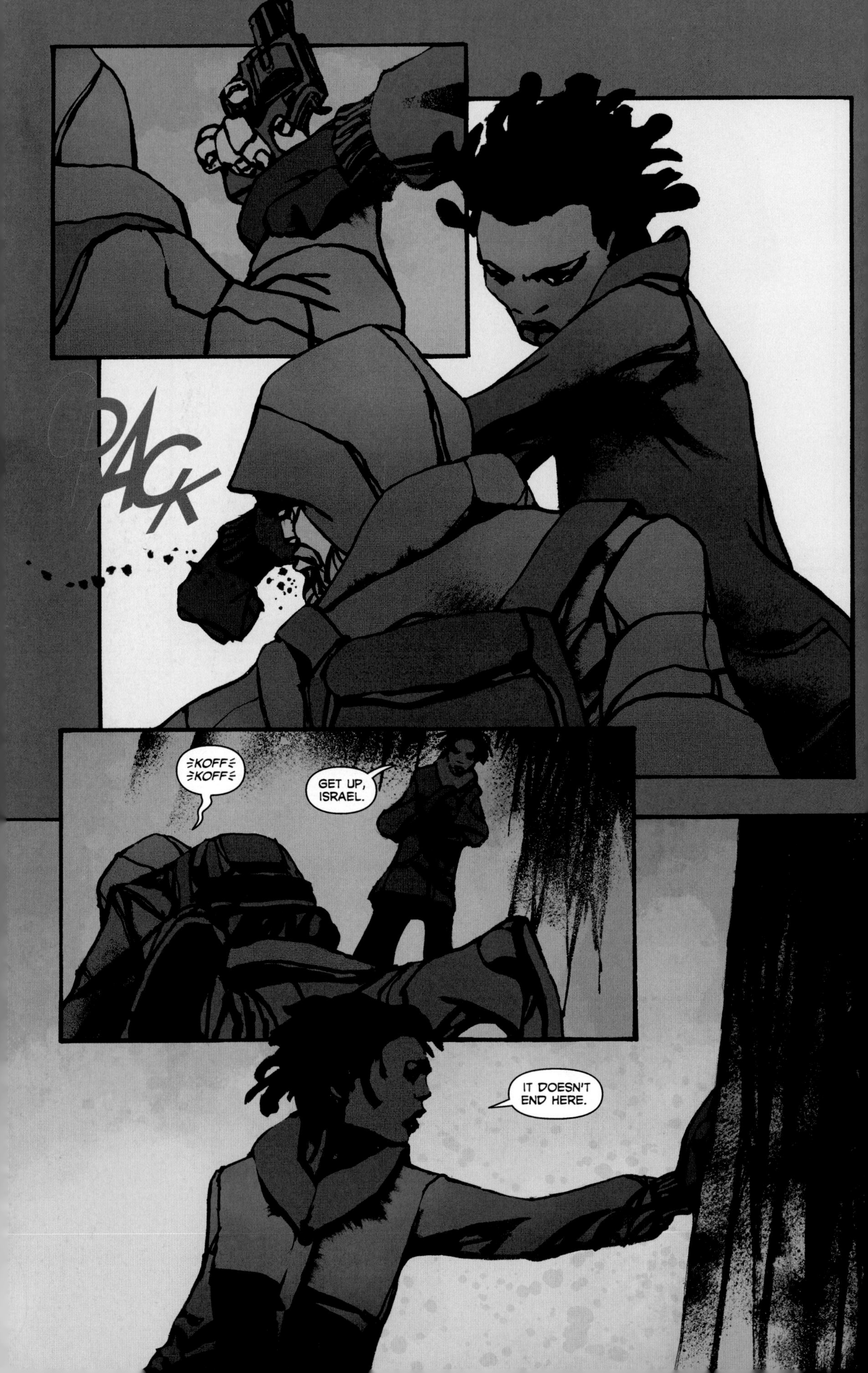

KRACK
KOFF KOFF
GET UP, ISRAEL.
IT DOESN'T END HERE.

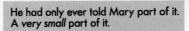

On the walk back to the *Kapital,* Callum confessed to it all. All the Blackbell missions, all the targeted killings, the kidnappings and the renditions. *Two decades* of it.

He had only ever told Mary part of it. A *very small* part of it.

Then he spoke about the North Sea oil rig, about the formation of Ninth Wave, about bringing Mag in. About using the skills and tools of conflict to fight a *nobler* war.

About the Crash and loss of mission clarity, the crew members deserting the cause...

...and the fact that, in his personal moment of weakness, he was willing to give up entirely.

ISRAEL

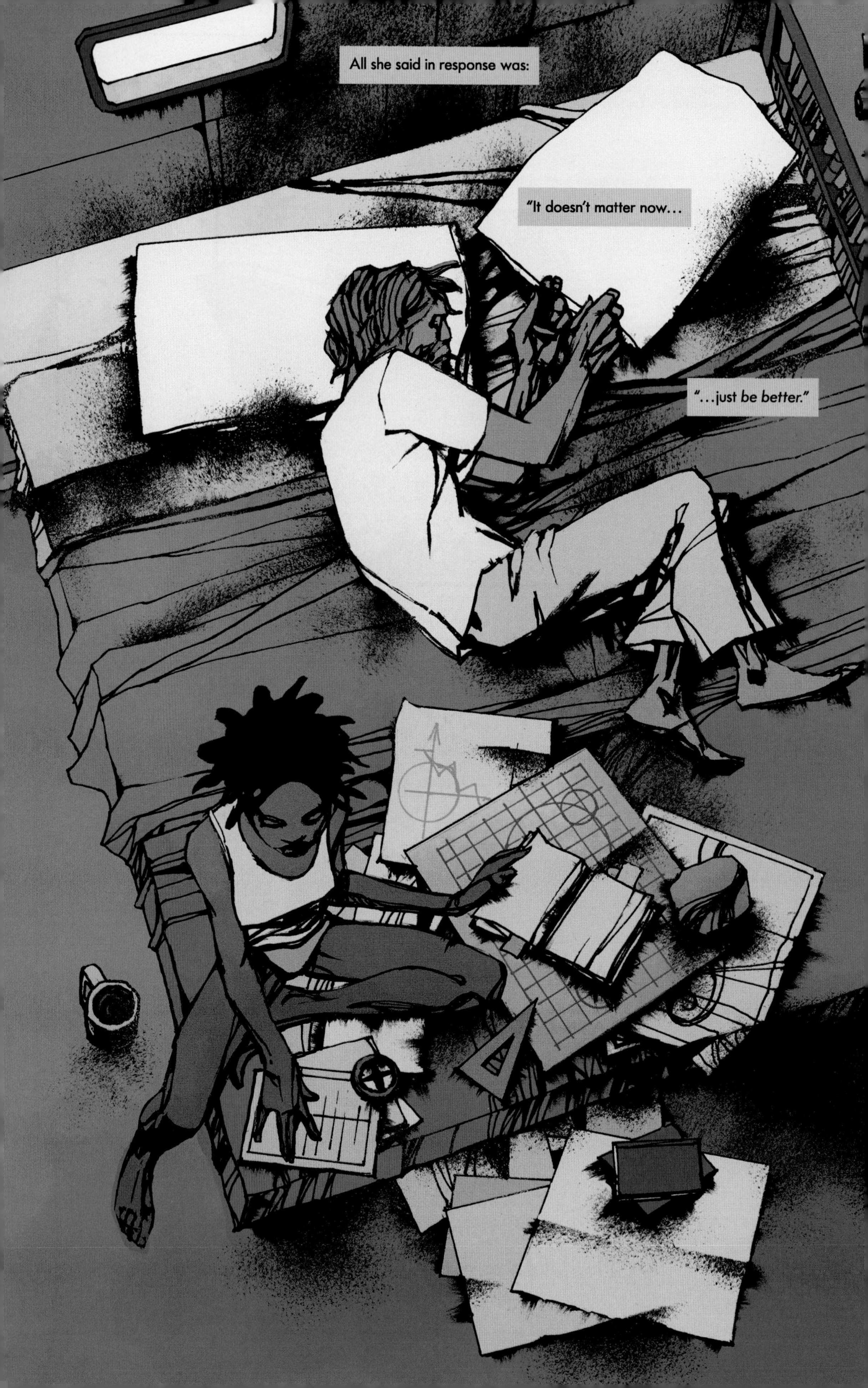
All she said in response was:
"It doesn't matter now…
"…just *be better.*"

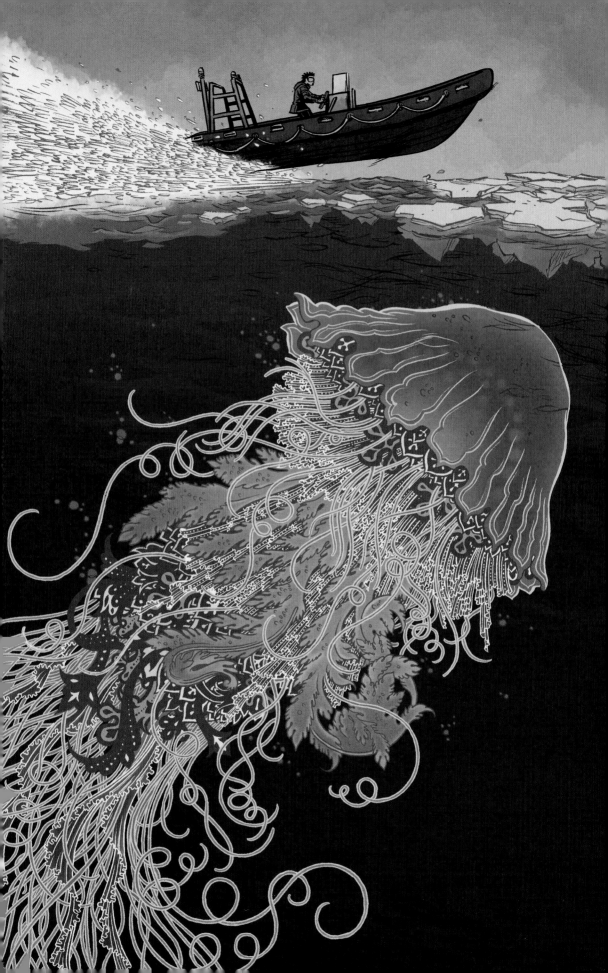

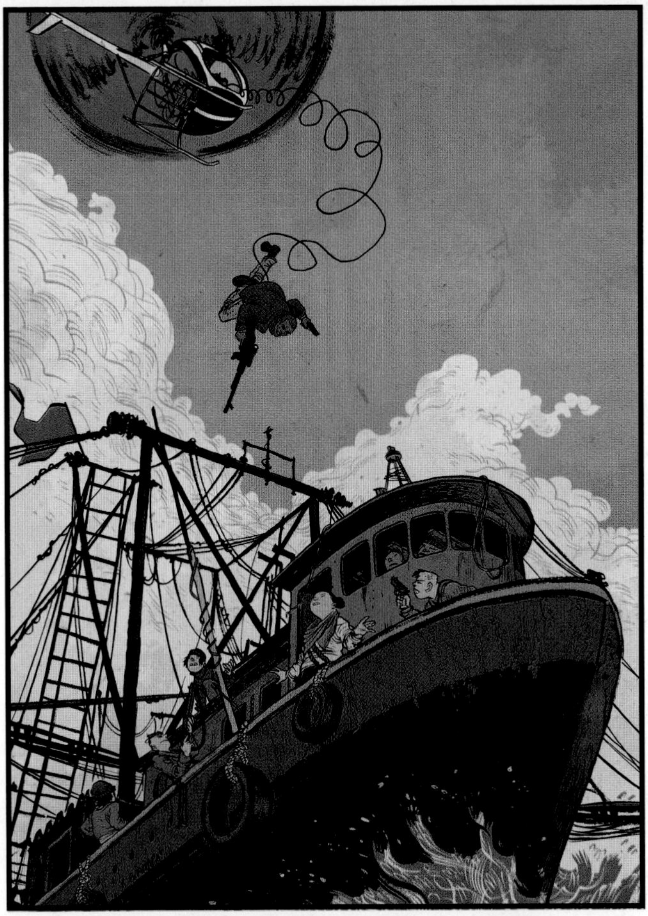

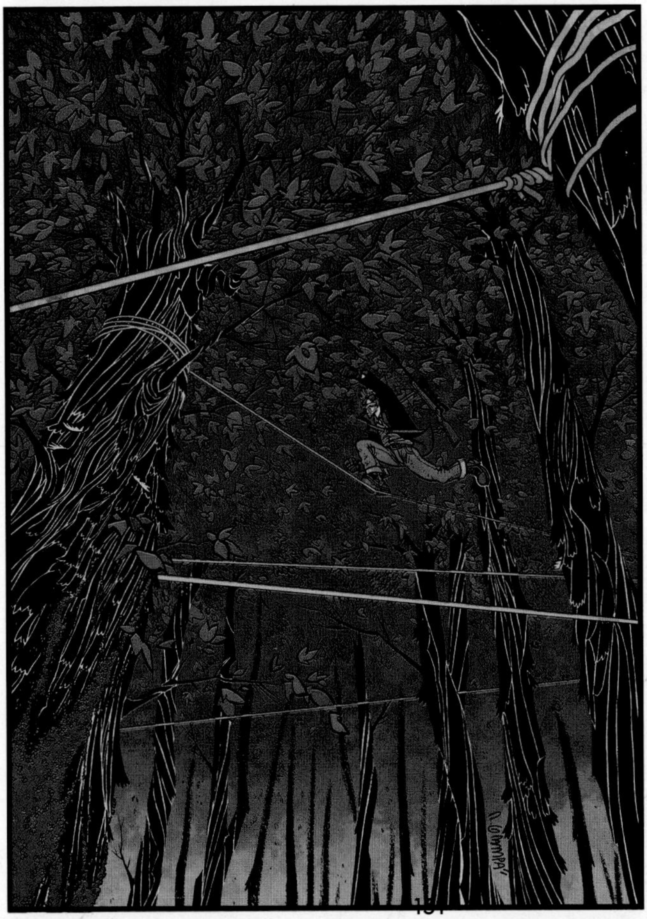

Artist Rafael Grampá's three variant covers for issues #1–#3 of the series.

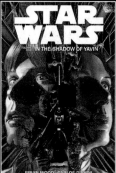